THE NEW
BOTTOM LINE

ALAN **MITCHELL** • ANDREAS W. **BAUER** • GERHARD **HAUSRUCKINGER**

THE NEW
BOTTOM LINE

Bridging the Value Gaps that are Undermining Your Business

CAPSTONE

Copyright © Alan Mitchell, Andreas W. Bauer and Gerhard Hausruckinger 2003.

The rights of Alan Mitchell, Andreas W. Bauer and Gerhard Hausruckinger to be identified as the authors of this book have been asserted in accordance with the Copyright, Designs and Patents Act 1988.

First published 2003 by
Capstone Publishing Limited (a Wiley Company)
The Atrium
Southern Gate
Chichester
West Sussex
PO19 8SQ
www.wileyeurope.com

CIP catalogue records for this book are available from the British Library and the US Library of Congress.

ISBN 1 84112 476 1

Designed and typeset by Baseline Arts Ltd, Oxford.
Printed and bound in Great Britain by TJ International Ltd, Padstow, Cornwall

This book is printed on acid-free paper responsibly manufactured from sustainable forestry in which at least two trees are planted for each one used for paper production.

Substantial discounts on bulk quantities of Capstone Books are available to corporations, professional associations and other organizations. For details telephone John Wiley & Sons on (+44-1243-770441), fax (+44-1243-770517) or e-mail corporate development@wiley.co.uk

Contents

Figures

Boxes

Tables

Designing value around people

Gondwanaland. You won't ever visit it, no matter how many frequent flyer miles you accumulate on your airline loyalty card. Gondwanaland was a massive continent that existed some 135 million years ago when Africa and South America were joined together as one, when Australia was part of the Antarctic, and when India was in roughly the same place as Australia is now.

However, continents drift. We humans don't notice such tectonic shifts because they unfold so slowly (usually about one centimetre a year). But as these huge land masses move they create huge tensions – tensions that can only be released through dramatic upheavals that transform the landscape. When continents drift apart, entire mountains can sink into seas or disappear into newly created valleys, for example, the Great Rift Valley of Africa. When they collide, huge new mountain ranges can be created, such as the Himalayas, which formed when India hit Asia.

This book suggests that something similar is happening in business. Long-maturing shifts in value – shifts that are all but invisible to those absorbed in the hectic hurly-burly of day-to-day bussiness life – are triggering an upheaval in the landscape. Old peaks of value are subsiding. New value peaks are thrust towards the sky. The value earth is moving under our feet. The old bottom line of corporate profitability is being superseded by a new bottom line, that of 'personal profitability' or 'value in my life'.

Figure 0.1 Our Value landscape is on the Move

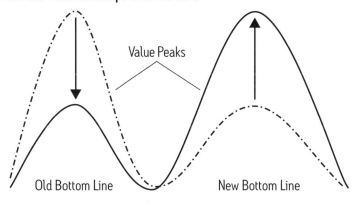

VALUE IN MY LIFE

Whew! That's a bold statement. No more bottom line? No more *profit*? How absurd!

Of course, that's not what we are saying. Every organization has to cover its costs. Every business has to make a profit. But what we *are* saying is that the necessary requirements for doing so are changing. The title of this chapter says it all: companies need to start designing value around people.

That's not the same as saying 'design value around the customer' or 'find out what your customers want and give it to them', because 'the customer' and 'the person' are not the same.

Take a simple example. As a leading consumer marketing company Procter & Gamble is forever researching the needs of its target customers, mainly housewives. In such research it often ends up bumping its head against a fundamental problem: many of these housewives' greatest areas of need are not really addressed by P&G's products – or by those of its rivals, for that matter. One example, explains chief marketing officer Jim Stengel, is that often 'the head of the household – the woman who is leading the household – is feeling really stressed. She can't get enough time for herself.'[1]

Yes, P&G does its best to create ever better, more convenient, time-saving cleaning products. It may even send this housewife some CDs of stress-relieving music as a relationship building exercise. But when push comes to shove, all of P&G's horses and all of P&G's men cannot really touch her central need for stress alleviation. That's because P&G's operations and products are *not* designed to meet the needs of a *person*. They are designed to meet the needs of a *consumer*.

By definition, a consumer or customer is someone who buys what we make. So if you design value around the consumer, you are in fact designing value around your own offerings and your own operations. Helping people tackle stress however, requires a fundamental shift in focus – from the efficiency and productivity of the *corporation's* operations to the efficiency and productivity of the *person's* operations: how I spend my time, day to day.

But companies like P&G are not designed to do this. The very way they create value for consumers is by maximizing the efficiency and productivity of their own internal operations: by providing ever better quality products at lower cost. Anything that takes their eye off this ball actually compromises this role and threatens their survival.

The fundamental question, then, is how to address these neglected forms of personal value: forms of value that cannot be made in factories and sold in shops; that traditional 'value from our operations' companies cannot or do not want to address. How to help people maximize the value they make in their own lives in a commercially viable way? Here, we suggest, is where we'll find the next breakthrough in wealth creation.

And of course it requires a new type of business. Such a business has very different operational and infrastructure requirements. Its core assets are different: not so much corporate assets such as mines, factories, warehouses, offices, pipelines or shops but *personal* assets such as time, information, attention, money and emotion. It relies on different processes, driven much more by 'bottom up' flows of information from individuals to companies than 'top down' marketing messages from sellers to buyers.

It generates a different set of revenue streams and is driven by different key measures: not so much traditional corporate measures such as return on financial investment, corporate profitability or unit cost but personal measures such as value for time, return on personal information, return on attention and value for money (hence this book's title of 'the new bottom line').

And it builds different kinds of relationship. The new bottom liner earns his keep not so much by selling to the consumer but by acting as the consumer's agent, helping him and her deal with the world of outside suppliers. He builds a new level of 'on my side' trust. He treats individuals not so much as consumers or customers but as co-producers and investors of critical personal assets.

One way of seeing this shift is to stop thinking in terms of 'corporations' and 'consumers' as completely different entities, and to see each individual as a producer – a sort of private company in the business of making my life.

Instead of looking at me as a consumer of a particular product or service, let's look at me in the round, from a different perspective. Let's look at me as a company, for example. As an individual I do the same things as the biggest company in the world. I source inputs. I process them, using assets and infrastructure I have acquired – plus my own skills and labour – to produce more valuable outputs.

I plan ahead. I do administration. I do routine maintenance of my plant and equipment. I invest in this equipment. I face logistical challenges of moving people and things. I employ people (such as plumbers). I develop relationships with suppliers and trading partners. I search for, and use, information. I plan and deploy my financial resources, make savings, take out loans, deal with cash-flow issues, pay taxes, etc. I sell my wares (such as my labour) on the open market. And so on, and so forth.

I also plan ahead, set personal priorities and goals (many of them emotional), and devise strategies to reach them. But I do all these things alone, as an isolated, amateur individual. Unlike companies, I do not have complete, organized professional departments and armies of consultants to make sure these things are done as efficiently and effectively as possible. Enter the new bottom liner.

In simple terms, we see the emergence of three main forms of new bottom line business, each of which parallels the main functions of any business. The first function is sourcing inputs: in this case, helping individuals to source the inputs of their lives in the form of products and services. We call this function trading agency. The second function helps individuals maximize the efficiency and productivity of their personal operations – to 'make' their lives better and cheaper. We call this function solution assembly. The third main function is to help individuals realize maximum value in their lives: reaching personal goals, attaining personal and emotional fulfilment. We call this passion partnership.

Separately and together, we suggest, these three forms of new bottom line business model will act as catalysts of far-reaching change. They will unleash the pent-up stresses and strains generated by old bottom line firms and markets to transform the commercial environment for all consumer-facing firms, whether in manufacturing, retailing, media, financial services, utilities, services, or transport.

'The new bottom line' sums up the two key elements of this tectonic shift. First, that critical shift in the prime location of wealth creation from 'our operations' to 'my life'. And second: a related shift in the focus of alignment.

Traditional old bottom line businesses created the richest, most extensive and dynamic wealth creating system the world has ever seen. Wherever there are new economies of scale to unleash or new technologies to apply, this model still has enormous potential. For many firms, their best future lies in extending and deepening its benefits. Indeed, it's only because old bottom liners have been so successful at addressing those forms of value that they are good at addressing that we have the luxury to turn our attention to the forms of value that they cannot reach. The enormous successes of the old bottom line have created the foundations for a new leap forward, just as many years ago advances in agriculture created the foundations for an industrial age.

Agriculture did not decline with the rise of industry. It had to grow, in order to feed the towns. Likewise, traditional suppliers will not decline with the rise of the new bottom line. The best suppliers will soon discover that new bottom line models open up new opportunities for growth.

Nevertheless, when industry created a new centre of commercial gravity, agriculture did decline in relative importance. Agriculture now had to find a new role for itself within an industrial environment. Likewise, with today's old bottom line businesses.

Currently, old bottom line businesses simply assume they are the centre of commercial gravity. Their core 'value from our operations' imperatives drive them in a quest to align individuals to their own operational needs and goals. Employees work for the company; the company does not work for its employees. When the company goes to market, its fundamental aim to is to change consumer perceptions and behaviours to do what the company wants her to do: buy our products and services! The purpose of building a strong brand is precisely this: to get consumer perceptions and behaviours orbiting the company's offerings. And, of course, the underlying purpose of all this activity is to maximize the company's profits.

To be welcomed into my life, however, I have to be confident that you will align your efforts to my purposes and goals; that you will work to boost my personal profitability. If you do so efficiently and effectively, I may reward you handsomely. But from now on, your bottom line is dependent on mine.

It's these two tectonic shits – in the operational location of wealth creation and the alignment of goals – that constitute the core of the new bottom line.

But why should these tectonic shifts be happening now? To see why, we need to look again at value peaks and the tectonic shifts that create, and destroy, them.

THE NEW HIMALAYAS

What, exactly, do we mean by 'value peaks'? A value peak occurs when a firm's (or supply chain's) productive ability (assets, infrastructure, skills, know-how, etc.) aligns as well as possible to people's needs and wants. It's when one tectonic plate – 'what I need' – collides with another – 'what you make' – to unleash the greatest possible wealth creation, given the circumstances prevailing at that time. This idea is illustrated in Figure 0.2.

Figure 0.2 When Tectonic Plates Collide

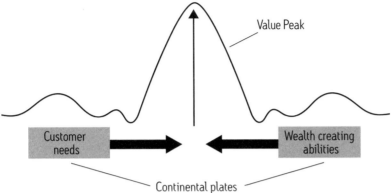

Different industries and products are continually climbing different peaks. Car makers cluster around one set of peaks connected by ridges of common attributes and technologies (with each individual peak representing, say, the 'best' SUV, off-road vehicle, classic sedan, estate, sportster, etc.). Cleaning products represent another cluster of peaks, and so on. Every company's ideal is, of course, to climb to the pinnacle of its particular value peak, where the alignment of what it makes to what its customers want is so perfect that profits flow quickly and easily.

Perfect alignment is very rare, however. Customer needs are always changing. So are economic circumstances. And technologies. And competitors' offers. So companies have to work hard just to avoid slipping down their value peak. The nightmare: to sink into a value valley – where the most important customer needs are not met and/or when productive capacity and assets are misdirected, misused, or neglected and left underutilized.

How to conquer your particular value peak is the subject of countless books. Quite rightly. But that's not our focus. Our focus is not the tops of those lofty peaks but their foundations. When we examine these foundations, we notice two things. First, just as rabbits, human beings, elephants, porpoises and dogs are all mammals, no matter how superficially different modern business models may be – manufacturing, retailing, banking, media, etc. – they all share the same old bottom line foundations and characteristics. They are part of the same mountain range.

Second, the very foundations of this *entire mountain range* are cracking and crumbling, as the tectonic plates upon which they rest drift apart. The big issue is not which individual peak happens to be higher, or which individual player is currently closest to his particular pinnacle. The big issue is that the mountain range itself is subsiding. And that's because the new bottom line needs of value in my life are moving centre stage – while old bottom line business models' capabilities, priorities and attention are focused elsewhere. As we've seen, this mismatch is not an accident. It is a product of the very nature of the beast. Deep. Long-term. Inexorable. *And with accumulating impact.*

Figure 0.3 When 'Tectonic Plates' Drift Apart

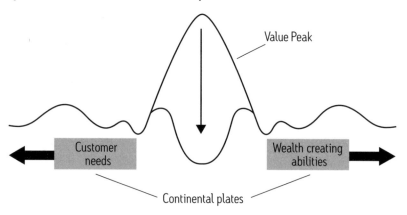

Hence the challenge we have set ourselves in this book: to show why and how this seismic transformation is occurring, what it means in detail, and how its problems and opportunities can be addressed so that both people and companies benefit.

We start out by identifying the parts of value in my life that traditional, old bottom line organizations are either *unable* or *unwilling* to meet – *the parts of value that old bottom line business models cannot reach*. 'Value gaps' we call them, and we identify seven of these in Chapter 1. They're all related to things we need to do to make our lives better, cheaper and simpler.

Also in Chapter 1, we identify 'seven deadly sins' that are driving old bottom line value subsidence. These are *systemic* problems: problems that are beyond the power of individual companies (who have to work *within* this system) to resolve; problems that are *insoluble* because they are a product of how the system itself works. Overcapacity is one example. It's a natural result of how competitive forces play themselves out. It's like the climate: it affects you, but you can't control it.

Another example is the ongoing crisis in marketing. A hundred years ago, roughly a quarter of all economic activity was taken up with the core marketing tasks of matching supply to demand and connecting buyers to sellers. The other three quarters was invested in actually making stuff. Since then, this 3:1 ratio of 'making' to 'matching and connecting' has been transformed into a 1:1 ratio. The costs of matching and connecting now account for a half, or more, of all economic activity.[2] The more efficient we become at 'making' the more complex and costly 'marketing' becomes.

This is why A.G. Lafley, CEO of Procter and Gamble now says that marketing has to be 'reinvented'.[3] And why his Unilever counterpart Niall Fitzgerald describes his company's current go-to-market costs as 'crackers'. Thanks to ongoing crises like these, we suggest, old bottom line value peaks are not only struggling to rise higher, in many cases they are actually sinking under the weight of their own accumulating costs and inefficiencies.

Incidentally, we take one important, underlying factor as read. New technologies are an inevitable part of this cocktail. New information technologies in particular are creating all manner of new opportunities, not only to cut costs but to change the way things work – by reversing the flow of information from buyer to seller, for example. As technologies, their impact has been discussed widely elsewhere. We don't bother repeating any of these discussions. We simply take this impact for granted and focus on how it helps to make new business models viable.

In Chapter 2, we explore the other side of the value gap coin. The most neglected, underutilized, undeveloped source of potential wealth creation today is what we call 'people assets'. We use the acronym OPTIMAL to list them: Operations or work, Passion, Time, Information, Money and Attention … in my Life. These OPTIMAL assets are the wherewithal with which we make our lives. But compared to the effort and attention that has been devoted to developing the value and productivity of *corporate* assets, they're still all but ignored.

Yet, we also discover that to fend off the consequences of value subsidence, today's major corporations desperately need access to these OPTIMAL assets – because *these assets are also becoming the key to corporate competitive edge*. Among employees, these 'people assets' include things like creativity, motivation and commitment. Among customers, it's their willingness to invest in a relationship and all that flows from such relationships: not only exchanges of money for goods, but exchanges of information, of value for attention, and so on.

What's more, unleashing the potential of these assets raises that thorny question of who is actually serving whom. In fact, we suggest, as owners and controllers of these OPTIMAL assets individuals – yes, individuals, are becoming the critical *investors*, investing their personal assets in companies, both as customers and employees. And as investors, they will only invest these assets when and where they are going to get an excellent return on their investment.

This, we suggest, is the dynamic driving the new value accommodation we call the new bottom line. In order to access my personal assets (as well as do traditional things such as win me over as a customer) companies need to start addressing 'value in my life' as well as 'value from our operations'. This requires climbing a completely different value peak. And that, in turn, requires new business models.

In Chapter 3, we look at the collision of these tectonic forces and examine new business models that can *both* address the seven key value gaps *and* unleash the potential of OPTIMAL assets. A new form of alignment, in other words, which brings together new dimensions of value, new *sources* of value, and new win-wins between buyers and sellers, to create new virtuous economic spirals. We also explore (in generic terms) how new bottom liners earn their keep. Basically it's from three sources: from people paying more (for more value); from improved ability to monetize personal assets such as information and attention; and from new economies of scale and efficiencies, such as slashing the cost of traditional matching and connecting.

While old bottom liners look *down supply chains*, from the point of view a seller trying to sell a product or service to a buyer, then new bottom liners look *up demand chains*, from the point of view of the individual trying to create value in my life. While the old bottom liner lives and breathes 'make and sell', these emerging business models are more concerned with 'sourcing and integrating'. In Chapters 4, 5 and 6 we turn our attention to three specific new business models. Roughly speaking, they address old bottom line value considerations of price, quality and emotional added value but as these apply to 'my life' rather than 'your product'.

The first of the three is *Trading Agents* (Chapter 4). To put it crudely, these are the consumer's professional purchasing department. Their job is to help buyers to buy, rather than help sellers to sell. They open up a completely new market: the market for 'go-to-market services' – services that help me maximize the value and minimize the cost of the stuff I buy (not just money costs, but time and hassle costs too). Crucially, they also have another – 'selling' – role. They help me take valuable personal assets such as information and attention to market, to maximize the value they can generate in the marketplace.

Solution Assemblers (Chapter 5) come next. Their focus is maximizing the efficiency and productivity of my personal operations, the things I have to do to 'make' my life. Things like running a home, keeping it replenished, organizing my personal finances, sorting out my personal transport problems, and so on. They add value by helping me spend less time and effort doing the chores I don't want to do, so that I can spend more time doing the things I do want to do. To do so, solution assemblers source and integrate the many different ingredients offered by traditional old bottom liners.

Passion Partners (Chapter 6) meanwhile help me maximize the returns I generate on my emotional investments. They help me to invest my precious personal assets – time, money, emotional commitment, the lot – in the things that really matter to me; and to maximize the returns I generate on these investments. In doing so, they help to unleash the full *economic* (as well as personal) potential of human emotions which have long been stunted and deformed by an economic system that was unable to recognize their true value.

Chapter 7 then takes stock. It examines some of the common characteristics of new bottom line business models. For example, instead of exchanging value along just one dimension (of money for goods or services) they trade in the many currencies of value in my life. Yes, value for money is important. But so is value for time, return on attention, return on information invested, returns on emotions invested and so on. We also see how the new business models 'reach back' into old bottom line value, subsuming what traditional brands have to offer, trumping them with new layers of value, and transforming the context within which they operate and go to market.

This brings us to the dilemma facing old bottom liners. They desperately need growth. They desperately want to get closer to their customers. To build brand loyalty. And so on. Yet a clear pattern of growth seems to be emerging. Fast, sometimes meteoric, growth is being experienced by companies that successfully address the key value gaps and rise to the challenge of personal asset productivity and maximization. Stagnation and value subsidence is the common theme among those failing to do so, as customers, employees and investors lose interest – a torpor broken only now and again as pent-up stresses explode in a new earthquake or avalanche, as a new bottom liner moves in for the kill.

The question is then: if I am an old bottom liner, how do I make the journey to these new value peaks and start climbing? If I'm a fish, how do I start breathing air? If I'm land-bound, how can I learn to fly? The trouble is, like jumping half way across a raging torrent, half-way houses are fraught with risk: there's a good chance you'll end up with the worst of both worlds. Somehow, old bottom liners need to build a bridge across the chasm generated by their very different business models, but how?

It won't be easy. But it can happen. There are many things that companies are *already* doing – things they originally started doing to make their *existing* businesses more efficient and profitable, which could be used for a new and different purpose: to 'reach out' to the new bottom line. Feathers weren't originally invented for the purpose of flight. They were originally invented for the purposes of thermoregulation: maintaining the right temperature. But they helped form a bridge to something completely new. Likewise, many of the things currently being 'invented' by forward-looking businesses could form the supports of a bridge to the new value peaks.

In Chapters 8 to 12 we look at five such potential bridge-building supports: use of information *from* the customer; organizing operations around customer, rather than corporate 'convenience'; organizing business partnerships around the requirements of the first two; becoming a company that works for its people; and building relationships by making marketing a service to the customer.

We show how the new bottom line throws each of these central business concerns of information, operations, partnerships, human resources and marketing into a new light, how current changes *begin* to address new bottom line considerations, and what further changes need to be made if they are to be successful.

But supports alone are not enough. They need to be brought together – connected – to actually build a bridge between point A and point B. That's the issue we address in Chapter 13: the need for a new, uniting vision of value that integrates and connects these different pillars to form a definite strategy for crossing from one value peak to the other.

We believe the new bottom line represents a huge opportunity. But our purpose in examining the new bottom line isn't because we think it's a 'nice' or 'good' idea. It's because we think it's a simple, hard *fact*. As we said at the beginning of this introduction, those tectonic plates are shifting whether we like it or not: the ground is moving beneath our feet, whether we like it or not. No 'consumer-facing' business in whatever sector – whether it's manufacturing, retailing, media or financial services – is immune.

Threat or opportunity, there is only one question to answer. It is not *whether* to respond. It's *how*.

1. The Value Gaps

In many ways, this book is about reaching the parts of value that 'customer focus' can't reach. The diagram to the right sums it up. On the one hand, today's businesses are finding it ever harder to add extra value for their customers. In fact, in many cases their ability to add such value is actually subsiding. At the same time, there are also some huge value gaps: areas of 'value in my life' that are simply not being met.

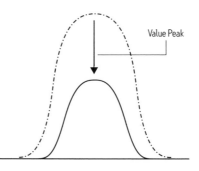

We have, in other words, a growing disconnect between 'demand' and 'supply' – a disconnect that reaches right into the heart of business as we know it: the old bottom line.

'Be customer focused'; 'Get closer to your customers'; 'The secret of success lies in understanding consumer needs and meeting them'; 'Be more customer-centric'. If the number of times businesses used phrases such as these was any indication of the real state of affairs, there would be no need for this book.

In fact, they're part of the problem, not the solution. Nine times out of ten consumer-focus rhetoric is just a smokescreen for an all-pervading seller-centricity that is now so deep that it is all but unconscious. Consumer focus is a sophisiticated exercise in organizational narcissism, where the organization peers into a mirror – 'the consumer' – that reflects the organization's own needs and preoccupations.

TASKS FOR THIS CHAPTER

1. Introduce the seven value gaps created by the old bottom line.
2. Show why the old bottom line's value peaks are subsiding.

THE MYTH OF THE CONSUMER

In fact, there is no such thing as a consumer. When we look at the world around us, we see millions of *people* and yes, an awful lot of consumption. But no matter how hard you look, you will never find a 'consumer'. Because the consumer is a fictional entity invented by producers: 'the consumer' is a unit of demand for the producer's products.

When a soap company looks at me, it's not really interested in *me*. It's actually looking in a mirror – at a reflection of its own needs: its need to close sales. The only parts of me it is really interested in – that it really looks at – are those parts that affect the likelihood of me buying its soap. When it sees me, it doesn't see *me* at all.

The same goes for every product and service. When a car company looks at me, it's searching for a unit of demand for its cars. When a bank looks at me, it's looking for a unit of demand for banking services. When an airline looks at me, it sees a potential unit of demand for flights. When each and every of these companies 'focus on the consumer' they are in fact focusing on how to meet their own need to find a market for their products. In the process, I am fragmented into a thousand and one separate 'markets' – for beer, cheese, sneakers, make-up, deodorants, holidays, bank accounts and so on. And the real me disappears from view.

This would not be a problem if together all these companies addressed all my needs. But they don't. As members of the same 'family' of business beasts they share the same dimensions of value none of them address.

INTRODUCING THE NEW BOTTOM LINE

We think there are seven main gaps, as follows:

The seven key value gaps

1. Transaction costs
2. Integration costs
3. Standardization versus customization

4. Seller versus buyer-centric information
5. Functional versus emotional needs
6. Where economies of scale fail
7. Neglect of personal assets

1. Transaction costs

When a seller-centric producer of products (or services) thinks 'price' it naturally thinks in terms of the price it charges for its product – the money the consumer will pay for it. But view of the world ignores other dimensions of cost incurred by the consumer in the course of the transaction. The price of a packet of soap powder in a shop may be ten Euros, for example. But in order to acquire that packet of soap powder, I have to spend time and money travelling to and from the shop, searching for the product, queuing, paying etc. The real price paid by consumers for products and services is invariably higher than the monetary price levied by sellers. *Seller 'price' is just one element of buyer cost.*

Every year, for example, European spends approximately 34 billion hours shopping for groceries. Fifty-seven percent of that time is spent in cars and other forms of transport, and 43 percent is spent in shops. If you charged these hours at minimum wage rates, these transaction costs equal 20 percent of the total value generated by European grocery value chains.

Such buyer transaction costs tend to be ignored by sellers, for a number of reasons. First, they have zero immediate impact on the seller's sales revenues or profits, so they simply don't impinge on the seller's consciousness. Second, specific 'divisions of labour' between buyers and sellers emerged in the mists of time and have become so 'normal' that we take them for granted. We just assume for example that 'it's the job' of the shopper to shop. Because shopping is such a 'natural' part of everyday life, as consumers, we don't stop to measure how much time, money or effort we invest doing it – or how good a return we get on this investment. Likewise, it's the producer's job to worry about his own costs, not other people's costs.

Third, most attempts by sellers to reduce buyers' transaction costs involve renegotiating these divisions of labour, which is complex and difficult. Usually it involves sellers taking on more work and cost, for very little obvious return. Just look at the difficulties grocery retailers have had trying to make money out of home delivery. Finally, it's often beyond any individual seller's ability to address these transaction costs. The soap powder manufacturer can't address my overall grocery shopping costs single-handedly, for example. Equally, an individual insurance provider will find it difficult to reduce the time I have to spend comparing different providers' policies.

In short, there are many excellent and deep-seated structural reasons why seller-centric marketers have not addressed consumers' transaction costs. But that's precisely the point. There's a big need out there, and it's not being met.

2. Integration costs

A frighteningly high proportion of today's value propositions take the form of *ingredients* to solutions rather than the solutions themselves. Take the simple example of a pizza. I can, if I want, go to a store to buy all the separate ingredients of a pizza (thereby incurring significant transaction costs). I can then invest a significant amount of further time and effort preparing these ingredients, putting them together, cooking them to get my desired end-result: a delicious, piping hot pizza, ready to eat. Alternatively, I can pick up the phone, order from a local pizza parlour and have it delivered right to my door.

This difference between buying a range of separate pizza ingredients and ordering a freshly made, home-delivered pizza sums up the difference between making and selling ingredients and offering complete solutions. Old bottom line businesses excel at making and selling ingredients – and avoid solutions – for a simple, basic reason. They are *asset-centric*. They make their money by investing vast sums in specialist, productive assets and by 'sweating' these assets to produce as much as possible. That's how they add value for consumers: by using these assets to drive up the quality and drive down the cost *of what these assets are best at making*. If you've invested your particular fortune in cheese making equipment, you live and breath the making and selling of cheese. Likewise, if you are in tinned tomato business, cars, airlines or retailing.

As long as each of these businesses focuses on doing what it does best (and why shouldn't it?), they will all focus on making and selling ingredients, leaving consumers with the job of assembling their own solutions. And like transaction costs, there are some very good reasons why old bottom line businesses continue to avoid solutions.

If you define consumer needs in terms of solutions such as say, personal financial management rather than financial services products, such as loans, savings, current accounts, plastic cards, mortgages, pensions and so on, then suddenly your 'market' evaporates before your very eyes. A whole host of potential new competitors materialize in front of you. And you face the prospect of your precious product being rendered invisible: who cares what brand of mozzarella the pizza parlour uses?

Addressing a solution also requires heavy investment in new skills and infrastructure – which reach way beyond your existing 'core competence' – while downgrading the value of your existing 'core' assets. Just look at the difference between the skills and assets of that mozzarella maker and that pizza parlour. Moving from ingredients to solutions is, therefore, an expensive, high-risk activity. A case in point is Ford under Jacques Nasser, who moved into a whole range of car-related businesses such as Kwik Fit the roadside repair service – only for his successor to incur enormous losses reversing the strategy. It takes guts and boldness to move from ingredient production to solution assembly. Few try. Even fewer succeed. But that doesn't make the need disappear.

3. Customization versus standardization

Industrial-age value creation lives and breathes standardization. It is only by standardizing inputs (such as raw materials), processes and outputs that you can replicate routines, automate and drive down unit costs. Yet, by definition, each individual is unique and different – so what is required to create value in my life is unique and different too.

'Choice' between a range of standardized offers is a wonderful thing. But value in my life is not about choice. It's about being able to get exactly what I want and that goes against the grain of everything standardized mass producers have been trying to achieve internally for the last hundred years. Real customization means, therfore, transforming the way they do business. It may involve additional cost and complexity rather than lower unit costs and cost cutting. It may mean reversing the flow of the entire business. Instead of making many units in batches and then trying to sell them, you might have to wait for orders from customers, and then make individual units to order. This, in turn, implies a completely different set of go-to-market strategies and different types of customer relationships. What's more, there are few viable half-way houses.

Once again, these are all very good reasons why old bottom liners have stuck with standardization. But the net effect is the same. From food to financial services, from cars to computers to clothing, the value gap is there. And it's growing.

4. Seller- versus buyer-centric information

Product-centric companies may do their best to address the needs of their customers as *users* of their products. This is in their interests because it helps them to sell more, more efficiently. But once they have made the product or service in question, then a completely different imperative takes over. Now, their over-riding priority is to cover their costs and realize a profit by selling what they have made.

So when they go to market to sell their wares, they do not attempt to provide the impartial, objective, easy-to-use comparative information that would help would-be buyers make the best choices and get the best deals. Instead, they do advertising: sending out information which is by definition partial and biased and designed to persuade the buyer to buy their particular offer.

It's a simple and obvious point. But it also runs very deep. The *rhetoric* of marketing is about identifying and meeting customer needs. But when seller-centric companies go to market, their marketing activities focus on the needs of the seller: how to sell more, more profitably. The *rhetoric* of marketing tells us that by focusing on the needs of the consumer, the company changes what it does (e.g. by tweaking what it makes) to suit the needs of the consumer. But when seller-centric companies go to market, their marketing activities are designed to get consumers to change what they do, to suit the needs of the company: 'buy my brand!'.

Seller-centric marketing, in other words, is about helping sellers to sell, and it does not even attempt to help the buyer buy.

Helping buyers to buy rather than helping sellers to sell, then, requires a completely different set of objectives, such as the provision of *buyer-centric* information and advice: impartial, objective, easy-to-use comparative information that helps us make the best choices and get the best deals.

Once again this value gap is enormous. And once again, the reasons for its existence are structural. At the risk of sounding like a stuck record, there's no reason why old bottom liners should ever address it. Indeed, as we'll see below, the gap is growing ever larger.

5. Functional versus emotional needs

Mass production is very good at meeting functional and physiological needs. It's not so good at addressing people's emotional needs. You can't make happiness in a factory, and you can't sell it through a retailer's shops. The only place you can make happiness is in your own life.

That's about all we need to say in introducing this value gap – with just one clarification. Various traditional offers and brands do provide consumers with some of the ingredients individuals use to 'manufacture' emotional value in their lives: the media with entertainment; brands that help consumers make statements about themselves; bars and restaurants that provide a platform for socializing, and so on. But this emotional added value tends to be limited or distorted in one of two crucial ways,

First, it's limited to the form of what can be packaged, mass-distributed, purchased and consumed – such as a Disney film. Second, it's distorted by seller-centric objectives. There's many a seller-centric marketer who appeals to peoples' need for a sense of community, self-esteem, identity, belonging or meaning as a means of attracting them to their brand and closing a sale. But *using* people's emotions as a means to an end is very different to helping them maximize the emotional value they *make* in their own lives. We explore this difference in detail when we look at the rise of the passion partner.

6. Where economies of scale fail

This value gap is slightly different. For decades, industrial-age businesses have added huge amounts of value by finding new and better ways to improve 'personal productivity': helping us to do more, in the same time, or with less effort. Running water, gas and electricity have boosted our personal productivity no end, for example. The average European household now uses the energy equivalent to 150 domestic servants by running electrical appliances in their homes.

There have been many waves of industrial age-generated personal productivity. Basic infrastructure such as the utilities, roads and railways created the springboard and platform for the consumer-goods revolution. This triggered a massive wave of 'outsourcing' of tasks to manufacturers, as consumers discovered that things that they used to make in their own homes – such as clothes or loaves of bread – could be made much better, and more cheaply, in mass production factories. A further boost came after the Second World War when 'home automation' began and labour-saving devices such as the automatic washing machine, the refrigerator and the toaster transformed our daily lives. They, in turn, created a platform for yet more labour-saving products. The chilled ready meal, for example, was only made possible by the existence of the fridge, the freezer and the microwave.

Looking back, it is breathtaking how much value these successive waves created. Nevertheless, over recent years, this hundred-year personal productivity revolution has begun to run out of steam. We've managed to automate the washing cycle, but not the loading, unloading and ironing. No clever machine has (yet) been invented to sweep floors, clean surfaces, make beds, fix faulty appliances and so on. Automation – the product of industrialization and economies of scale – worked as long as it could be made 'in our operations' and embedded in a mass-produced product like a washing machine. As soon as the delivery of value moved out of the factory into the home – ironing those clothes, making those beds – the revolution ran into sand. As *Financial Times* writer Richard Tomkins put it 'the last big inventions to have significantly changed our lives – television and the passenger jet – came half a century ago.[1]

That's why, for the most part, running a home (the 'factory' of wealth creation in my life) remains a cottage and craft industry that's largely untouched by ongoing technological revolutions elsewhere. Economies of scale and centralized mass production got us an awful long way. But at a certain point they hit the buffers. We not only need new technologies to address this value gap, we need new business models too.

7. Neglected personal assets

Old bottom line businesses create wealth by investing in productive assets (plant, machinery, infrastructure, know-how, etc.) and sweating them to the full, to produce the best possible products and services as cheaply as possible. Their natural operational focus is to maximize the productivity of these assets.

The assets that really matter to me, however – the ones that I use to make my life – are personal assets. They include traditional physical assets like money, my house and my car (if I own them). But many of the most important personal assets take a different form: my time, my attention or the returns I get for investing emotionally in relationships. Helping me maximize the value, potential and productivity of my personal assets is, for want of a better phrase, 'the mother of all value gaps' encompassing most of what we've discussed above.

Old bottom liners neglect this task for a very simple reason - 'They're not my business, and I'm not set up, or organized to do it.' Indeed many of the things old bottom liners do when they go to market positively waste my time and abuse my attention.

That's where new bottom liners enter the fray: to help me make the most of my personal assets – a role so economically significant we devote the next chapter to it.

A CONTINENTAL SHIFT

Now let's step back and put these seven key value gaps in perspective. They range far and wide in nature, from accessing the inputs I need to create value in my life, through the processes I use to do so, to the final outcome of emotional fulfilment.

They are created by a mixed bag of causes. In some cases (e.g., buyer-centric information), the gap has emerged because it's simply not in the interests of suppliers to fill it. Other cases such as emotional fulfilment simply lie beyond the old bottom liner's reach. In others, (e.g., domestic chores) traditional suppliers would love to fill the gap – if only they could work out how. And yet others, such as transaction and integration costs, are the product of deep-seated structural factors: addressing them is just 'too big' a challenge.

The value gaps summed up

- The value gaps exist because old bottom line businesses are unable or unwilling to address them. They are the product of deep-seated structural barriers and marketing myopia.

- Separately and together, they represent a huge untapped business opportunity.

- Addressing this opportunity, however, requires a different type of business.

- Every consumer-facing industry is affected by these value gaps.

- Successfully addressing them will transform the economics, criteria for success, value offerings, infrastructure and culture of each and every one of the industries concerned.

But whatever the cause, the value gaps exist (see the Roland Berger Profiler, Box 1.1) and their potential effects reach both wide and deep. Wide, because every sector suffers from them, from one degree to another. Everyone is affected from food to financial services, from consumer durables to utilities to retailing/shopping. From health and transport through to leisure and entertainment. Deep, because a large percentage of each of these industries' income is involved.

Take the simple example of 'fast food'. Fast food is an early attempt to address consumers' transaction and solution assembly costs in the realms of food: the time and hassle of food shopping and preparation. In the US, it has already grabbed over 50 percent share of stomach. Europe is following

BOX 1.1 THE ROLAND BERGER PROFILER

Evidence of the power of unmet consumer needs comes from a unique research project undertaken by Roland Berger. This was an open-ended research programme, with no particular issue in mind. It simply asked consumers 'what is important to you?' Answers ranged over a total of 1,600 statements which were then analyzed and grouped together by common themes. These themes were distilled further and re-researched – and refined down to 20 broad themes.

These are:

Rational needs and value propositions: quality, service, 24/7 - Protech, comfort and convenience, customized, proven, price awareness, smart shopping (i.e., bargain hunting) and total cost (shopping systematically on price).

Emotional needs and value propositions: carefree, clanning, new and cool, classic, vitality, thrill and fun, passion, fair, nature, tranquil and purism.

The results are striking. Classic marketing battlegrounds around product quality and price make their appearance. So does an emphasis on classic design and tradition that makes some luxury brands so powerful. But the majority of identified desires, needs and dreams fall outside these classical marketing battlegrounds and into the value gaps discussed in this chapter. Key themes include 'customized' (the desire for controllable exclusivity, uniqueness, variety and flexibility), 'protech' (fast access to information) and 'comfort and convenience' (time efficiency and 'pro-active support').They chime with the themes of transaction and integration costs, customization, and buyer-centric information.

Emotional value gaps loom largest, however. Some of them revolve around themes such as 'vitality' (a need for physical and mental fitness and mobility), 'thrill and fun' (adventure and risk seeking, and rebellious escapism), and 'carefree' (a need for spontaneity and easy-going optimism). Others – like the groupings 'fair', 'nature', 'tranquil' and 'purism' – represent consumer desires not to exploit people or nature and to have high ethical standards, to work in harmony with nature, or to slow down, de-stress and find inner peace and simplicity.

Many marketers have nodded towards these emotional needs in their marketing communications imagery, but so far few companies have actually attempted to build businesses that address these needs as the central core of their value offer.

fast in these footsteps. By focusing on traditional seller-centric value – and failing to address crucial value gaps – traditional food manufacturers and retailers saw half their market evaporate before their eyes.

When push came to shove, better 'value in my life' beat 'better products and services' hands down. Or to put it another way, better products and services are *just one part* of helping to create better value in my life. This new bottom line habit of subsuming the value offered by old bottom liners represents its greatest threat – and opportunity.

WARNING! VALUE SUBSIDENCE!

Remember the notion of the value peak. The higher it is, the more value it offers. Competition drives businesses to climb such peaks, because that's the way they acquire and keep customers. Slip too far down a value peak and you risk your survival.

If consumers have a choice between two peaks representing two different types of value offering, then clearly they tend to opt for the highest one. As long one peak remains higher than another, it's safe. It doesn't really matter if it's 1km higher or 1cm higher: as long as it is higher, consumers will tend to choose it.

But what happens when one value peak keeps on rising, while the other keeps on falling? In this case, at some crucial point, the tables are turned: 1cm higher becomes 1cm (or 1km) lower. The value scales tip, and all the momentum of competition flows in the opposite direction towards the new, rising peak. From now on, it's the new peak that sets the competitive agenda.

This is our suggestion. We've reached a tipping point where the potential value offered by new bottom line business models reaches higher than that offered by the old. We've examined some of the reasons already.

When it comes to identifying and meeting consumer needs via the making and selling of products and services, old bottom line companies are geniuses, forever discovering new market opportunities and rushing to seize them. But the value gaps represent those needs that have fallen through the net; the needs that have been left to fester.

The old bottom liner is also a victim of its own success. Thanks to old bottom line wealth-creation, in advanced Western industrial economies at least, we are more affluent than ever. Our basic needs are met, we have more 'discretionary' money to spend, we are healthier, we live longer, we are more educated and more sophisticated. All of this gives us the luxury of being able to start climbing up Maslow's famous hierarchy of needs: to reach beyond the quest for physical security and sustenance for higher goals such as 'self-actualization'. Yet as we've seen, old bottom liners are not designed to address these higher-order needs. But there's another, crucial side to this coin. The old bottom line wealth-creating system has passed its prime and diminishing returns are setting in: far from creating ever more value, it's in danger of actually producing less.

THAT AWFUL SINKING FEELING

The causes of these diminishing returns are very familiar. They're the subject of endless academic and consultancy research – and endless managerial fretting. Yet they persist, because they are *systemic*. They are a product of how the system works and *cannot be resolved or solved within the confines of that system*. Let us remind ourselves of some of them.

The Seven Deadly Sins of the industrial age

1. Overcapacity
2. Product parity
3. Innoflation
4. Over-satisfied customers
5. Information overload
6. Marketing overload
7. Tangibles focus

1. Overcapacity

When markets are fresh and new, investment in additional productive capacity generates enormous value for consumers – and sometimes stupendous returns for investors and producers. But as markets mature, they reach a tipping point where supply begins to outstrip demand. In industry after industry, overcapacity is now the norm, not the exception.

Even 'star' sectors such as personal computers and mobile phones have discovered, to their cost, how quickly overcapacity can set in.

The onset of overcapacity has a crucially damaging effect on the win-wins that form the foundation of the old bottom line business model. These win-wins revolve around developing 'New! Improved!' products and bringing them to market, thereby stimulating demand which earns a return on the investment, and which provides an incentive for the producer to invest even more in productive capacity and R&D. The win for the producer: growing revenues and lower unit costs. The win for the consumer: 'New! Improved!' products at lower prices.

When overcapacity sets in however, that win-win dynamic evaporates. Companies focus their attention on rationalization and cost-cutting, not new value creation. Costs actually rise, and companies naturally try to pass these costs on to their customers. In this way a hugely powerful, dynamic win-win tips over into lose-lose. Overcapacity destroys the win-win heart of old bottom line production.

2. Product parity

Every marketing person will tell you: innovation is the key to growth and improved customer satisfaction. They are quite right of course. But no company would dare let a competitor get ahead on product quality or attributes, so each attempt at innovation is quickly matched – and the net competitive benefits cancelled.

As time-to-market cycles are compressed, product parity becomes a major headache for any would-be innovator. Many companies now despair of ever gaining, or keeping, a sustainable competitive advantage for their products or services. The effects run deep.

Product parity undermines the logic – and payback – of sustained innovation. It also undermines the win-wins central to brand-consumer relationships. In the early days of the old bottom line, marketers invented brands as ambassadors for 'unique selling propositions': clear points of differentiation built around clearly identified points of sustained superior consumer benefit. These brands acted as signposts of value for consumers, pointing them easily, quickly and efficiently to the sources of value most appropriate to them.

As product parity sets in, however, marketers have found themselves turning this original purpose of branding on its head. Today, increasingly, marketers seek to build brands in order to *hide underlying sameness rather than express important points of difference*. This destroys the win-win heart of branding.

3. Innoflation

In their desperate attempt to tackle the curse of product parity, firms have pushed 'innovation' higher and higher up their corporate agendas. They've looked to more, better innovation as a way out. What they've created instead, is innoflation. This happens when firms start throwing ever more superficially different products at the market, in the desperate quest for a point of difference. The net result is counterproductive. The proliferation of products and variants creates layer upon layer of extra production, distribution and marketing cost and complexity, without adding benefit for consumers. In fact, consumers lose out as costs, and therefore prices, rise and as choice descends into confusion and becomes a chore instead. Once again, with innoflation win-win tips over into lose-lose, as the win-win benefits of old bottom line innovation and choice evaporate.

4. Over-satisfied customers

A customer is 'over-satisfied' when a further improvement along a particular dimension no longer adds any real value. If a car breaks down every ten thousand miles, then improving reliability to a breakdown say, every fifty thousand miles is a major benefit. But once reliability reaches a level where few customers ever experience a breakdown during the time that they own the car, further improvements in reliability do not add to the customer's experience of the product.

As Harvard Business School professor, Clayton Christensen points out, over-satisfaction spells disaster for any company that grows prosperous on the back of a particular improvement, such as reliability. Suddenly its 'secret' of success evaporates and it becomes a victim of its own success as value subsidence sets in.

5. Information overload

The mass production of products such as soap powders, automatic washing machines and motor cars created an awesome value breakthrough. But it's not the only breakthrough generated by old bottom line business. Another awesome value breakthrough came with the mass production of information and entertainment. First, the printed word. Then the radio. Then television. Then cable and satellite. And the Internet. And so on. Result: ever-richer 'content' made ever more freely available.

But all of us have only so much attention time. The more information that's thrown at us, the more we suffer from information overload and attention poverty. This has huge long-term implications for the two key players in the media industry: media owners and advertisers.

Media owners face the unpalatable fact that content, far from being 'king', is becoming commoditized. The commercial, marketable value of most of what they offer is falling, inexorably. They're finding it ever harder to win the war for people's attention. Advertisers face the equally unpalatable fact that the more information overload sets in, the less effective advertising becomes. One counterproductive result is that advertisers find themselves forced to invest ever more money, on ever more intrusive advertising initiatives designed to 'cut through the clutter' to get their message through – thereby intensifying the very information overload that they're trying to overcome.

Information overload means that the hugely powerful win-win dynamic that has driven advertising-funded media is now stalling. It also elevates 'return on attention' to an important economic dynamic in its own right, placing a big question mark under the future role and value of traditional 'push' marketing communications. Another old bottom line win-win is turning into another lose-lose.

6. Marketing overload

The combination of all of the above factors is the source of another crucial piece of value subsidence. Industrial-age wealth-creation revolves around standardization, automation and economies of scale. Companies' endless quests for improved productivity have pushed production costs down ever lower. The other side to this coin, however, is that while production costs have fallen, the relative costs of going to market – of identifying, communicating with and transacting with customers – have risen.

A hundred years ago, about a quarter of all US economic activity was devoted to what the economists John Wallis and Douglass North called 'transacting' – which includes all the costs incurred by companies in taking their goods and services to market.[2] By 1986, the figure had nearly doubled to 45 percent and was rising. Over a half of all US labour activity is now focused on 'the searching, coordinating and monitoring that people and firms do when they exchange goods, services or ideas'.

The result of this pincer movement in relative costs is devastating. While overcapacity, product parity, oversatisfaction, etc., mean that the value creation has hit diminishing returns, the costs of realizing this value on the market are still rising, inexorably. The effects reach right to the heart of the old bottom line business model.

Old bottom line businesses try very hard to make sure that *what* they sell represents good value for the consumer. But they don't judge *how* they go to market – their marketing spend - by the same criterion. Marketing itself is not meant to add value for the consumer; its job is to *realize the value that has already been created*. As far as the consumer is concerned, for the most part marketing is non-value adding. Yet, this non-value adding element of the old bottom line package is growing proportionately larger every day. So consumers are paying less for what does add value, and more for what doesn't. This is value subsidence with a vengeance. Yesterday, marketing was a win-win exercise because it helped to cement the virtuous circle of improved supply and rising demand. Today, it too, is tipping over into a lose-lose exercise.

7. Tangibles focus

At the same time, the very economic logic at the heart of the old bottom line business is changing fundamentally. It's not uncommon nowadays for only 15 to 20 percent of the stock market value of the company to be accounted for by hard, physical, 'tangible' assets such as plant and machinery. The other 80 percent is delivered by so-called intangibles.

Intangibles come in many forms: staff skills and know-how, brands and customer relationships. We'll return to this in more detail, especially in Chapter 11. But for now we need only note one core effect. The industrial age lives and breathes automation as the means of producing more at lower cost: it is the essence of 'value from our operations'. Yet the counter-intuitive effect of the relentless advance of automation is that increasingly, competitive edge comes not from what we *can* automate (because that's easily copiable) but what we *can't* automate (because that's harder to copy).

Hard-to-copy things are, almost by definition, 'people things'. Things like sensing, making judgements, imagining, creating and inventing, amusing and engaging, building relationships, motivating other people, setting goals, being dedicated and determined, and so on. They're all things created by 'people assets'.

What unites these 'people assets' is that the real source of value is located in people, not in things, machines or processes. Companies cannot 'own' these people assets or control them as they do things, machines and processes. Indeed, to a large degree, people own their own people assets. And they invest and allocate these assets according to their own personal criteria. Result: the proportion of economic activity which is effectively owned and controlled by old bottom line, tangibles-driven logic is shrinking – and the proportion which necessarily revolves around the optimization and maximization of people assets (the new bottom line) is growing.

The old value peak is sinking under the own accumulated weight of the 'seven deadly sins' just discussed. We need only remember three key points about them.

1. Separately and together, they're all the unavoidable consequences of a system at work; they're the product of the system's own unfolding inner logic.

2. Separately and together, they all have the same underlying effects: of diminishing returns and value subsidence.

3. Because they're the product of a system at work, it is beyond the power of any individual firm to address them, as long as it keeps working within the constraints of that system. Indeed, many such attempts may have completely the opposite effect: of actually intensifying and exacerbating the problem they're supposedly trying to address. Increased marketing spending adding to information overload is just one example.

Overcapacity, product parity, innoflation, over-satisfaction, information overload, marketing endgame, and the intangibles crisis. Of course, each one of these forces affects different industries and companies to different degrees. But they are unavoidable. They are why the old value peak is declining. Today's business obsessions – lower cost production, better, faster innovation, better marketing, 'culture change' – may address the symptoms of this decline. Temporarily. But they are not a cure.

STUCK IN FLATLAND?

This does not mean that seller-centric companies haven't created untold wealth for consumers. Of course they have. Indeed, over the last hundred years or so they've presided over the richest explosion of wealth creation mankind has ever seen. Indeed, it is precisely because they've been so successful in the past that they have begun to reach a point of diminishing returns. Thanks to everything they've done for us in the past, we now have the luxury to sit back and worry about what they're *not* doing.

It's also true, however, that no matter how successful they have been in meeting certain types of need, there are some dimensions of value in my life that they hardly touch – *and will never touch*. Here's a simple parallel. Earlier this century, some teachers taught school kids basic geometry by taking them to flatland: an imaginary two dimensional world where the notion of height – the third dimension – didn't exist. In this two dimensional world there is an infinite range of beasts. Straight lines, squiggly lines, squares, circles, triangles and so on. But you won't ever find a cube, or a sphere. Because that involves leaping to the third dimension.

Seen from the perspective of a rich, three-dimensional world, flatland seems, well, awfully flat. Awfully limited. But flatlanders don't feel this way at all. There's an infinite variety of two dimensional shapes for them to play with. And because flatland extends forever in every direction – north, south, east and west – they're able to continue exploring forever.

At the same time, they simply cannot understand notions like 'sphere' or 'cube', because they've evolved to live in a 2D world and they can't think in 3D terms. Indeed, they even have difficulty understanding 2D notions such as 'square' and 'circle' in the way we understand them: because that involves looking down on them from above. Which flatlanders can never do.

The new bottom line is about making the leap from flatland to 3D richness – to new dimensions of value. The question is, how? To start answering this question we need to look at the other side of the coin of new bottom line value – new bottom line, or personal assets.

Summary

Most modern businesses work according to a 'value from our operations' model. They invest significant amounts of money, skill, energy and time in productive assets – whether it's say, factories, bank branches, pipelines or retail outlets – which they use to create value. They then sell this value to customers, hopefully for a profit.

'Value from our operations' wealth creation is driven by the need to maximize the productivity and efficiency of infrastructure and to maximize the value of its output in the marketplace. These imperatives create a business logic which we call 'the old bottom line'.

Old bottom line firms have been enormously productive, creating the foundation and springboard of all that is to follow. However, the very way in which old bottom liners add value for customers – via their intense focus on 'value from our operations' – also creates certain value 'blindspots': dimensions of consumer value that they either cannot, or do not want to, address.

These 'value gaps' lie in the arenas of: consumer transaction costs; customization to fit personal needs; integration of ingredients to create desired outcomes; the need for buyer-centric information; services where traditional economies of scale fail; authentic emotions; and improving the productivity of personal assets such as time, attention and information.

The value gaps create a distinct new opportunity for value creation: 'value in my life' as opposed to 'value from our operations'.

Old bottom liners' inability to deliver 'value in my life' is not their only problem, however. They also face *systemic* challenges, such as overcapacity, product parity and information overload, which are created by the combined actions of many firms and cannot therefore be addressed by any one firm alone. These systemic problems are serving to undermine old bottom liners' ability to create and realize value.

Precisely because firms' ability to address these issues is limited, the pressures generated by the value gaps and the systemic flaws are mounting inexorably. Both companies and consumers could benefit from a new value breakthrough – a new model of wealth creation. This is the opportunity for a new bottom line.

2 Untapped assets

Think about your own life for a moment. The things in which you find pleasure and fulfilment. The things that worry and concern you. If you look at your life as a business – with certain inputs and outputs – you will quickly see that you invest certain 'personal assets', such as time, money and emotional commitment in doing things that you hope will generate 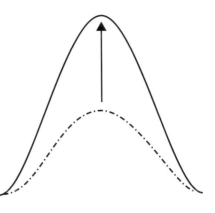 high returns. In other words, you are always looking for the best possible value for money, value for time, return on attention, return on emotional investment, and so on.

But there is no business *that makes it its business* to achieve these things. Many companies may offer you bits and pieces which help you along the way: a rewarding chocolate or film, more convenient shopping, a place to meet with friends. But no one dedicates themselves to helping you make the most of these personal assets, invest them wisely, maximize their productivity or generate maximum returns. Until now.

A NEW OPTIMA

The defining feature of the new bottom line business model is that it organizes itself around such personal assets. While old bottom line businesses organize themselves around corporate productive assets such as factories, shops, offices, infrastructure and so on – and focus on getting the best possible returns from these assets – the job of the new bottom

---

TASKS FOR THIS CHAPTER

1. Examine the nature and importance of the six main personal assets.
2. Explain their crucial importance to emerging business models.

liner is to maximize the value and productivity of personal assets – to generate maximum value in my life.

The OPTIMAL assets

1. Operations
2. Passion
3. Time
4. Information
5. Money
6. Attention
7. ... in my Life

Personal assets come in six main forms: Operations or work, Passion, Time, Information, Money and Attention – or OPTIMA for short. We discuss them in detail below. But for now, let's focus on what makes them special.

First, they have a triple role:

- As an 'input'. We invest time, work, accumulated knowledge, commitment and so on in doing things in order to get the outcomes we desire.
- As 'profit'. We rarely measure the rewards, or outcomes, that we are looking for in purely financial terms alone. When it comes to measuring our personal profitability we instinctively measure it in the currency of core assets. Did it represent 'value for time'? Was it worth the bother, or work? Was it 'emotionally fulfilling'. And yes, of course, did it represent value for money?
- As an 'output', which can be traded on the open market. Companies 'buy' our money with goods and services. They buy our time, work and skills when they employ us to do work for them. They may also buy our attention and our personal information too.

Separately and together these personal assets are the currency of value in my life. But there's something else that makes them special. They are also increasingly valuable: valuable to companies which need them to solve their problems.

Look at any consumer facing company today, and study its obsessions. It wants to make products and services that customers really want – that they'll choose in preference to those of any competitor. For this it needs genuine, superior consumer insight: information from and about that consumer. It wants to go to market efficiently and effectively, which means attracting the attention of its target customers and persuading them of the merits of its offer. As we saw when discussing information overload, winning customers' attention is now a key challenge for every marketer.

It goes without saying that the company desperately needs its customers' money. Less obvious, however, is its equally desperate need to win the battle for a decent share of that customer's time. Because, again and again, how people choose to spend their time determines how they spend their money.

Then, of course, it also desperately wants some form of emotional commitment or bond with that customer: to build brand loyalty, to encourage word-of-mouth recommendation, and so on. What's more, when the company looks inside itself, at its employees, it needs to maximize its access to (and the productivity of) exactly the same set of personal assets. It needs to tap its employees' know-how, creativity, commitment, motivation, etc.

However, it's in the nature of these assets they cannot be owned or controlled by any company. Individuals own and control their own assets, and choose when and where to invest or trade them, on what terms. Naturally, individuals will choose to invest and trade their assets in ways (and with organisations) that generate maximum returns. And precisely because of the old bottom line's systemic crisis, the 'market value' of these assets is soaring.

This is where new bottom line business models emerge: the intersection of personal assets in their role as the key source value in my life, and their role as a 'way out' for companies facing old bottom line value subsidence.

We discuss these new business models in detail in Chapter 3 to 6. But first, to really understand their nature and potential, we need to look closer at the personal assets that drive them.

MY OPTIMAL ASSETS

1. Operations

To achieve the things I want to achieve in my life I have to work at them. In this arena of work, new bottom liners do two main things:

■ improve the productivity of my operations – to reduce the amount of work I have to do to 'make' my life, and to increase the value of that work.
■ improve the value I realize for my work on the open market.

Personal productivity improvements come from two key sources. I might outsource non-core, low-value jobs such as shopping for routine replenishment items or home cleaning, maintenance and decoration. This covers value gaps such as transaction and integration costs, plus 'where economies of scale fail'. I might also retain an organization to help me get more 'bangs for bucks' from the work I retain 'in-house', such as helping me to better plan and organize my personal finances, or working with me to achieve personal goals and objectives such as to get fit or lose weight.

My ability to work is also, of course, a highly tradable asset. I sell my work on the labour market, to earn money – and clearly I want to maximize the value of this asset on the market. We discuss this in more detail in Chapter 11.

I also 'trade' work with companies in connection with their products and services. We often take this for granted. But the fact is, every existing product or service assumes a certain division of labour between supplier and consumer and between seller and buyer. As new technologies, consumer priorities, cost structures or business models emerge, new win-wins can often be found in renegotiating these divisions of labour.

Many companies seek to 'outsource' work to consumers, often in exchange for lower prices. Ikea transformed furniture retailing by passing the work of furniture assembly back to the consumer. On-line banks look to on-line 'self-service' to get consumers to do work such as inputting transactions and updating records free – work that was once undertaken by paid staff.

Likewise, consumers seek to outsource work to companies. Home-delivered groceries and ready meals are obvious examples: consumers pass back a task they once undertook (travelling to and from the shop, assembling the ingredients and cooking the meal) to the supplier.

The ideal is a sort of 'mutual process re-engineering' where both sides adjust their own internal operations and processes to save the other side time, money or hassle. In the case of on-line banking, for example, consumers 'pay' more by doing previously paid work for free. But they also 'get' more, in the form of easy, 24-hour access and far greater flexibility.

For new bottom liners, unleashing new win-wins by such mutual processes of re-engineering is one of the key ways they add value. The bottom line remains very simple, however. While the old bottom liner's over-riding priority is to maximize the productivity of its own operations – its factories, offices, shops and so on – the new bottom liner's job is to help me maximize the productivity of the operations I undertake to make my life. If it succeeds in that task, it has a role to play.

2. Passion

Let's be blunt. If our emotional 'profit and loss account' is negative – if we're really unhappy and unfulfilled – then we don't find life worth living. In the end work, money and just about everything else is all about maximizing our personal emotional bottom line.

We invest emotionally in virtually everything we do. We invest emotionally in relationships that we hope will be rewarding, in hobbies and pastimes, in causes and beliefs, in the work we do. (The 'rational economic man' beloved of twentieth-century economists was always a fiction). One form of new bottom line business addresses emotional added value directly: the passion partner, who we discuss in more detail in Chapter 6.

But our emotions and passions also have a certain 'open market exchange value'. Marketers have long known that there is an emotional dimension to everything; that our emotions play a huge part in our perceptions of value, what we choose to buy, at what price, and so on. It's a fundamental building block of modern marketing theory that brands represent bundles of functional and emotional attributes. That's why marketers are forever trying to appeal to these emotions: because our emotional investment in their brand is extremely valuable to them.

If we invest emotionally in a brand, for example, we are far more likely to become 'loyal'. And overall, loyal customers tend to be more valuable. What's more, if we're truly committed to the brand, we're likely to act as its 'ambassador', spreading the word among friends, family and acquaintances; doing its marketing for it. In fact, there's no stronger recommendation for a brand than a positive reference from a trusted friend. It is far more likely to influence a purchase than an ad campaign.

Old bottom line brands, then, are desperate for such emotional investment. By shifting the goal-posts of trust and value new bottom liners help consumers maximize the returns they can expect from brands for such emotional investment: they force companies to fight much harder for loyalty and affection. They also, by the way, compete with each other (and everyone else) to maximize their own 'share of heart'.

3. Time

If we look back at economic history, value for time arguably comes before value for money. We traded time – via things like barter and divisions of labour – long before money was ever invented. If I could make a good quality pot in less time than you, and you could make some cheese in less time than I, it made sense for us to trade pots for cheese. In fact, we only really invented money to make time trading easy.

As individuals we have three core value-for-time requirements:
- To spend less time doing the things that give me low value for time.
- To invest more time doing the things that give me high value for time
- To improve my time productivity, whether invested in low or high value for time activities.

Time and work go together: work takes time. As we saw in our value gaps discussion, old bottom liners often ignore or neglect value for time – say, in transaction and solution assembly costs – because it doesn't affect their financial profit and loss account. What they're concerned with is turning products and services into cash. For new bottom liners providing improved value for time is key.

Value for time is already having a major impact on traditional markets. Just look at food, where the market is rapidly splitting into two different segments which revolve largely around value-for-time considerations. There is the high value-for-time segment (gourmet cooking as a hobby, eating out at restaurants, food as part of a broader leisure experience) and low value-for-time segment (outsourcing 'chore' cooking to the fast and convenience food providers). The message: increasingly, share of purse follows share of time. For many consumers nowadays, 'value for time' is more important than straightforward price.

Helping me maximize the productivity of my time is a key plank of all three main new bottom line business models: trading agency, solution assembly and passion partnership. The other side of the coin is my willingness to invest my time with you – as an employer, a product or a brand. How much time I have to invest, with what return, is an increasingly important bargaining ticket in buyer/seller relationships. Time, as well as money, is a central currency in value in my life.

4. Information

There are two sides to the coin of information trading. To maximize value in my life I need better information. I need to know which companies and brands are offering me best value, for example, and how to get the best from my dealings with them. That's one of the roles of trading agency.

On the other hand, I am also a source of valuable information. Information (especially finely grained, detailed information about supply and demand) is the invisible black gold of the information age. It lubricates the economy. It's a precious resource in its own right. The fact is, however, if information is the 'oil' of the information age we as individuals own the most valuable oil wells. *We*, as individuals, are where the most valuable information comes from. Only when we volunteer information does it really flow.

As we'll see, consumer ownership and control of information is one of the decisive factors in the shift from an old bottom line economy to a new one. Companies are prepared to pay good money for information from and about consumers: what they want, in what form, at what price, etc. One of the trading agent's main jobs (and to a lesser extent solution assemblers) is to gather up such information, slice and dice it, and pass it on to the right people in the right form. We look at this in detail in Chapter 4.

5. Money

We all seek to maximize the income we generate from the work we do. We all invest our hard-earned money in precious assets: cars, homes, clothes, appliancies, etc. In addition, we want to maximize a) what we get for our money and b) the value of the stuff we buy. (Important assets such as houses and cars have high tradable value in their own right.) We also want to maximize the value of our savings and to minimize the costs of our borrowings. Each one of these different priorities represents a huge business in its own right.

The big difference between the old bottom line and the new is that the old bottom liners' key priority was to maximize the amount of money they got *from* consumers – by successfully closing sales for example. The new bottom liners earn their keep in a very different way: by optimizing the efficiency with I use my precious financial assets (when buying and when saving); by getting the most for my money when sourcing goods and services on the open market, and by maximizing the money they make *for* me (when selling assets such as information, for example). In other words, new bottom liners see my money as an asset to be maximized rather than as a market to be tapped. The better they are at adding value for me in these ways, the more I am prepared to pay them.

6. Attention

Attention is like time. We only have so many waking moments, only so much attention to invest: it's a very scarce and precious asset. Whether or not I invest my attention wisely, and how effective I am at maximizing my return on attention is a critical contributor to my personal bottom line. All three new bottom line business models – trading agency, solution assembly and passion partnership – help me avoid wasting my attention on things that don't deliver high returns, to focus my investment on the things that do. Like value for time, the dynamics of 'return on attention' are transforming today's markets, especially marketing itself (as we'll see). Do I want to bother thinking about your offer, or communicating with you? What return on attention are you offering? (In the case of a lot of advertising, for example, the honest answer is 'zero'.)

Precisely because it is so scarce and so valuable, the market price of consumer attention is rising rapidly. To get a glimpse of its commercial value just look at the billions of Euros spent by advertisers and media owners in the battle for consumer 'eyeballs'. Why? Simply because companies and brands desperately need consumers to pay attention to their brands, offerings and communications if they are successfully to close sales.

New bottom liners transform the market for attention by claiming a share of this value for the owner of the attention, the consumer. We'll see in Chapter 4 how trading agents in particular create new liquid markets that help consumers to capture the market value of their attention. In Chapter 5 we'll also see how solution assemblers draw attention to themselves, away from traditional ingredient providers.

7. in my Life

Value in my life revolves around making the most of each and every one of these OPTIMAL personal assets because they are the currency, or the medium, through which I live my life. Enrich them, and you do me a great favour. Waste or abuse them and you do me harm. These simple facts lie at the heart of what we believe is a looming and far-reaching economic transformation.

When old bottom line businesses make and sell valued products and services, invariably they are valued because they help me make the most of one or more of these OPTIMAL assets. When they fail to add value – as per the value gaps discussed in Chapter 1 – it's because they are wasting, neglecting or abusing these assets. Likewise, the test of the new bottom liner is its ability to make more of these assets *for* and *with* me than any would-be competitor.

In the next chapter we'll begin to answer this question: how and why can new business models do this? But before we do, let's quickly conclude with two crucial observations.

Multi-dimensional exchange

First, recognizing the importance of OPTIMAL assets also involves recognizing the importance of *multi-dimensional exchange*. Traditional firms focus on just one, narrow dimension of exchange: money in exchange for goods and services. Only recently has it begun to dawn on them that they are also effectively trading other assets such as information, time, emotional investment and attention.

Multi-dimensional exchange may be far more complex and much harder to measure. But it's also far richer. It means that we judge the value of a relationship across many criteria, not just one. It demands a far more sophisticated balance between different ways of offering value and different ways of receiving value. One of the things that makes trading agency, solution assembly and passion partnership so powerful is their ability to take full advantage of the richness of such multi-dimensional exchanges of value.

New economies of scope and scale

However, there's something else that makes new bottom liners powerful. Look at Box 2.1. It lists many of the richest and most powerful, influential types of organization to flourish in modern economies. They are united by one common factor. They all trade in one or other OPTIMAL asset.

OPTIMAL asset trading is already an awesomely huge business. Yet, we believe, its true potential has yet to be unleashed. The forms of business we see today – in banking, media, retailing, marketing communications, etc. – are just a pale precursor of what is about to emerge with the new bottom line.

They are flawed and limited in the following ways.

BOX 2.1 THE POWER OF 'THE ORGANIZED CONSUMER'

- What makes financial services such a huge industry? The aggregation of consumer savings.
- What makes retailers so powerful? The aggregation of consumer buying power.
- How do multi-billion dollar media empires make their profits? By aggregating and selling consumer attention, to advertisers.
- How do market research, database marketing and a large swathe of the IT industries earn their keep? By gathering, storing, analyzing and distributing information from and about consumers – another personal asset.
- What makes pressure groups so influential? Their ability to organize and channel people's passions.

- They each focus on just one asset, in isolation (banking on savings, retailers on buying power, media owners on attention). They are therefore unable to generate any 'synergies' between them, either in terms of cost structures or asset deployment.
- They deploy these assets incredibly inefficiently, often extracting just a fraction of their potential value. Just look at the waste in modern advertising and direct marketing, for example.
- They do so in a thoroughly seller-centric old bottom line way, seeking to harvest this value *from* consumers, rather than maximizing its productivity and value *for and with* them.
- For all these reasons, individuals see little reason to increase their investment of personal assets beyond a bare minimum.

In other words, today's personal asset traders are actually stifling these assets' true potential, not unleashing it. Now imagine the power of an organization which gathers and trades a range of these assets, in a combined and integrated way, with my expressed knowledge and permission, on my behalf – so that I have a positive incentive to invest ever more money, information, attention, time, work, and/or passion with it. That organization is the new bottom liner.

Summary

Old bottom line firms generate value from corporate assets such as farms, mines, factories, offices, shops and so on. Their overwhelming priority is to maximize the productivity and value of these assets.

Individuals depend on a different set of core assets to create 'value in my life'. These personal assets include: operations (our energy or work); passion; time, information, money and attention.

To maximize 'value in my life', we need to maximize the productivity and value of these personal assets. That is how new bottom liners earn their keep: by helping individuals generate better value for money, better value for time, better return on personal information, on attention, etc 'in my life'.

Personal assets have more than just personal value, however. They also have a high – and growing – market value. When traditional sellers go to market, they increasingly want more than a simple exchange products or services for customers' money. To succeed, they also need preferential access to customers' time, attention, information, emotional commitment etc. And they are prepared to pay for this access.

Already, many of today's biggest businesses trade in different types of personal asset. The financial services industry aggregates and trades in consumers' aggregated savings; retailers aggregate and trade in consumers' buying power; the media and advertising industries in consumers' attention; market research and database companies in consumer information.

But they often do this inefficiently and are not focused on maximizing the value of these personal assets 'in my life'. This is the special role of the new bottom liner.

The old bottom line 'took off' when breakthrough business models such as Henry Ford's found ways to organize and aggregate industrial assets to create new economies of scale. They unleashed the potential and economic value of *things*.

A new bottom line is poised to take off as new breeds of business find new ways to organize, aggregate and drive personal asset productivity and value. This new bottom line unleashes the true potential and economic value of *people*.

3 The New Bottom Line

Connecting need to opportunity

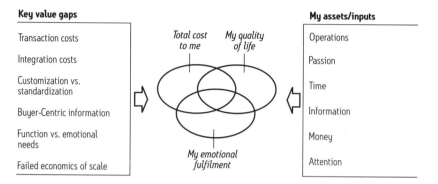

Key value gaps	My assets/inputs
Transaction costs	Operations
Integration costs	Passion
Customization vs. standardization	Time
Buyer-Centric information	Information
Function vs. emotional needs	Money
Failed economics of scale	Attention

In one of his stories about the English detective Sherlock Holmes, Arthur Conan Doyle has Holmes solving the mystery by referring to the dog that didn't bark: the thing that didn't happen, when you would have expected it to. With the new bottom line we face a similar mystery. Here, on the one hand, we have a range of huge value gaps – unmet needs which, you would have thought, present a huge new market opportunity.

On the other hand, we also have a wide range of increasingly important, untapped assets and sources of value. What's more, they both revolve around the same entity – 'the consumer'. So they come together naturally.

Table 3.1 outlines some of the new forms of value that emerge when this 'coming together' happens. Our suggestion: the services in the left-hand column naturally come together in a new bottom line function which we call trading agency. Those in the middle column come together to create solution assembly, and those on the right-hand side come together to create passion partnership. Some of these individual services are self-

---

TASKS FOR THIS CHAPTER

1. Explain why the new bottom line didn't happen earlier.
2. Clarify key differences between new and old business models.

explanatory, others less so. We'll discuss them all over the next three chapters, where we look at these functions in more detail.

First, however, we need to answer an obvious question. If there is such demand for these services, why haven't market forces already reacted to fill the gap? Why haven't hundreds of 'consumer-focused' organizations already rushed to offer these services as extra layers of value, in addition

Table 3.1 New Forms of Value from New Types of Business

Trading agency	Solution assembly	Passion partnership
Buyer-centric information (e.g., comprehensive, impartial price/product comparisons)	Address coordination/ integration challenges	Authenticity/ shared interest
Expertise of products, suppliers etc.	Expertise of products, suppliers etc.	Passion-related expertise
Search/navigation services	Reduce time spent achieving objectives	Passion-related community
New negotiation/ market mechanisms	Reduce money spent achieving objectives	Passion-related information
Provide consumers with voice, as well as choice	Reduce work needed to achieve objectives	Passion-related activities/ events
Aggregation services (e.g., buying power)	Provide additional products needed to achieve objective	Provide additional products
Information, attention and other trading services	Provide additional information needed to achieve objective	Passion-related services
Fulfilment services	Provide additional services needed to achieve objective	

to their existing offerings? Why do we need new business models to do so? And what's so different about these new business models?

We've begun to answer this question already. The seven value gaps only emerged because they represent forms of value which old bottom liners cannot or do not want to address. Likewise, OPTIMAL personal assets are neglected and underdeveloped because they are not central to the old bottom liners, who naturally organize themselves around maximizing the productivity and value of their own assets, not those of a third party.

Result: both the market and the key means of addressing it remain overlooked. Asking an old bottom line organization to prioritize new bottom line services is a bit like asking a fish to explore the land and expecting it to start breathing air along the way. The fish may be supremely adapted to its particular environment, but this very strength also brings limitations:

- Operational limitations which mean there are some things it's not built to do;
- Mindset limitations which mean there are some things it's not really interested in doing.

To see the full scale of the new bottom line challenge, we need to explore these limitations a little further.

OLD VERSUS NEW

The limitations of the old bottom line business model are a product of its enormous strengths. The following is one way of summing up its core characteristics:

1 The old bottom liner is organized around maximizing the efficiency and productivity of core industrial assets – mainly various forms of infrastructure. **Value from our operations** in other words. The new bottom liner is organized around maximizing the efficiency and productivity of personal assets such as time, information and attention. **Value in my** life is its watchword.

2 The old bottom liner is focused on achieving **economies of scale** in its operations to bring down unit costs. It tries to sell more of the same thing to as many different people as possible. The new bottom liner seeks **economies of scope**. It tries to funnel as many different transactions as possible through the same relationship.

3 The old bottom liner is funded by investments from **financial investors** who own the company. Individuals invest key personal assets in a relationship with the new bottom liner, and look for a return on this investment. With the new bottom line **'the consumer' is also 'an investor'**.

4 The old bottom liner draws back from doing things where it cannot unleash economies of scale, thereby creating very specific divisions of labour between producer and customer. The new bottom liner negotiates new and different **divisions of labour** with consumers: consumers may work harder within this relationship, inputting more time and effort, but at the same time they outsource more.

5 The old bottom liner brings these different aspects together in a powerful set of **win-wins** which revolve around **making more, better stuff (products and services) at lower cost**. The new bottom liner's win-wins are driven by **better, cheaper matching and connecting**.

Table 3.2 New and Old Bottom Liners: Systemic Differences

Attribute	Old bottom line	New bottom line
Core assets	Industrial: value from our operations	Personal: information, time, attention,etc.
Wealth creation	Economies of scale	Economies of scope
Divisions of labour driven by needs of . . .	Vendor efficient supply	Customer efficient demand
Win-win	Better, cheaper making	Better, cheaper matching and connectng
Main investor	Financier	Customer

Let's look at the old bottom line characteristics in a little more detail. The old bottom line is a product of an industrial age which created untold amounts of new wealth via new ways of making things – mass production, distribution and advertising. Old bottom line firms are effectively defined by the assets that make this possible. The car company is defined by its car factories; the airline by its planes and landing slots; the retailer by its stores; the bank by its branches, and so on.

Such companies naturally focus on the productivity of these core assets, and over the years a whole series of technological revolutions – from the first non-animal energy such as water mills and steam power through oil and electricity, via internal combustion and jet engines, the telegraph and telephone, television and the computer, and so on – has helped them do so. Each new wave of technology has allowed firms to create ever more value from their operations, via ever higher quality, new, better and cheaper products and services.

To maximize the value they create from their operations, old bottom liners have had to do other things as well. None of their wealth creation could happen without sometimes huge up-front investments of capital from financial investors, for example. As firms have raised capital from these investors, they became driven by the need to repay and reward these *capital*-ists: shareholders. When push comes to shove they make their money *from* their customers, and *for* their investors – a key influence on their mindset.

To do so, however, firms have had to draw a clear line between activities that help them improve the productivity and profitability of their operations, and activities which do not. Anything that undermines operational productivity is bad – *even if it improves the productivity of the customers' operations.*

Grocery home shopping provides a classic example. Retailers have spent decades trying to improve the productivity of their core assets – their stores – focusing on key metrics such as sales per square foot, footfall and basket size. It has not entered their heads to do anything that might encourage consumers *not* to visit their stores.

That is why Internet home shopping represents such a challenge. When consumers order a basket of groceries on-line, *not* only do they *not* go into the store (so that they are not influenced by a whole battery of carefully crafted merchandise and promotional tools designed to get them to spend more), they also hand over some extremely expensive activities to the retailer. Activities such as picking the items off the shelf and delivering them to the door.

Worse, consumers are not prepared to stump up the full cash costs of someone undertaking these tasks for them. So grocery home shopping – a service that addresses the consumer's transaction costs, our value gap number one – goes against every traditional grain of traditional retailing; potentially undermining the viability of the retailer's core asset, while adding more cost than direct revenue. Not surprisingly, most retailers have made a complete hash of it.

The few retailers (such as Tesco) that have been successful in grocery home shopping anticipate many of the key themes of this book. First, Tesco has been prepared to invent a new business model to make it work, with new divisions of labour, new cost structures and new revenue streams.

The delivery fee it charges helps to cover some of the extra costs it incurs, but not all. By reducing customers' transaction costs however, it unleashes a different source of value: customers spend far more at Tesco than before, and they are far more loyal. In other words, by addressing its customers 'operational productivity' rather than just its own, it wins competitive edge.

Second, it has worked extremely hard to find a 'migration path' to this new business model – one which uses its existing assets (its stores) to new purposes rather than investing huge sums up front in new infrastructure. Such migration paths – and the ability to use old assets and skills for new purposes – are the main theme of Chapters 8 to 12.

Finally, the nature of the system's win-wins are crucially important. The old bottom liners invests in making 'New! Improved!' products and services, and in stimulating demand via marketing. Because it is adding new value via its products and services, consumers flock out to buy them and become 'brand loyal', thereby generating not only pay-back today, but relatively secure revenues tomorrow. This provides the firm with the incentive and confidence to invest yet more money and effort in new productive infrastructure with even greater economies of scale and lower unit costs, leading to even cheaper, better, new products, to repeat the circle over and over again.

This win-win system is a hugely powerful magnetic force. And it pays – both companies and customers – to keep working within the system, and not to challenge or undermine it. Yet, as we saw in Chapter 2, these win-wins are subsiding while the new bottom line offers powerful new ones elsewhere.

CORPORATE NARCISSISM

Old bottom line operations, then, form a sort of hermetically sealed system, and considerations that reach beyond or across it – like our value gaps and OPTIMAL assets – tend to compromise its efficient working, thereby creating less value, not more. The old bottom line's marketing mindset is an integral part of that system.

1 The purpose of finding out what customers want and need is to help firms concentrate on making stuff that's going to sell, rather than wasting efforts and resources making stuff that's not going to sell.

2 Via the device of marketing communications marketers then help complete the circle by stimulating demand for the products in question.

Like a Chinese puzzle, in other words, the beauty of this system is that each part helps lock the others snugly into place. Operational necessities create a certain mindset, and this mindset in turn helps focus attention on operational necessities. Hence, the knee-jerk marketing reaction that more, better marketing is the answer to every problem. With their customer-oriented rhetoric marketers like to believe they provide an antidote to its inherent producer-centric tendencies.

But from the perspective of the new bottom line, such seller-centric marketing is likely to be part of the problem, not the solution.

1 As we've seen, when it comes to the product, marketers tend to focus only on those consumer needs which relate to what they are trying to sell.

2 When it comes to taking this product to market, all pretence at meeting the consumer's needs go out of the window. When in go-to-market mode, the marketer is firmly focused on meeting the needs of the seller, not those of the buyer. The real purpose of marketing communications, for example, is not to provide useful information to consumers, but to provide consumers with information that's useful to producers; information that will influence potential buyers to buy their brands.

The same goes for consumer understanding. When sellers go to market, they deploy consumer understanding *for the purposes of control* – they want to understand which buttons to press and which triggers to pull in order to get consumers to do what they want them to do. Thus, the purpose of building a strong brand is not to get the company's actions orbiting the consumer, but to get consumers' thoughts and actions orbiting the company – to get them to be 'loyal' to the brand. To this degree, seller-centric branding is simply an extension of the industrial age command and control mindset, applied beyond the corporation's formal corporate boundaries into the marketplace; into other people's minds and actions.

We can see the same corporate narcissism in familiar terms such as 'value for money' and 'quality'. All these terms revolve around 'what we make', not value in my life. Value for money relates to the seller's price not the buyer's cost (this is the source of one of our key value gaps). Quality

Figure 3.1 A New Focus of Value

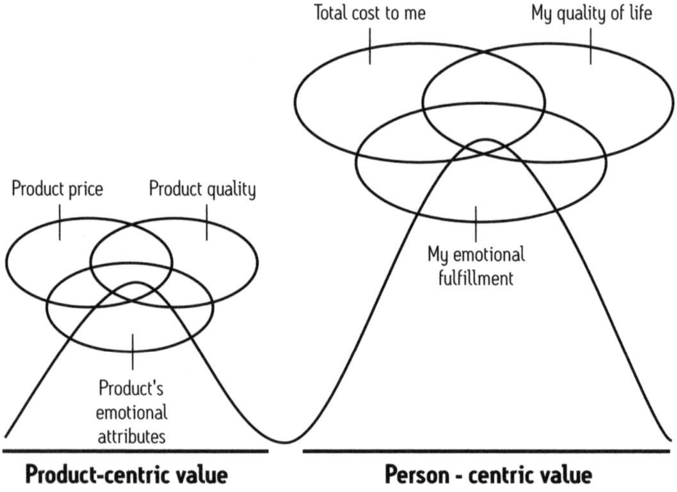

Product-centric value   Person - centric value

relates to the attributes and qualities of the seller's product, not the quality of my life. Emotional added values relate to the emotional associations triggered by the seller's brand, not my personal emotional rewards or satisfaction. Each one of these core marketing notions are actually product- and not 'consumer'-centric.

In contrast, as Figure 3.1 shows, the three new bottom line business models shift the focus entirely: trading agency focuses on my total costs, solution assembly on my personal productivity and better use of time (quality of life), and passion partnership on personal emotional fulfilment.

For all these reasons the new bottom line simply doesn't fit the old bottom line agenda. That's why addressing the new bottom line isn't just a matter of incremental change. For deep systemic operational and mindset reasons, the new bottom line represents a break from the past. There is a deep ravine between these two very different value peaks.

BOX 3.1 THE IDEOLOGY OF MARKETING

In our experience, the greatest resistance – and the greatest degree of incomprehension – to the new bottom line comes from those ostensibly most committed to the theory and practice of 'customer-focus': marketers. Why is this? Is it because marketers are somehow dishonest, incompetent or driven by the wrong motivations? Of course not. It's because of the way their ideology works.

Ideologies work by rendering any possible alternatives invisible, impossible and/or undesirable. Mediaeval cosmology before Copernicus and Galileo provides a good example.

1. *Invisibility.* The pre-Copernican theory accorded with what people saw in their everyday lives. They literally could not see any evidence of the earth travelling around the sun. What they saw – right there, before their very eyes – was the sun travelling around the earth. Why should they believe the opposite of what their eyes tell them?

Likewise, say marketing traditionalists, what we see around us is the eternal truth of marketing at work: Look at any and every successful brand, and it's as clear as daylight that success comes from finding out what consumers want and giving it to them. You can see the evidence right there, before your very eyes. What possible alternative is there: *not* finding out what consumers want, and *not* meeting their needs? Yet, as we've seen the very notion of 'the consumer' is an expression of a seller-centric worldview.

2. *Impossibility*. When Copernicus proposed his alternative theory his set-up seemed impossible. The Church had already provided a coherent explanation for our seeing the sun during the day and the stars at night. The heavens were a 'firmament', which was a solid vault extended above the earth, and heavenly bodies such as stars were lights hung by God from this firmament. As St Philastrius explained, God brings the stars out each night from his treasure-house, while the sun and the planets are 'windows of heaven' opened and shut by angels appointed for that purpose. (Later, as the theory developed, the movement of various planetary bodies was explained in terms of successive transparent spheres rotated by angels specially appointed for this task.)

When Copernicus suggested that the sun was the real centre of the universe, his theory raised more intractable questions than it seemed to answer. If the stars are not lights hung out by God, then what are they, who moves them, and how? If the firmament is not a solid vault, then what is it? If the earth moves around the sun, what force is making the earth move? And why can't we feel or see that movement? In the absence of clear, incontrovertible answers to these questions, it was Copernicus's theory, not that of the Church that seemed impossible and ridiculous.

Likewise, to a marketer brought up with the assumption that good marketing is about helping sellers to sell, the mere suggestion that it should perhaps focus on helping buyers to buy, seems absurd. If the angels are not moving the stars at night, then what is moving them? If we focus on helping buyers to buy, how on earth are companies to sell efficiently, effectively and profitably?

3. *Undesirability*. Meanwhile, there were vested interests and deeply held convictions which made Copernicus's theory undesirable to the powers that be. His theory challenged the authority of the Church, as he was well aware.

That's why he kept his opinions to himself for thirty years, waiting until he was close to death before publishing – and choosing to publish in Poland rather than in Rome (where he had worked). It also raised unsettling questions about religious truth. As one Father Lecazre worried on seeing the evidence for the Copernican theory 'If the earth is a planet, and only one among several planets ... [then] how can their inhabitants be descended from Adam? How can they trace their origins back to Noah's ark? How can they have been redeemed by the Saviour?'

Likewise, the business models we outline in this book may threaten some companies with loss of control, authority and perhaps even prosperity – if they fail to adjust. To them, the idea of corporations orbiting the consumer at the consumer's convenience doesn't only seem impractical, it is positively undesirable.

Nevertheless, that's where we're headed.

BEYOND SELLING

The new bottom line represents the beginnings of a different *system*: Like the old system, all the different parts naturally 'fit' together. If the old bottom liner is a fish breathing water, the new bottom liner is land-based mammal breathing air. The beast works to a different logic. We saw some of the key differences in Table 3.2 above:

■ From an industrial centre of gravity to a personal centre of gravity.
■ From economies of scale and low unit costs to economies of scope and high added value.
■ New win-wins: from better, cheaper making to better, cheaper matching and connecting.
■ From the unquestioned primacy of the financial investor to the consumer as investor

Now let's look at some of these aspects in a little more detail. Under the new bottom line the *central unit of wealth creation and goals* shifts from the firm to the person. It's as if the individual has become the corporation, so all efforts are now focused on maximizing his personal productivity and profitability.

This isn't just an empty metaphor. It's real. As individuals we do all the things that firms do. We source inputs, process them to create additional value, and seek to realize value in the marketplace. We seek to maximize the efficiency of the processes we undertake along the way and to maximize the final benefits we gain.

As individuals, therefore, we are all 'mini-corporates'. Like corporates, we buy products and services; we hire and fire staff; we plan and forecast; we set priorities and goals; allocate scarce resource; manage cash flows; make savings and investments; work; invest in skills; do financial planning and management accounting; build relationships with suppliers; coordinate activities; face logistical challenges; and so on. Indeed one way of looking at the new bottom line is that its new business models seize upon all the tools, techniques and professionalism developed over a century of corporate business – including all the functional specialisms such as accounting, marketing and human resources – and apply them to 'my life': to help me boost my personal productivity and profitability.

As we've seen, old bottom liners make their money by accumulating, aggregating and tapping the potential of corporate, industrial assets such as plant, machinery and infrastructure. New bottom liners, on the other hand, accumulate, aggregate and tap the potential of *personal* OPTIMAL assets. Of course, new bottom liners need plant, machinery and infrastructure. But these are important only in so far as they help to maximize the potential of the core asset – the customer relationship – just as for old bottom liners consumers' money, time and attention is important to realizing the value generated by their operations. The relationship between the two is simply inverted.

The old bottom liners' relationship with me is primarily as a customer for their products or services. The new bottom liners see me much more as an investor – investing my assets in a relationship with them. (Or, perhaps, in the case of a passion partner, a member, supporter, fan, or believer.) It follows that for the new bottom liner, provding a decent return to these personal investors is paramount. This doesn't mean new bottom liners cannot return profits to traditional shareholders. After all, the fact that the old bottom liner serves his shareholder investor doesn't stop him delivering value to customers. The one is merely a means of achieving the other.

Some of the other main differences outlined in table 3.3 include:

■ *Raison d'Être* From maximizing the value of, and return on, corporate assets to doing the same for my personal assets.
■ *Value focus* From value 'from our operations' to value in my life; from corporate productivity to personal productivity.

Table 3.3 New and Old Bottom Liners: More Differences

Characteristic	Old bottom line	New bottom line
Central unit of wealth creation	The company	The individual
Goal	Corporate profitability	Personal profitability
Personal profitability	'From our operations'	'In my life'
Raison d'etre	Maximise value of, and return on, corporate assets	Maximize value of, and return on, personal assets
Operating focus	Corporate productivity	Personal productivity
Exchange	One dimensional: money for goods	Multi dimensional: money, information, attention etc.
Mode	Make. Then sell.	Sense and respond
Measures	Financial	Personal: e.g. value for time

- *Mode* The old bottom line goes beyond making, selling and consuming to helping me make value in my life. The alignment is not so much of 'product' to specific consumption 'need' but of the firm's total capabilities to the needs of 'my operations'.
- *Mindset* This means moving beyond producer push and command and control, to 'consumer pull' and 'sense and respond'.
- *Type of exchange* From the one dimensional exchange of money for goods or services to multi-dimensional 'trading' in many assets such as money, time, information and attention.
- *Measures* Not just financial, but personal.

A NEW BUSINESS MODEL

So here we get to the nub of it. We are faced with a huge, untapped opportunity to create new dimensions of wealth and value. Yet there is a deep gulf between the sort of organization needed to unleash these opportunities and those that currently exist. The new and old bottom lines represent different wealth creating systems; different business models. And like jumping half-way across a river, a half-way house between these two very different value peaks will probably result in the worst of both worlds, not a happy compromise. This raises three questions:

- How, then, do we get from one value peak to another?
- What are the connections/overlaps between the two systems; how do the two business models relate to each other?
- How, exactly, do the new models earn their keep?

Chapters 8 and onwards address the migration issue. For now, let's outline an answer to questions two and three.

How new bottom liners earn their keep

1. By creating new revenue streams from additional services which customers are prepared to pay for
2. By subsuming old bottom line value into their offerings
3. By tapping, organizing and monetizing personal assets such as information
4. By driving new efficiencies and creating new win-wins
5. By cannibilizing the revenue streams of old bottom line players which fail to add enough new bottom line value
6. By integrating all the above

1. By *creating* new revenue streams. The new bottom liner offers new dimensions of value, for which people are prepared to pay more. It creates *new revenue streams from new services* (such as those listed in Table 3.1) which consumers are prepared to pay for. Sometimes consumers pay in straight cash. Often, however, they pay by handing over valuable assets such as information and attention, which the new bottom liner can then monetize. Usually 'payment' comes in the form of a combination of the two.

To this degree, new bottom liners represent a new layer of economic activity, just as industrial production represented a new layer on top of agriculture.

2. By *subsuming* old bottom line value. The new bottom liner does not replace traditional products and services, he incorporates them into a

bigger, broader offering. When a trading agent helps its clients source items on the marketplace, it effectively incorporates these products and services into its offering – just as retailers incorporate manufacturers' brands into their overall offerings today.

Likewise, an electrical retailer might move towards home maintenance solution assembly by supplying electrical goods *plus* breakdown insurance, preventative maintenance and emergency repairs. Somebody still has to make the electrical goods and underwrite the insurance, however.

This is one way in which old and new bottom lines connect and relate. New bottom liners have a habit of 'ingredient-izing' old bottom liners' offers (and, sometimes, brands). In turn, many traditional suppliers of these ingredient products and services may see new bottom liners as 'just another distribution channel'.

3. By *monetizing* personal assets. The new bottom liner unleashes the full economic potential of personal assets such as information and attention, and uses them to generate new win-wins. For example, it involves consumers in the process of marketing by unleashing a flow of information *from* consumers about what they want and when. We return to this in detail in Chapter 4.

4. By driving new *efficiencies* and creating new win-wins. We've already seen how, nowadays, the costs of going to market – matching and connecting costs – account for around half of all economic activity, and that these go-to-market costs are growing inexorably compared with the costs of actually making the stuff that's being sold. New bottom liners add economic value by removing this bottleneck. They use their access to personal assets such as information and attention to revolutionize the whole matching and connecting process, in two ways. They:

■ Enrich its content, so that a greater proportion of total consumer needs are met far more accurately and sensitively.
■ Slash its overall costs, by bringing buyer and seller together more efficiently

The old bottom line's win-wins revolve around producers' ability to supply products and services better and cheaper. Old bottom liners organize more *efficient supply*. The new bottom line's win-wins revolve around better, cheaper matching and connecting. New bottom liners organize more *efficient demand*.

This creates another crucial connection between old bottom line and new: the effects of the new bottom liner reach back into the supply base by revolutionizing traditional companies' go-to-market practices and strategies *in a way which potentially benefits all parties*.

5. By *cannibalizing* old bottom line revenue streams (in some circumstances). For instance, instead of complementing old bottom line business models, they create a better, richer, cheaper substitute – and 'steal' its revenue streams. At present, for example, advertisers pay vast sums of money to media owners to deliver consumer 'eyeballs' to their messages. They also pay vast sums of money to market researchers to ascertain consumers trends. By connecting want and need – and buyer and seller – more efficiently, trading agents and solution assemblers stand to win a significant share of such spends.

6. By *integrating* all the above. New bottom liners integrate all these different approaches into one seamless, easy to understand and use service. Just one of the above, alone, is probably not enough to create a viable business. It's only when they're all brought together, combining a range of different revenue streams into a coherent whole, that a new value peak begins to emerge. In doing so, it creates a new centre of gravity.

A NEW SYSTEM OF WEALTH CREATION

Tectonic shifts like the new bottom line don't happen often but we have seen one before: the shift from an agricultural age to an industrial age. The rise of industry made manufacturing, as opposed to agriculture, the new centre of economic gravity. This was true operationally: how people worked, what they made and where. Everything was reorganized and reconfigured around 'the factory' rather than 'the farm'. This new centre of gravity also changed relationships between people. It needed employers and employees rather than serfs and landlords. It required new institutions such as the limited liability company. It even reconfigured the landscape, changing its geography via mass population movements and urbanization.

The new subsumes the old

The change to industry also prompted people to think differently. Before the industrial revolution, wealth creation was equated with 'the land'. People of such a mindset simply couldn't see how machines, factories and trade could ever become the new centre of gravity. After all, doesn't everyone have to eat? And isn't eating the fundamental of survival?

Of course, we still had to eat. When we moved from an agricultural society to an industrial one, agriculture didn't disappear. We used the old (agriculture) as the foundation and springboard of the new (industry). In fact, as we industrialized, agriculture became *even more important* because now 'the farm' had to feed not only itself but the towns too. Even as agriculture lost its *relative* position as the centre of economic gravity, its *absolute* importance grew. Farming was industrialized.

Likewise, with traditional products and services. The new bottom line may become the new centre of gravity, but, if anything, this shift will create even more demand for an ever more dazzling array of new products and services. Yet in the process, the making and selling of products and services will be reconfigured around the requirements of the new bottom line.

It's also true that elements of the new can always be found nestling among the old, in some prototype form or other. People had always done manufacturing of pots, harnesses, ploughs, weapons and so on. But this manufacturing orbited the needs of the farm – to make it more productive – and it was organised in a farm-like way, using craft methods. What we didn't have was an *economic system* built around mass manufacturing. Likewise, the demand for 'value in my life' has always existed. But it has been addressed in such a way that it orbits the old bottom line – 'consumer-focused' marketing that translates consumer needs into demand that feeds factories with sales, and makes them more productive. And it is organized in an industrial, not a personal way.

Organization is crucial

Looking back at some accounts of the industrial revolution, it's very easy to believe it was driven by new technologies like the steam engine, the railroad and electricity. Likewise, looking at today's economic changes, it's very easy to believe they're driven by technology too: the Internet, satellite communications, fibre-optic cable, and so on.

Yes, these are a crucial enabler of many new bottom line business models. Even so, they are an enabler and nothing more. A particular technology may be a *necessary* pre-requisite for a particular economic revolution. But it's never the whole explanation. *Without new attitudes and institutions, organizational structures and relationships, new technologies hardly ever flower.*

Take the motor car. The core technologies of the motor car – internal combustion, the pneumatic tyre, etc. – were around for decades before the car really reached critical mass to change society. The breakthrough didn't come from the technologies themselves. The breakthrough came from a change *in the way production was organized.*

As long as people continued to produce motor cars in the same way as they had produced everything else – in a one-off, bespoke, craft fashion – cars remained extremely expensive to make and repair. They were stuck in a niche as a plaything of the very rich. It was only when Henry Ford introduced standardized, interchangeable parts and mass production that the new system took off.

The new technologies needed his system for their real potential to be realized. Likewise, new information technologies need new organizational structures and relationships for their potential to be realized: those of the new bottom line.

Having a changed mindset is not enough either. As we've seen, the mindset change needed for the new bottom line reaches further and deeper than appears at first sight. It takes us beyond 'consumer focus', beyond selling and marketing. Even so, a new 'ideology' by itself won't deliver. Before the industrial revolution, there were many entrepreneurial, profit-focused farmers trying to transform farming. But they weren't the ones to create a new industrial system. Likewise, today, there are many customer-focused producers. But they haven't managed to address their system's value gaps.

Technologies and mindsets – a vision of the opportunity – are essential ingredients of chemical reaction in economics. But a new way of organizing production is the catalyst that sets them off. That's our task in the next three chapters: to outline the three main catalysts, each of which addresses a key dimension of the new bottom line.

Summary

The big question is this: how to address the value gaps discussed in Chapter 1 in such a way that the value of individuals' personal assets is maximized – in a commercially viable way.

Three new business models are emerging to tackle this challenge:

- Trading agents, which help me source the inputs I need to create value in my life, and to conduct other exchanges (e.g. of information and attention) with my personal trading partners.
- Solution assemblers, which help me maximize the efficiency and productivity of the personal operations I need to undertake in order to make value in my life – things like running my home and organizing my finances.
- Passion partners, which help me maximize my personal 'profitability' – the 'outputs' of my life such as achieving personal and emotional goals.

Old bottom line businesses focus on *consumers* as buyers of the value they create 'in our operations'. Ultimately, old bottom line marketing rhetoric about 'consumer focus' is seller-centric: it focuses on a consumer as a potential unit of demand for what the seller is trying to sell.

In contrast, new bottom liners relate to individuals as *producers* of 'value in my life' and as investors of personal assets – *investors* expecting a return on their investment. They represent a different type of business with different goals, imperatives, cost structures and revenue streams.

New bottom liners earn they keep in a number of ways. These include:

- Payments from individuals for added value services

- Using new information and communication technologies to reduce the costs of integrating and coordinating activities in my life, interactions between buyers and sellers, and between different ingredient suppliers.
- Generating new economies of scale around individuals and their localities rather than around 'our operations'
- Monetizing the value of personal assets such as information and attention, for and on behalf of individuals.
- Using higher levels of trust, new technologies and detailed information about demand to drive down both individuals and suppliers' matching and connecting costs.

The new bottom line is the product of a collision of a range of deep 'tectonic' forces. These include mounting pressure to address neglected value gaps, the need to transcend intractable systemic problems, the quest to maximize the productivity and value of personal assets (for both individuals and companies), and the emergence of new information and communication technologies which facilitate all the above.

The leap from 'value from our operations' to 'value in my life' is rather akin to the leap from agriculture to industry. Agriculture provided the foundation and springboard for industry. But at the same time, industry created new and different forms of value, via new and different forms of organization.

New bottom line business models will act as a similar *catalyst for change* within our current industrial wealth creating system.

4 Trading agency

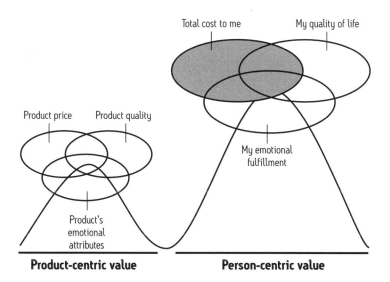

Total cost to me

My quality of life

Product price

Product quality

My emotional
fulfillment

Product's
emotional
attributes

Product-centric value

Person-centric value

Every self-respecting company has its own purchasing and sales departments – staffed by experts who are focused on getting best value and who pursue this goal in a dedicated, organized, professional manner.

As consumers, however, we go to market as isolated, amateur, individuals. We undertake all the same basic tasks as companies. We gather information about what's on offer, make comparisons and trade-offs, enter negotiations, close transactions, ensure fulfilment and so on. But we do so without any organized, expert, professional assistance and as a result, we often don't do these things half as well as we could.

Marketing departments help companies go to market to get best value from the market place. Trading agents are the marketing department's mirror image 'in my life'. Instead of helping sellers sell, they help buyers

---

TASKS FOR THIS CHAPTER

1. Explain the nature of trading agency, and ...
2. ... why it is potentially so powerful.

buy, to access and realize best value in the marketplace. In doing so, they have the potential to transform byer/seller relationships acrosss *all* consumer-facing industries.

The motif for this chapter (above) shows how trading agency fits within the new bottom line. Broadly speaking, trading agents add value in my life by helping me source better, richer life inputs at lower cost. Solution assemblers, on the other hand, focus on my internal operations and personal productivity – how efficiently and effectively I use these inputs to run core operations such as running a home or owning a car. Passion partners focus more on my personal output – my emotional bottom line. (As the chart suggests, in reality all three tend to overlap, but we'll keep that for later.)

The trading agent's closest parallel within the traditional marketing mix is 'product price' – except that with trading agency the real remit is much broader. Trading agents may or may not help me reduce the actual price of the things I buy. That depends on my particular priorities and market circumstances. What they must do, however, is one or both of the following:

1 Help me source better and richer: to find exactly what I need; to fit my needs and wants better than I could do alone.

2 Help me reduce my total go-to-market costs: not only 'product price', but the time, money, hassle, etc., that I have to invest in the whole process of going to market.

THE CONSUMER'S GO-TO-MARKET PROBLEM

As consumers we all face the same basic set of go-to-market challenges. Table 4.1 summarizes some of them. The way markets currently work, we face significant hurdles with each. Searching, for example, can be a time-consuming, expensive process especially if the market is unfamiliar to us and we lack specialist expertise. So, often, we do not search as thoroughly as we could to find the best deal or the most appropriate product.

Sifting can be hard work too, especially if the market is complex and requires specialist expertise. How can you make informed comparisons if

---

Table 4.1 The Consumer's Go-to-Market Challenge

Search
- Find out what is available
- Ascertain terms & conditions (price, service, delivery etc)
- Identify special offers and deals etc.

Sift
- Relate answers to how this fits my needs/wants
- Identify trade-offs between alternatives

Negotiate
- Make enquiries, ask 'what if' questions etc
- Bargain, make counter-offers etc

Transact
- Close deal, sign contract etc
- Make payment
- Ensure delivery etc

---

you don't know the ins and outs of the category? How can you make informed judgements about value if you are not aware of underlying cost structures or margins? Often, the sheer hassle of truly understanding what's on offer (think of small print and insurance contracts) means we end up making less-than-perfect, short-cut decisions.

Negotiation represents yet another hurdle. Many consumer markets work on a simple take it or leave it basis. The seller sets the price, and the consumer simply chooses whether to accept that price or not. Where negotiations are entered into – such as in car show rooms – many consumers find the whole process extremely stressful because they lack confidence, real bargaining power, or they don't really have the necessary information or expertise to negotiate effectively.

Transactions can represent another important hurdle. I may know there's a much better offer on the other side of town, but the hassle of getting there means I opt for a worse deal anyway: wherever transaction costs are high, 'perfect' decisions are distorted.

As isolated, amateur individuals, consumers face these problems alone: sellers rarely provide much help. Indeed often, they make these problems worse. The win-win side of branding is that brands represent easily identifiable, beacons of unique, trustable value. They help consumers streamline the process of search and choice, and reduce risk. But as we saw in Chapter 1, many of the seven deadly sins of the industrial age are working to undermine such win-wins.

Product parity means that instead of building brands to signpost genuine product and services differences, many marketers now turn to 'branding' as means of hiding underlying sameness. Innoflation means that far from being a boon, choice is becoming a hasslesome chore. Besides, while the mantra 'find out what your customer wants and give it to them' may apply to *what* companies are trying to sell, it doesn't apply to how they take their wares to market. When the marketer goes to market, his job is to help his employer – the seller – to sell better, not to help the buyer buy better.

Marketing Practices that Add to Consumer's Go-to-market Problems

- 'Smoke and mirrors' branding to justify excessive price premiums
- Building brands to hide underlying sameness, rather than articulate genuine difference
- Advertising as partial, biased seller-centric information
- Advertising overload
- Inertia selling
- Taking advantage of consumer ignorance (price, quality, appropriateness)
- Channel strategies designed to restrict choice and/or competition

Thus, for many companies the real purpose of 'branding' is not to deliver superior value to the customer but to 'justify' a price premium – to charge more. And this is why they deploy branding techniques such as special imagery, associations, emotional cues, etc. Likewise, the purpose of a marketing communication such as an advertisement is not to help the buyer make the best possible choice, but to influence him to buy that particular seller's product. Seller-centric marketing information, in other words, is inherently partial and biased.

Meanwhile, information overload means that consumers are bombarded ever harder with ever more such partial and biased information, which makes the whole sifting process even more arduous and complex.

And there's more. Many companies positively rely on customer inertia (high transaction costs again) to get away with offering low value. How many times do people say 'It's too much hassle to make a change'?

Others positively rely on 'information asymmetries' between seller and buyer to get away with selling low-value items or charging excessive prices. Just look at the pension and mortgage mis-selling scandals in the UK. Yet others rely on stranglehold control of distribution channels to make 'shopping around' more difficult, and to make sure they keep full control over what information is made available, to which consumers, when. Look at the history of car selling in Europe. The result is that time and again 'better marketing' and long-established selling practices may be part of the problem for the consumer, not the solution.

HOW TRADING AGENTS HELP

Trading agency is a new type of business that addresses individuals' needs along a new dimension: not their needs as *consumers* of specific products and services, but their needs as buyers; their *go-to-market needs*. Before looking in detail at what trading agents do, let's put their role in perspective. Trading agents mark the beginning of an era buyer-centric commerce. They upset the status quo in three crucial ways.

- **Technically**, they reverse the flow of information at the heart of the marketing process.
- **Politically**, they leverage the crucial bottleneck resources in modern marketing – consumer information and attention, to add value for the owner of this resource: the consumer.
- **Structurally**, they look at and organize markets according to the point of view of the buyer, rather than the seller.

Let's look at these three key characteristics in a little more detail. Marketing, as we know, has always been a 'top down' activity. Information has flowed just one way – from seller to buyer – as sellers send 'here we are, this is what we have to offer' messages to buyers via media such as the press, television and direct mail. Trading agents enable consumers to reverse the flow of information by sending, 'Here I am, this is what I want' messages to sellers: expressions of interests, requests for information, requests for offers or bids, purchase orders, and so on.

Until very recently, trading agency would not have been a technical possibility: it is only becoming economically and technically viable thanks to the emergence of new technologies, especially the Internet and e-mail, but also to a lesser extent, the call centre. In the process, it helps tease out better value from the market, and helps change the 'balance of power' within the market.

Marketing is about matching and connecting: matching supply to demand and connecting buyers and sellers. Ultimately, this matching and connecting process is driven by information about demand (who and where are our customers, and what do they want from us?) and attention (no 'connecting' is possible if the buyer is not aware of what the seller has to offer).

Traditional marketing solves this problem in two ways. It gathers information about consumers mainly via market research. And it sends information to consumers, hoping to grab their attention via devices such as the 30 second television commercial. By reversing the flow of information, and sending 'Here I am. This is what I want' messages from buyers to sellers, trading agents short-circuit both these processes. What's more, they add an enormous amount of value to such information, because they can elicit much richer, more detailed, timely and relevant expressions of interest than any database model or advertising initiative.

Table 4.2 illustrates the richness and range of the sorts of information that could be volunteered by individuals to agents if (and remember 'if' is the biggest word in life, love, politics, war and business) they can trust this agent *not* to mishandle, misuse or abuse it and to use it *on their behalf*, to help them solve their go-to-market and other problems.

Sellers' ability to access such information – usually only in disguised, non-attributable form and only after the client has given permission – opens up huge opportunities for them to enrich their understanding of

---

Table 4.2 Examples of the sorts of data trading agents might collect (with permission)

- Who am I? Name, address, age, sex, occupation, income etc.
- Who are my family? Their names, addresses, age, sex, etc.
- Who is my extended family?
- What is my potential word-of-mouth network? (e.g., who do I communicate with on a regular basis) What groups and communities am I member of?
- Health. Ailments, operations, treatments etc.
- Interests. Hobbies, pastimes, leisure pursuits.
- Beliefs. Causes (for and against), memberships, religious affiliation, political affiliation, etc.
- Current life concerns. Personal financial affairs, work, health, relationships.
- Likes and dislikes. Fashion, food, brand preferences, lifestyle preferences.
- Current ownerships. How many cars, televisions, computers etc., how recently purchased, what brands and models.
- Current purchasing profile. Items purchased over last period.
- Current purchasing plans. E.g., house, car, holiday, pension, furniture, home-improvement project.
- Relationship management preferences. E.g. by phone, mobile phone, face-to-face, PC, interactive television; best times to contact, etc.
- Current information-needs and interests.

---

their target markets and to streamline their go-to-market process. This is the source of huge new win-wins (see below).

Like oil companies sucking black gold out of the earth, trading agents 'mine' and trade the critical resource that fuels modern commerce. The politics are, that unlike the earth, these oil wells are living human beings, who own and control this resource, and will only sell it to those who pay for it. Trading agents organize and make this new market for consumer information and attention.

The structural change to markets follows these technical and political changes. All of modern marketing (no matter in what form: traditional advertising and direct marketing; customer relationship management;

permission marketing or whatever) assumes the vantage point of the seller trying to sell to buyers. Its perspective is seller-centric: it's driven by sellers worrying about how to sell more, more efficiently and more effectively.

Traditional marketing sweeps the market of buyers to pinpoint and target those most likely to add value to the company, by buying its wares and becoming loyal customers. Trading agents sweep the market of sellers to pinpoint those most likely to add most value to the buyer. They reorganize the go-to-market process from the point of view of a buyer looking out on to a world of sellers. So what does this mean in practice?

TRADING AGENCY FUNCTIONS

Here are some of the things tomorrow's trading agents will do, on a professional mass-scale – with some examples of early experiments along the way.

Information flows

Reversing the flow of marketing information lies at the heart of most trading agent business models. For example, BT, the UK telecoms giant, has developed a prototype car buying system that enables consumers to build up a list of specifications for their 'ideal' car, and lets them list things that are really important (say, price bracket, engine size, sedan, station wagon or SUV) and things which are less important (e.g., colour). It then sends this specification to sellers inviting them to make offers.

Experiments with this process have thrown up some interesting learnings. Often, for example, consumers aren't clear about the benefits of certain features such as air bags or air brakes. They need educating. And when they receive offers from companies, often, they realize it wasn't exactly what they were looking for. They don't like that particular car brand or design, for example. In other words, the new buying process not only helps consumers get a better deal, it also helps educate them about the market, and to clarify their own often-hazy preferences.

One company that is focusing on the buying agency market – and developing the infrastructure and the interactive networks necessary for buying agency – is the UK-based Conciera. Working with businesses which have strong, existing trusted relationships with their customers ('Agency Providers') and with a broad mix of retailers and service providers ('Sellers'), Conciera aims to put buyers in control of the buying process. Box 4.1 sums up its model.

BOX 4.1 CONCIERA BUYING AGENCY MODEL

1. Agency Providers host a customized Conciera consumer agent service ('Fetchmax') on their web site and/or via a managed call centre. The service allows an agent's customers to specify decision preferences relating to a desired product purchase (say, price range, purchase timing, preferred size, colour, brand, feature and delivery requirements for a widescreen television) as well as key additional attributes (such as preferred transaction channel, purchase context and willingness to receive other communications relating to special offers and promotions).

2. Once completed, the detailed purchase specification (but not the prospective buyer's name or address) is immediately sent to a network of relevant Sellers. Using an online response system called Partnermax, each seller is able to view the consumer's request in order to decide whether to respond, at what price and with what conditions. Each interested seller can construct a response from pre-defined template libraries or they can construct a personalized reply.

3. Responding seller offers are immediately posted to a secure, personalized section of the Agency Provider's Fetchmax service. Here, the consumer can inspect and compare the incoming offers after being notified of their availability by email, text message or any other means.

4. If the buyer wants to pursue a particular offer, he signals his intention, at which point the name and contact details are revealed to the Partnermax seller and the normal process of purchase (via the customer's choice of channel) follow.

This sort of model provides a number of potential wins for each party. An Agency Provider may offer a service like this in order to deepen existing relationships, brand values and trust among existing customers. Whether it is a financial services institution, a telecoms company, a retailer or a media owner, for example, the fact that it is offering an additional service that clearly adds value for its customers may help it to fend off competitors, and to build 'closer relationships'. In addition the service should deliver new revenue streams, from customer usage and from on and offline permission based advertising and targeted marketing services (more on this below), while providing access to consumer profiles and purchase data (on a strict, permission-only basis).

Buyers benefit because the service provides a convenient means for them to find the right seller, deal, product or service to match their individual requirements, particularly in complex product categories (such as mobile phones). It also offers added convenience because all relevant information and offers are collated at single site – which in turn helps them to make effective comparisons. It also puts them in control of marketing communications and seller relationships: letting them specify which marketing promotions and offers they wish to receive, about what subjects and categories, from whom, when. The service also provides a trusted environment for sourcing information from, interacting and trading with sellers, marketers and other partners.

Sellers meanwhile benefit from access to a new channel to sell products and services, perhaps via many new Agent Providers. The service gives them the opportunity to respond to direct and information-rich purchase requests from interested buyers, plus the ability to interact directly with buyers through their preferred channel to close the sale. It also gives them the option to perform dynamic pricing and promotion tests as well as manage product inventory, and to gather consented personal buyer profiles as well as access to important purchase decision data and criteria – information that can be used to improve the performance of other marketing channels.

As the infrastructure and service provider, Conciera earns its keep (in this model) from fees paid by sellers. Conciera's *'Seller Response Fee'* pricing mechanism is levied just once – when a seller responds to a consumer request. If the seller decides not to respond to a consumer request, no fee is incurred. In this way Conciera (and the Agency Provider who takes a cut), only earn money by providing a win to both sides. Buyers get information and offers about relevant sellers about things they positively want to buy, when they want to buy it. Sellers get the chance to communicate and sell to people who have already identified themselves as being in the market, now, for their particular products. Once the model gains critical mass, Conciera expects revenues to rise rapidly, as many small fees from many transactions mount.

However, response fees are only its first level of value. A lot more potential value lies with the consumer data that Conciera captures on behalf of its Agency Provider clients. By aggregating and analyzing detailed consumer preference and permission data, Conciera aims to become the owner of a highly valuable market knowledge and research resource.

Search costs

Sending out requests for information – Conciera's approach – is one way of reducing buyers' search costs. Another way is to develop services that aggregate 'everything you need to know' about a category in one place. A classic example is MSN's Carpoint, which provides price, feature and other comparisons of cars (updated weekly) plus independent auto reviews. It also enables buyers to sift through a range of competing 'no-fee, no-haggle, no-obligation quotes' from affiliated dealers.

Information content

Another aspect of buying agency is the provision of easy-to-understand, useful *buyer-centric* information. Think of it as the opposite of seller-centric advertising: relevant, comprehensive, comparative, objective and impartial information, that helps the buyer make the best possible choice. Early prototypes of this element of the total trading agency service can be seen in the many web sites that now offer price and product comparisons. MySimon and Kelkoo use 'intelligent' software agents to search the Internet for price comparisons across a range of categories. US-based, peer-to-peer product and store review service BizRate.com ranks online stores on the basis of twelve quality ratings ranging from price through product selection and information, to ease of ordering and on-time delivery. 'We are', it says, 'dedicated to providing consumers with unbiased information to make more informed and confident online buying decisions'. The ratings come from customer 'votes' – the actual experience of users – and stores can be listed according to each rating, thus addressing the needs of both price and service sensitive buyers.

More up-market agency services might provide far more personal and specialist advice. The independent financial advisor or travel agent (when he's not captured by seller-commission fees or other selling incentives) provides an early example of this function. In the UK, the AA (Automobile Association) – part of Centrica – has a service whereby its qualified car mechanics inspect second-hand cars for buyers before they buy.

Another service, which combines reduced search costs with a degree of 'information reassurance' is HomePro. Its target market is home improvements and building works: a market full of risk, stress and 'cowboy builders'. HomePro.com tackles the cowboy builder by putting consumers in touch only with approved local builders. That sounds simple, but to be approved, builders not only have to have a clean legal history plus Dun & Bradstreet-vetted financial health, they also have to agree to a HomePro vet of their past work – by calls to ten previous customers, all randomly selected from the company's books by HomePro itself.

In addition, they have to commit themselves to a nine-point customer service charter, including promising to turn up on time, keep to schedules, be polite, and clean up at the end of each day. On completion of a job, each builder's work is rated by the customer. Those who come top of the list of aggregated customer ratings are the first to be contacted when new work comes in: they get the best pick of the best contracts. Those with less-than-glowing customer ratings fall to the bottom, or may even be excluded.

The win for the consumer is almost hassle-free access to a choice of (usually) two or three reliable builders chosen because their expertise fits your particular project. The win for builders is that HomePro effectively organizes their customer acquisition for them – a service which they pay HomePro for. These new win-wins are generated from a new set of go-to-market processes (HomePro-organized matching and connecting), new market dynamics (builders' need to compete for good consumer reviews), and new forms of buyer-centric information, such as the HomePro vetting and peer-to-peer reviews.

Negotiation

'Take it or leave it' pricing mechanisms have their advantages. They are quick and simple. They're transparent, above board and fair (in the sense that every consumer pays the same). By adding *voice* to *choice*, however, buying agents can add extra value for their client/consumers.

- By arming consumers with richer, more comprehensive information they enable consumers to negotiate more effectively. It can be quite astonishing how flexible a car salesman's prices can become when you tell him the prices other dealers happen to be offering.
- By aggregating and deploying buying power they can help to negotiate better terms.
- By introducing new pricing mechanisms such as reverse auctions, reverse spot markets, requests for bids, name-your-own-price, etc., they can tease out better value offers.

Request for bid or offer systems such as those being pioneered by Conciera, BT and – of course – 'name your own price' services such as Priceline, open up the opportunities for dynamic pricing systems. (The win for the seller is the opportunity for much more finely tuned yield and stock management.) There is also enormous potential in new 'consumer' spot markets.

One pointer to the future comes from UK supermarket Sainsbury's. In the mobile phone market, competing sellers have created mind-bogglingly complex tariff structures which vary dramatically depending on how often you use your phone and at what time. The differences between these tariff structures make it almost impossible to make straightforward price comparisons. Sainsbury's is trumping such efforts however, by offering a mobile phone deal that works as if it were a mobile phone tariff 'spot market'.

Each month Sainsbury's tracks how you have used your phone over the billing period, compares this usage to the main providers' tariff structures, and charges you the lowest from among them. By sweeping the market for you, on a regular basis, it cuts across individual sellers' attempts to 'lock' consumers into particular contracts. How could other long-term contract markets – such as energy supply, mortgages, loans and credit cards be transformed by a buying agent deploying a similar spot market approach?

On the other side of the coin, how could markets dominated by traditional short-term, arms length transactions be transformed by turning them into long-term contracts? How much would a consumer-products company such as Procter & Gamble, Nestle or Unilever be prepared to pay to secure an 'annual supply contract' across the complete range of its goods with a particular consumer? How could it use such annual supply contracts to reconfigure its promotional and other marketing strategies?

Meanwhile, as every retail buyer knows, buying power works wonders when you're trying to negotiate on price. In Germany, the UK and Letsbuyit.com offers 'co-buying' services which deliver discounts related to volume – the number of buyers joining that particular co-buying circle. And other services wait in the wings.

For many years, the price of cars sold in bulk fleet deals in the UK was often 30 percent or more below the price paid by individual buyers at manufacturer-controlled dealers. In the late 1990s, the Woolwich – a UK bank – came up with a smart way of selling car loans to consumers. 'If you take a car loan from us,' it told consumers, 'we will source your car via a fleet buyer, thereby delivering you a fleet discount'. This particular service never took off, thanks to prevailing 'block exemption' legislation giving car makers control over their distribution networks. As the fleet buyer in question, PHH Europe Ltd, later complained to the UK's Monopolies and Mergers Commission, 'In most cases manufacturers would not sell, and would not permit dealers to sell, at prices reflecting the volume of PHH's purchases, particularly if the cars in question were to be sold to individuals'. However, the service did highlight the opportunity which, no doubt, will be taken up by others in due course, if and when legislation allows.

SELLING AGENCY

So far, we've talked solely about helping buyers to buy. But there is another side to trading agency, and that is 'selling' agency. As individuals, we each go to market with many things to sell. One of the most important is our ability to work – that is so important we discuss it in a separate chapter (Chapter 11).

We also have *things* we might want to sell. E-bay has created a flourishing new market by enabling individuals to sell to each other on a peer-to-peer basis. Amazon is moving in to the same space, by offering second-hand books, computer games, etc., alongside new. But crucially for trading agents, we also have information and attention to sell too.

Currently, companies invest vast sums of money and effort sourcing information about customers (both gathering this information from customer transactions, and buying it in from third parties), processing and analyzing this information, and using it for various activities such as product development and marketing.

Most of this information is gathered and traded without our permission or even without our knowledge, hardly ever with our involvement, and virtually never for our benefit. 'List broking' where, for instance, a magazine sells the names and addresses of its subscribers to third parties, is a significant mini-industry in its own right. The sale of such lists, to third-party direct marketers, generates an incremental revenue stream for the magazine – and unsolicited junk mail for its subscribers.

The irony is that this massive investment in the gathering and use of consumer information is currently executed in an extraordinarily inefficient way. Companies invest vast sums in sophisticated data-mining and data-handling techniques – data warehouses, relational databases, expert systems, genetic algorithms, pattern-recognition systems and so on and so forth – to generate ... guesswork. Ultimately, these massively expensive and complex activities generate only poorly fitting models about likely or predicted consumer behaviour. That's because they deal in information that has been gleaned *about* consumers, not in information fresh *from* them. It is shot through with holes: it is too partial, it is out of date, it is incorrect, etc.

What's more, the uses to which this information is put are often even more inefficient. Today's direct marketing industry, for example, often celebrates 2 percent response rates – e.g. 98 percent waste – as success. Mass mailers are happy with a response rate of just one or two percent. Such waste occurs not just because the quality of the data is suspect. It is because, for the most part, the content of the messages sent is of zero value to the recipients.

Under the old bottom line, then, the entire approach to the vital consumer asset of information seller-centric. Data is gathered *about* customers, and targeted *at* them mainly *without* their permission. Selling agents turn this on their head. They generate more, richer, better, more timely information *from* consumers, and use it *for* them and *with* their permission.

We've already seen one way in which buying agents do this. When a buyer sends a message to his agent saying 'I want to buy a new washing machine', the buyer is volunteering a very specific and highly valuable piece of information. But that's just the first layer. There are many more. Instead of telling my buying agent that I want to buy a washing machine now, I might tell him 'I'm thinking about buying a car/holiday of this sort some time over the next three months'. This enables my agent to solicit messages about this sort of car/holiday over a specific period of time, thereby creating the opportunity for much more relevant, targeted and timely advertising and promotion than any other traditional marketing channel could possibly offer. In this way, the trading agent is not only selling direct, explicit information about demand, it is also selling pre-qualified, permission-based attention.

But it doesn't stop there. I might also tell my trading agent that I have an enduring interest in gardening, or classical music, or mountain climbing, and that I am open to messages on these subjects all year round. Yet more highly valuable pre-qualified, permission-based attention.

In addition, over time, my agent will accumulate a very detailed picture of my transactions, lifestyle, interests etc., which he may use to proactively suggest new products and services – things I haven't asked for but in which I might be interested (again, only on a permission basis).

And at yet another level, I might be happy to let my agent sell aggregated market research data, analyzing patterns of spending, consumption and interests on an anonymized basis (as many companies already do), but on a more up-to-date, rich and detailed basis.

BOX 4.2 THE NEW WIN-WIN

Old bottom line marketing is driven forward by a hugely powerful supply-side win-win. The better marketers match what firms make to what consumers want, the more value consumers receive and the more sales the firms realize. But it is a commonplace in business circles nowadays that marketing is getting less effective. Many reasons are put forward to explain these problems: media fragmentation and inflation, increasing consumer sophistication and marketing literacy, for example. They have their role. But the real reasons for the crisis in marketing effectiveness reach right to its very heart. Because it is done by sellers for sellers, it provides little value to buyers – who invest little time or attention in sellers' marketing efforts. Result: they go to waste. We've already seen the three big lose-loses in modern marketing. They are:

■ Its seller-centric nature. While old bottom liners try to make *products* that meet the needs of consumers, they do not make *marketing* that meets the needs of buyers. Their marketing programmes are entirely self-interested and are therefore ignored by buyers or taken with a pinch of salt. This creates a vicious circle (see negative system effects below)

■ Lack of information about demand. The linchpin of successful marketing is timely, detailed, relevant information about which consumers want exactly what. But for historical reasons, old bottom line marketing is a top-down, producer-push process with information flowing only one way: down, from seller to buyer (more on this in Chapter 8). Seller-attempts to gather such timely, relevant information – via mechanisms such as market research – are poor substitutes for data direct 'from the horse's mouth'.

■ Negative system effects. We discussed these in Chapter 1. They are the irrational outcomes that occur as the net result of many individually rational decisions. Information overload is a classic example. One seller 'ups the ante' of his marketing programmes in an attempt to cut through the clutter and grab consumers' attention. So in response his competitors also up the ante. Net result: the consumer is bombarded with even more messages, pays even less attention to each one of them, while sellers' costs soar. Another example is product parity, where each attempt to innovate is quickly neutralized by competitor responses.

Each of these lose-loses is deeply embedded within the old bottom line system. By working 'outside' this system trading agents offer sellers the opportunity to break

> free of these lose-lose dynamics and create new win-wins based on the flow of information *from* consumers and the provision of useful, relevant information.
>
> This points to a root-and-branch reengineering of go-to-market processes. We've already touched on the 'big picture' economic importance of this. Around a half of all economic activity is now devoted to matching and connecting tasks, ranging from market research through marketing communications to distribution and retailing. Trading agents open up the opportunity to massively reengineer these processes, to huge benefits to both buyers and sellers.

Put together, such rich, detailed, accurate, timely, relevant information – plus guaranteed attention from interested buyers – is the holy grail of modern marketing. It offers immense value on two counts:

■ Massively streamlining sellers' go-to-market costs.
■ Opening up rich new sources of information to drive more aligned new product development: simply having a better idea of what the market is looking for, right now.

It is this merging of database and direct marketing, with media advertising and traditional marketing communications, with retail around a new centre of gravity – customer information and attention – that makes trading agency so immensely powerful.

There is one hugely important caveat however. For any of this to work, consumers must be prepared to invest time and effort in making information available to their agent. 'Invest' is a crucial word here. The owner of the vital 'bottleneck' assets of information and attention is 'the consumer', and trading agents must provide a superior return on investment to make the whole process worthwhile. The promise of 'relevant offers' is unlikely to be enough. A significant saving of time and/or money and hassle, plus the opportunity to access products and services that better meet my needs are crucial. And a new level of trust between individual and agent is critical. To unleash more value, in other words, trading agents have to offer more value. They have to start addressing those value gaps.

A NEW BUSINESS MODEL

So how do trading agents make their money? By fulfilling a combination of roles. Trading agents:

- **Open up new markets** for buyer-centric information and services. Because they save me time and/or money and hassle, while (perhaps) enriching the value I access from the market may be, I am prepared to pay up-front for these services. This is the first revenue stream: cash payments from consumers for information, services, advice, expertise etc.
- **Complement existing markets**, in particular by making more, richer information available to existing suppliers, and by reducing their go-to-market costs. This generates payments from sellers, for example, in the form of commissions, transaction fees, Conciera's 'seller response fee', etc.
- **Compete with existing markets.** To the degree that trading agents provide matching and connecting services – for both buyer and seller – that are better or more efficient than existing providers (say, in advertising, direct marketing or retailing), they are competing with these providers for revenue streams. Their crucial weapon in this battle is a resource to which traditional providers have no access: information *from* consumers and permission-based attention. Consumers effectively 'pay' agents for their services by making these resources available.
- **Subsume existing markets.** If I source a washing machine via a trading agent, the value created by the washing machine supplier remains exactly the same, and it is an open question as to whether my 'brand loyalty' is to my agent, to the washing machine supplier or to both. This debate is hardly new. It has raged for many years across all intermediary markets, including traditional consumer-retailer-manufacturer relationships. But trading agents do tilt the balance further, because they broaden the value equation. Before, it was just the price or quality of the item being purchased. Now it is the price or quality of the item being purchased *plus* the price or quality of the total go-to-market process.

This combination of four sources of value – cash payments from buyers; non-cash payments from buyers (e.g., information and attention which can be monetized); cash payments from sellers; plus the simple battle for share of total transactions – provide the foundations for successful trading agency.

There are many possible permutations and combinations, and many issues. Some trading agents may strive to offer 'free' services – e.g., relying solely on their ability to monetize the information they glean to generate cash payments from sellers. Other models may require a cash input from the customer. For example, grocery home shopping (a stepping stone towards agency in the grocery industry) saves buyers time and labour which they are prepared to pay for.

The danger with 'free' services – i.e., where cash flows come entirely from sellers – is that they may quickly be 'captured' by seller incentives, or be perceived as being influenced by seller incentives. That's why, for example, Conciera links its seller payments not to closed sales but to seller responses. This way, Conciera has no incentive to favour one seller against another, or sellers generally against buyers.

Whether or not consumers are prepared to pay for trading agency services will also depend on a certain degree of market education. As individual buyers, we already invest significant amounts of time (researching, travelling to and from shops, etc.), money (researching, travelling); stress, etc., sourcing the inputs we need to run our lives. But we rarely sit down to calculate these costs. Until we do, we may not be aware of how much time, money and hassle we could save by adopting a different approach. Online retailers such as Amazon, which also trade time for money (the cost of shopping for the book vs delivery charges), are part of this education process.

A more subtle – but equally important – piece of education is the realization that as consumers, we all pay for sellers' go-to-market costs anyway. The seller's marketing costs are subsumed into the final price we pay. It is therefore in our interests to help reduce these costs (as long as we get a share of the benefit).

Retailers and manufacturers are used to thinking of the retailer's gross margin – the difference between the 'factory gate' price of the item and the price at which the retailer sells it – as a form of payment by the manufacturer to the retailer for selling the product. In earlier days, manufacturers deliberately built this 'selling fee' into their marketing considerations, setting a recommended retail price to cover it.

However, you could look at exactly the same process from the other end of the telescope, to see it buyer-centric terms. The retailer's gross margin is effectively what consumers pay the retailer for finding the item in question and making it available: a sourcing fee. What would happen if retailers – or trading agents – separated out these two charges (factory gate or item price and sourcing fee) for everyone to see? It would focus everyone's minds on two things: a) how effectively is the retailer/agent buying for me (e.g., is he using his buying power to bring the factory gate price down)?, and b) how much is he charging for his sourcing activities?

If these sourcing costs were more visible, consumers might pay more attention to what exactly they are getting for their money here. Efficient trading agents might find this to be a useful marketing weapon. Indeed, that is exactly what successful retailers like Tesco have been doing over the past decade: pushing as hard as possible to reduce supply chain costs and reinvesting these savings in the form of lower prices. Tesco has been rewarded with rising market share as a result (see below).

SO WHO IS GOING TO DO IT?

Earlier in this chapter we gave many examples of possible elements of a complete trading agency service: reverse messaging; new search mechanisms; 'permission attention'; price and product comparisons; independent, expert impartial advice; new market mechanisms, etc. However, like the separate parts of an aeroplane – an engine here, a tail there, a wing there, a fuselage lying next to it – if they are not put together in the right way, the chances are they will never fly.

Offering an isolated ingredient of trading agency is probably not enough. The whole idea of using a trading agent is to save me time, hassle and money – not to increase it. But as long as, say, logging on to a separate price comparison web site involves me in a separate, additional time-consuming task on top of 'normal' shopping, take up will be limited. Only when agents bring all these elements together in an integrated, seamless, easy to use way are they likely to achieve real critical mass.

That's precisely the problem with today's market set up. If we look around today's markets, we find that many different players offer small, isolated elements of buyer-centric service – but in a half-hearted, isolated manner.

Some specialist media companies – such as 'Best Buy' magazines and some Internet sites – offer consumers a little comparative, objective information on what different sellers are offering. Newspapers and television programmes provide some product reviews. By providing competing products on their shelves, retailers enable consumers to inspect different offerings and make more informed comparisons. Retailers also deploy buying power to reduce prices (though they don't always pass these cost savings on to their customers). Independent financial advisors provide expert opinion on complex products such as pensions.

Figure 4.1 sums up some of the ways existing business sectors may provide 'buying assistance' to consumers. But to create a complete service the consumer has to go to each one in turn, and 'fillet out' just one element of what that business is offering. To access them all is a complete searching and sifting task in its own right.

Figure 4.1 Buying Agents: a new Convergence?

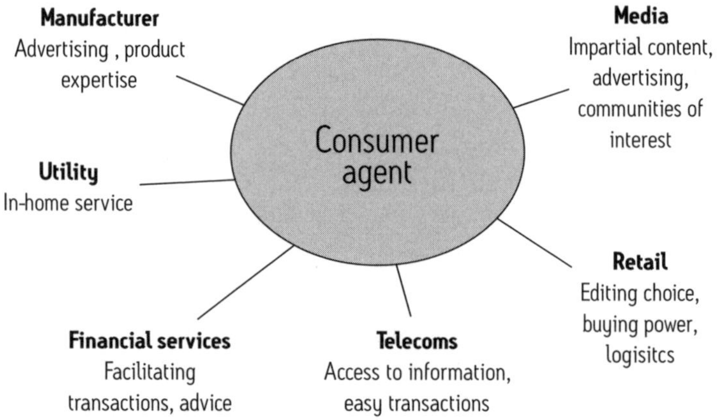

Manufacturer
Advertising , product expertise

Media
Impartial content, advertising, communities of interest

Consumer agent

Utility
In-home service

Retail
Editing choice, buying power, logisitcs

Financial services
Facilitating transactions, advice

Telecoms
Access to information, easy transactions

That is one reason why these services remain of marginal value to the buyer. Another is that they are not the company's core business, and do not, therefore, receive priority investment. The product review section of a newspaper is just one, tiny element of a much broader advertising-driven editorial offer, for example. Also, where these services are offered, they are compromised by the seller-centric context in which they are offered. Retailers are not in business to exercise buying power on behalf of their customers, for example.

The other side of the coin, however, is that such buyer-centric elements may become 'launching points' for a move into trading agency. A specialist media company may decide to offer reverse messaging and transaction services on top of independent editorial reviews, for example – thereby adding convenience for its consumers, and a new revenue stream for itself. A telecoms company might offer Conciera-style reverse messaging as an additional customer service which both boosts customer retention, while encouraging incremental use of its core business (e.g., in fixed and mobile telephony and Internet services). A loans provider might offer trading agency services as a 'plus' for customers choosing to take out loans from it, rather than one of its rivals (as the Woolwich bank tried with Motorbase). A retailer might decide that 'deploying buying power on your behalf' sounds like an attractive marketing message – and an idea it can extend into new sectors.

BOX 4.3 THE TESCO EXAMPLE

To see how an existing, established player might make the leap from old bottom line to new, let's look at what one highly successful company – Tesco – has already done, and what it could do in the future.

Tesco has flourished over the past decades by superb execution of a whole series of grocery retailing mini-revolutions including: the rise of out-of-town superstores and later, other convenience formats; supply-chain control; development of own label; use of growing buying power; extensive use of point-of-sale data; brand extensions (e.g., into areas like petrol and financial services); and the value of strong supplier partnerships.

Its experience with these developments has helped it to learn three hugely important lessons.

■ There are huge win-wins to be gained by continuously reducing go-to-market costs for both seller and buyer. Out of town superstores lowered costs for Tesco – the property was cheap, they were easier and cheaper to replenish than town-centre supermarkets. They also offered significant benefits to customers. By offering car parks and easy access, they reduced the time and hassle of travelling to and from shops carrying heavy loads. By offering a much wider range of products in store, they reduced the need to 'shop around', thereby saving precious time. And because they were a lower cost economic model, they could offer lower prices while still maintaining healthy margins.

■ Experience shows that one of the best ways of cutting cost is to move from 'push' supply and marketing strategies to 'pull' strategies. Generally speaking, it's more efficient to source goods that happen to sell well in your stores, rather than buy goods that are pushed at you by suppliers and then trying to sell them on. This move from 'push' to 'pull' has been made possible by the introduction of barcode scanning, sophisticated data transfer mechanisms and new supply chain practices such as 'just-in-time' replenishment.

■ Strong customer relationships have a high value in their own right: if you have a strong relationship with your customers you can funnel a widening range of transactions through it, which is why brand extensions work so well.

More recently, three further developments have begun to mark Tesco out from the retail crowd: the way it has been able to use loyalty card data to upgrade and transform its operations; its successful foray into home shopping; and its adoption of 'lean thinking'.

With its loyalty scheme, Tesco expanded its relationship with its customers who now provide it with the named, personal information with their expressed permission. It is, in turn, using this information to customise its offerings to them.

With home shopping, Tesco is migrating away from its previous focus on real estate to embrace new operational and marketing priorities. Operationally, for example, Tesco now needs new local economies of scale such as increased doordrop densities – the number of people it delivers to, in one street, at one time. We'll see later how crucial such new economies of scale are to new solution assembly offerings.

Home shopping also means that customers are becoming accustomed to richer interactions with Tesco – exchanging information online. It allows Tesco to extend its range even further – beyond what can be stocked physically in local stores. It would be a huge psychological shift (if only a small one in terms of total revenues) if customers were able to order specific items that were not a part of Tesco's normal stock. With new supply chain technologies such as radio-frequency identity tagging waiting in the wings, the supply-chain costs of offering such a service are set to plummet.

Finally, home shopping also dramatically reinforces a trend that's long been under way: the emergence of Tesco as a 'media owner'. The trend started a long time ago with the development of in-store and point-of-purchase displays and communications. It was reinforced by the launch of a mass circulation customer magazine – and by mailing activities driven by ClubCard data. Now, with an Internet site as well, Tesco is able to communicate with its customers in store, in car parks, in print, in direct mail, via e-mail, by online advertising and messages, etc. It is becoming a fully fledged media owner, in other words. What's more it can offer advertisers something traditional media owners cannot: direct, up-to-the-minute tracking on the effects of such initiatives on sales – via its loyalty card data.

In addition, because it has data about the individual it is communicating with (by mail or online) it can target the right individuals, tailoring the right messages to them. This is attracting the attention of traditional brand advertisers who are beginning to see it as a better way of targeting key customer segments, hereby opening up new revenue streams for Tesco. Tesco is also selling (averaged) data about shoppers to these brand manufacturers thereby creating new revenue streams from both customer information and attention.

Finally, 'lean thinking' is driving Tesco to eliminate any and every activity that does not add value to its end customers. This 'lean' approach is at the heart of Tesco's win-win strategy with its customers. By continually cutting its supply chain costs it frees up funds which it can reinvest in lower prices and/or better service. This extra benefit encourages them to shop more at Tesco, thereby spending more with it, and creating a virtuous circle of extra value for both sides.

With these developments, Tesco is continuing to reduce its customers' go-to-market costs, rounding out its services to become less of a grocery retailer and more of a 'sourcing portal' to the world of suppliers, and trading information and attention as well as money for goods. But all these developments have taken place within the shell of traditional, old bottom line retailing. What happens if we break this shell to let a new bottom line chick emerge? Here are some possibilities.

Rethinking its core business

Tesco chief executive Terry Leahy has already laid out his company's basic stance. 'We build our business back from the consumer. We try to operate the business as a genuine pull system,' he says. The core purpose of Tesco, he says, is to 'create value for our customers to win their lifetime loyalty'. And he defines loyalty in a very specific way: 'Loyalty is an emotional term, which means that there is a relationship of trust. The assumption on behalf of the consumer is that they can trust the retailer to *work in their interests*.' (Our italics.)

Given this vision – and the skills, relationships and infrastructure it has already developed – Tesco is well placed to make the transition from traditional 'retailer' to customer sourcing agent.

Additional trading agency services

As we've seen, trading agents work by gathering signals of demand from their clients and eliciting responses from competing suppliers. With its strong, trust-customer relationship and its intimate knowledge of them, why shouldn't Tesco take on such a function for them in a wider range of areas – from car purchases to mortgages to holidays to computers, mobile phones etc.? This would be a service (and revenue stream) in addition to all existing business.

Information and attention trading

Many suppliers would be willing to pay good money for the chance to access information from specific customers who signal an interest in their products (or who fit the supplier's criteria as a 'target market'), and for the chance to supply information and messages to these people. Using its data, infrastructure and relationships could Tesco organise this on a *permission-only basis* – the customers concerned would have to positively volunteer to take part – in return for additional benefits. If Tesco earns a fee for organising this streamlined matching and connecting process, it might incentivize customers to take part by sharing that fee with them in some way.

Special segment services

So far, Tesco has three clubs for mothers with children of different ages, a 'healthy living' club and a club for wine buffs. Already 40 percent of all UK mothers are a member of one of its baby, toddler or kids clubs. At present, these clubs revolve around special offers for grocery and related products sold in-store. But Tesco could evolve these clubs into fully fledged 'solution' providers, offering additional child-related information (health, child development, education, etc.), peer-to-peer support networks both virtually (e.g., chat forums) and physically (e.g., child-minding clubs for people living within a certain distance of a store), plus access to any and every product related to children, from prams to car seats, to clothes and toys, to child-friendly holidays, including impartial information about these products and services.

In-home services

Tesco has made a huge mental and strategic leap by moving beyond its store to bringing its service to the customer's door. But why stop there? If Tesco is already selling, for example, household appliances, why not extend the service to insurance contracts, preventative maintenance and repair? Why not evolve, like Centrica subsidiary British Gas (see next chapter), towards a home maintenance/replenishment solution assembly role?

Precisely because of its previous successes in areas such as the loyalty card and home shopping, Tesco is well placed to seize these opportunities. There are many reasons why Tesco might decide *not* to do such things, of course. It might feel it has enough on its plate improving existing operations, expanding internationally, and expanding from food to non-food, for instance. Embracing the notion of trading agency also implies significant changes to its underlying buisiness model. For example, it involves accepting that its most important asset is its relationahip with its customers, and that other assests such as stores are only there to serve this core (and not the other way round). It also involves accepting that Tesco earns its keep by sourcing value on behalf of its customers, rather than selling stuff to them.

OBSTACLES, PITFALLS AND CAVEATS

Trading agency represents a huge opportunity. It unleashes two of the most neglected assets of the information age: consumer information and attention. And it promises to deploy these assets to tackle the central bottleneck of modern markets: the costs and complexities of efficient, effective matching and connecting. But it's also something of a leap in the dark. It *is* a new business model and it does have many hurdles to clear before it reaches critical mass.

- **Consumer education** Precisely because it is new, consumers need to be educated about the new type of service, and to become familiar and comfortable with it. Educational areas might include: what are my current go-to-market costs? How could trading agents benefit me? How do they work? What is a fair price to pay for their services? Why should I trust them with my personal information?
- **Consumer habits** Being educated is not enough. Only when enough people start using the service regularly – as their first port of call for many key transactions – are trading agents likely to develop viable business models. Habits take time to change.
- **Convenience** Such regular usage will only occur when the service is extremely easy to understand and use. Anything that makes shopping even more time consuming or complex is unlikely to take off.
- **Trust** None of this can happen without high degrees of trust between consumer and agent, at a new level. Not just competence trust (which is a basic must) but 'on my side' trust too. Yet many consumers, rendered cynical by a life-time's experience of seller-centric marketing ploys, are suspicious of any claim from any company claiming to be taking the side of the consumer. They want to know: 'where's the catch?'

Trading agents have two possible responses. First, a demonstrable track record, which takes time to earn. Second: transparency. Traditionally, sellers go out of their way to keep costs, margins, business model details and profits opaque. Buying agents, however, may need to show consumers why and how what they do represents a win, not only for the consumer, but for the agent too. This may be the only way of overcoming deep-rooted scepticism.

- **Win-wins** Win-wins are closely linked to transparency. To succeed, trading agents need to generate clear, palpable wins for both buyers and sellers. This involves both education and 'proof in the pudding'.

- **Viable business models** When grocery retailers moved into home shopping they found that costs and benefits were so different to traditional retailing that they effectively had to rethink the business from scratch. It wasn't easy to get the right balance between new costs and new revenue streams. The same goes for trading agency, only more so. As a new business model it requires a steep commercial learning curve.
- **Crystal clear segmentation** Some sceptics remark that while trading agents appeal to the rational side of the buyer, most buyers actually make purchasing decisions on much more irrational grounds. They choose the car they like the look of, for example, not the one with the best engine performance, or lowest cost. They opt for the brand with the highest status cues or greatest sex appeal, not the one with the best quality-price trade off. Of course some people do this. Trading agents need to know who they are appealing to, and on what grounds.

Some consumers are obsessive control freaks. Others are relaxed outsourcers. Some love the thrill of chasing for bargains. For others, saving time is top priority. Some are confident, expert connoisseurs in certain categories. Others may be utterly ignorant of the same category and in desperate need of reassurance.

Likewise, consumers tend to approach different product categories very differently. The way we search out and buy big ticket items may be very different to our approach to low ticket items, or to high versus low emotional risk, frequent versus infrequent purchases etc. Trading agents will need to tailor their offers to both customer and product segment.

Likewise, some say, trading agency will never take off because consumers just *love* shopping, and don't see it as a cost or a chore at all. Indeed *some* do. They like shopping for many reasons: as a social occasion; a leisure occasion; a source of inspiration and ideas; a chance for bargain hunting, etc. On the other hand, others don't. And these responses vary by category. We may like shopping for, say, clothes or exotic food but not for other categories such as motor insurance or routine replenishment items such as potatoes.

So once again, crystal clear segmentation is crucial. In all likelihood, the rise of trading agents will simply accelerate an already well-established trend: the division of buyer/seller intermediary businesses into two very distinct categories: those offering high value-for-time 'retail theatre', inspiration and fun and those addressing low value-for-time sourcing issues where more instrumental considerations take over. One option is perfectly suited to a passion partnership role (see Chapter 6), the other to trading agency: the new bottom line takes many forms.

Likewise, the trading agent's 'core' service will depend on the priorities of the buyer. These may include: best value at lowest price; least hassle and most time saving; maximum hand-holding for a purchase in a category I am not familiar with; connoisseur sourcing for specialist, niche interests.

Trading agents target some, but not all, of the core value gaps we discussed in Chapter 1. They particularly focus on transaction costs and buyer-centric information. They help me maximize the value of some personal assets, particularly information and attention (and to a lesser extent time and money), but not others such as emotional fulfilment.

Nevertheless, the trading agency opportunity is huge. By merging key elements of the database, direct marketing, media advertising and retailing industries trading agency promises a shake-up in the way buyers and sellers relate to each other. It could overhaul the way many industries, such as retailing, financial services, consumer durables, cars, computers, telecommunications services and holidays go to market. But it is just a beginning. It is just one of the three dimensions of the new bottom line.

Summary

One of the three main forms of new bottom line business model is the trading agent. Trading agents fulfil two key functions for individuals. They help individuals buy better – more appropriate products and services, more efficiently, at lower cost etc. And they help individuals to sell personal assets such as information and attention on the open market.

Trading agents offer new levels of 'buyer-centric' value to individuals in the form of new market mechanisms and services and the deployment of personal assets such as consumer buying power, information and attention.

They fulfil a variety of different functions, including:

- Eliciting information about demand from consumers
- Searching markets for 'best fit' supply
- Signalling this demand to potential suppliers to trigger offers, information and value exchange
- When appropriate, to organize reverse markets or dynamic pricing mechanics to identify best value offers
- When appropriate, to provide independent, impartial buyer-centric information and/or advice to assist best buying decisions
- Organizing or facilitating efficient fulfillment
- When appropriate and only with permission, selling specified segments of consumer information and attention to sellers

By organizing 'efficient demand' in this way, they also open up potentially powerful new win-wins with suppliers – offering them new ways to reduce their go-to-market costs and new ways to gain a better understanding of their customers.

5 Solution assembly

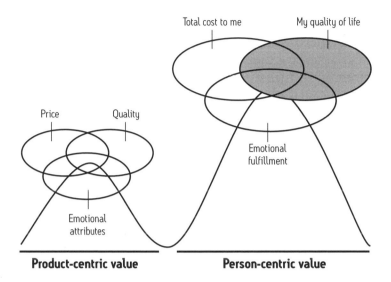

Total cost to me
My quality of life
Price
Quality
Emotional fulfillment
Emotional attributes

Product-centric value   **Person-centric value**

Let's not beat about the bush. The way companies and industries are organized today is not designed to maximize value to the consumer. Companies and industries are organized around the imperatives of efficient production, and efficient production does not always translate into optimum consumer value.

By definition, of course, every efficiently produced product and service adds *some* element of value: more than an inefficiently produced product or service. But look at any important aspect of 'my life' – my finances, my health, home maintenance, home replenishment, my transport/logistics – and what companies bring to market are the *ingredients* of the solutions I need. They only go some way towards meeting this need. Invariably, there is something else I have to do to get the outcome I really want – something

---

TASKS FOR THIS CHAPTER

1. Explain how solution assembly adds new value ...
2. ... and how solution assemblers earn their keep

that requires additional work, time, energy, expertise, expense, etc.; something that costs me more than the price of the product or service itself.

Solution assemblers go beyond the dictates of traditional vendor efficient supply to focus on customer efficient demand instead. They help me reduce these additional integration and coordination costs and/or improve the final result.

NEW DIVISIONS OF LABOUR

The value gap between product or service ingredient and desired outcome is deeply rooted in economic realities. Old bottom liners do their level best to meet customers' needs. Of course they do. But they only do so as long as what they offer stays *within* the limits set by their quest to maximize their own internal operational efficiency. Once they reach the point where meeting a customer need costs more than the revenues it generates, they draw back. Thus, soap powder manufacturers focus intently on producing ever better soap powders, ever more efficiently. But they have left consumers to do the washing and the ironing, because they can't find a way to do the washing and ironing at a price that enough consumers are prepared to pay.

In this way, every modern industry and product category has created a certain division of labour between company and customer: the customers' work begins where it's more efficient for them to do the work themselves than outsource this work to the company.

Solution assemblers renegotiate and recast these divisions of labour, drawing on three crucial factors to drive them forward.

- People are more affluent and can afford to pay for higher levels of service.
- The price they put on the time, energy, effort and stress they currently invest in assembling their own solutions is rising ever higher, so they are increasingly prepared to pay other people to help them with these tasks.
- New, more efficient ways of assembling solutions are emerging.

Solution assemblers, then, focus on a very different area of value in my life. While trading agents help me *acquire the inputs* of my life more efficiently, solution assemblers help me *make* a better life, more efficiently.

Trading agents help me make the most of my information and attention, and to a lesser degree time and money. Solution assemblers focus particularly on my operations and my time. They are about personal productivity: achieving more in less time – spending less time and energy doing the things I *don't* want to do, so that I can invest more time and energy doing the things I *do* want to do.

Table 5.1 Characteristics of solution assembly

Advanced solution assemblers:

- Focus on my operational productivity, not just my consumption needs or wants.
- Have open-ended 'contracts': most life operations (e.g., home maintenance or financial management) are continuous: the solution assembler's value cannot easily be embedded in a simple package
- Require a relationship: e.g., a high level of trust, a certain degree of information exchange, etc., on an ongoing basis.
- Are operationally local: where I am.
- Span diverse product and industry categories.
- Address specific customer emotions: e.g., trust, anxiety and stress relief, reassurance – but not 'meaning' or 'personal identity'.
- Are 'close' to their customers operationally, but rarely emotionally. Often the best solution assemblers are the ones we can take for granted and forget about, rather than feel a great emotional affinity with. It is a different model of branding.
- Go beyond 'balloon-squeezing' to generate richer and/or more efficient outcomes.

HOW LONG IS A PIECE OF STRING?

Words like 'solution' should come with a health warning. 'Solution' can be (and often is) used to mean almost anything: there is never a clear boundary between what is, and what isn't, a 'solution'. A good rule of thumb is that a fully-fledged solution encompasses:

- Content: expert information relating to the problem in hand.
- Products: tools, ingredients etc., to address the problem.
- Services: work, skills, expertise to deploy these tools and information.
- Information exchange: for the solution assembler to understand the client's particular problem/needs and to customise the solution accordingly.

However, there are many possible shades of grey. The typical motor car is an assembly of 10,000 or more ingredient components. To an important degree therefore, motor car manufacturers are solution assemblers. (Just imagine how many cars would be on the road if we, as individuals, had to undertake the task of assembling these separate ingredients, even assuming we had the technical capability.)

Yet, at the same time, owning a motor car goes only some way towards meeting my total, personal transport needs. I incur a whole range of extra costs managing my car, keeping it in good working order, insuring it, and so on. Indeed, industry estimates suggest that car manufacturers typically capture just 40 percent of the total amount of money consumers spend owning and running their cars.

The 'downstream aftermarket' takes up the other 60 percent. It includes car-related loans, insurance, taxes, maintenance and repairs, car washing, new tyres, extra accessories, breakdown services, in-car extras (such as audio), and so on. The balance between the two is also tilting – away from the car making section and towards the downstream aftermarket section. Some visionaries have even suggested that one day car companies could give away their cars for free, as long as their customers lock themselves into lucrative, long-term contracts, for example, for satellite navigation services. Also remember: this 40:60 division represents up-front money costs only. The calculations take no account of the time, energy and hassle that goes into car ownership – for example, when the car breaks down or when it has to be serviced.

So arguably, a personal mobility solution provider could address all these things (see below) And still it could do more, because there are many occasions – such as travelling to 'a night out on the town' or to catch a flight – when I might not want to use my own car at all. I might want a taxi service instead.

A solution, then, can be as long as a piece of string. Some 'solutions' are almost trivial: a prepared meal delivered to the door and costing a few Euros, for example. At the other end of the spectrum are hugely expensive, personally vital and ongoing life management tasks such as home management and maintenance, managing my personal finances, managing my health, and managing my personal mobility.

Some 'life critical' solutions

- **Home management and maintenance**
- **Home replenishment**
- **Personal mobility**
- **Personal health**
- **Personal finances**
- **Personal communications services**

Each one of these 'mega-solutions' are likely to involve costs/revenues of tens of thousands of Euros each year. They are 'mission critical' if I am to generate maximum value in my life. Table 5.1 indicates the vast range of ingredients that may be subsumed into such a mega-solution. These ingredients must be integrated into a seamless service if they are to add value. There must also be a high degree of customization, so that customers can choose which ingredients they do, and do not, want.

In between, there is a vast range of still important, but more-focused solutions such as managing my clothes (so that I always have fresh clean clothes, ironed and ready to wear), or 'keeping the house clean', or managing child care, or 'keeping the garden well stock, weeded and tidy'.

Clearly, there are many areas of potential overlap. Do car insurance and car loans fit best into a personal finance solution or a personal mobility solution? Is 'tending the garden' a separate 'mini-solution' or just one part of a much bigger home maintenance solution? The opportunities for both specialists and generalists – and for turf wars between them – are clearly huge.

Table 5.2 Ingredients Available To A Solution Assembler

Financial services	Health	Home maintenance
Money transmission services	Information about keeping fit, diet, ailments, treatments, drugs, etc.	Building /contents insurance
Savings	Medical diagnosis	Appliance, furniture,decorative materials sourcing
Mortgages	Drugs	Appliance repair and maintenance
Loans	Surgery, hosptial treatment	Appliance disposal, Indoor decorations, repair, maintenance, improvements
Credit cards	Physiotherapy, massage, etc.	
Credit facilities		
Pensions, Investments	Counselling/personal/ emotional advice	External decorations, repair, maintenance, improvements
Advice relating to all the above	Gym membership	
Financial analysis, highlighting trends and issues relative to above	Sports equipment, clothes, etc.	Design/architectural advice
Tax advice	Personal trainer services	Infrastructure repair/ maintenance e.g., plumbing, electricity
Financial planning	Dietary/lifestyle advice	
Administration	Related financial services,insurances, etc.	Information and advice relating to all the above
Coordinating all the above to best effect		Home cleaning
Information relating to all the above		Energy/water supply
		Home security management: alarms, locks, burglar bars, etc.
		Related financial services

SOLUTION ECONOMICS

How, then, do solution assemblers earn their keep? The simple answer is a) from people paying more, for higher levels of service, convenience and peace of mind, and b) from lower costs – being able to achieve what the customer wants to achieve more efficiently than he can. (To this degree, every solution assembler's main competitor is his own customer; the challenge is to be more efficient/effective/expert than your customer.)

Solution assembly economics

1. Balloon-squeezing: Do work for me that I don't want to do.
2. Sourcing expertise: Use specialist expertise of suppliers to source better than I can.
3. Execution expertise: Use specialist skills and knowledge to do things better than I can
4. Administrative efficiencies: Coordinate tasks and integrate ingredients more efficiently than I can.
5. Local economics of scale: to cut costs and add convenience.
6. Information logistics: Integrate the information I need to add value.
7. A gatekeeper role: Use their 'gatekeeper' role to generate more value.

1. Balloon-squeezing

The first and most obvious source of revenue is *up-front cash payments*. You get what you pay for: the more work somebody does for you, the more you have to pay them. The more affluent people are, the more they are prepared to pay for extra service. Unilever chairman Niall Fitzgerald once remarked that 80 percent of economic growth is coming from services; that 80 percent of this growth is concentrated in advanced industrial countries, of which 80 percent is driven by the most affluent 25 percent.

Increased affluence is a real and important factor driving the growth of solution assembly. Just look at the boom in home cleaning and other services in prosperous metropolitan areas. But it's also solution assembly's biggest limitation. As long as solution assembly consists simply of balloon-squeezing – paying somebody else to do work you don't want to do, without any overall efficiency gains being squeezed out of the process – it will always remain a marginal influence. Only the rich will be able to afford it.

'Balloon squeezing' work such as ironing clothes or weeding the garden or painting a wall, may well feature as one element of many solutions – a simple payment for work done. But the acid test for solution assemblers is whether they can surround such balloon squeezing with genuine added value/improved efficiencies.

2. Sourcing expertise

There is enormous value to be gained from specialization – and not simply reinventing the wheel. Packaged holidays were an early form of solution assembly. One of the extra bits of value they brought to the party was expertise about holiday ingredients such as locations, hotels, flights, transport providers, etc. It would take an enormous amount of research for each individual holiday maker to search out an appropriate hotel in Spain. By making it their specialism, packaged holiday companies could do this at a fraction of the cost.

Likewise, a key value-add for the lifestyle management company Ten (which stands for Time Energy Network) is its experience in dealing with life management issues, whether it's finding a reliable local cleaner or plumber, or hiring a marquee for a garden party. The first time it undertakes a task for a customer, Ten's learning curve is the same as that customers. The second time it is asked the question, it is already pretty close to an answer. 'It could take you three or four days to find the right cleaner for you in Shoreditch [a residential area very close to the City of London]', notes Alex Cheatle, CEO of Ten. 'But now we know every cleaner in the area. We can find the right one for you in three or four minutes'.[1]

3. Execution expertise

The whole point of my outsourcing building work to a builder is that he has the expertise to do a much better job than I can. Specialist expertise then, enriches outcomes while cutting costs. Where this combination matters, solution assemblers have an 'in'. Another special form of expertise is *customer* expertise – the ability to understand each particular customer's needs, preferences and circumstances to find the right collection of products and services 'for me'.

4. Administrative efficiencies

Coordinating things and people can be a nightmare. It takes time, costs money, and can be extremely stressful. Anybody who can lighten these time, money and stress costs is often welcomed into open arms.

Before the packaged holiday came along, the sheer hassle of trying to coordinate flight bookings to hotel bookings to airport transfer arrangements, and so on, meant that few people ever went on holiday abroad. By undertaking this task for thousands of people, packaged holiday companies drove these coordination costs down. They took the hassle out of arranging a holiday.

Solutions and services

- A solution is not the same as a service.
- The trouble with the word 'service' is that it is meaningless. It covers everything from burger flipping, to the professional advice of a lawyer, to a utility such as the supply of gas or the running of a bus service. It doesn't tell us anything specific.
- Most so-called 'services' are made and sold just like 'products'. We therefore avoid the word 'service' unless in the most general way, as in 'products and services'.

Improved planning is a key source of administrative and operational efficiency. As every factory owner knows, planned and preventative maintenance of machinery is usually far more efficient than crisis repairs. Planned maintenance nips problems in the bud, before they become too big. And because it is planned, work can be coordinated. If an engineer can address two jobs in one visit – because they have been planned ahead, and the information has been collated properly – time costs are slashed by nearly 50 percent. Ditto, if the operative can visit ten homes in the same postcode, for example, rather than rushing from one emergency to another.

That is why modern communications and information infrastructures – rich customer databases, customer contact strategies plus the mobile phone – are a crucial platform for many solution assemblers.

5. Local economies of scale

Local economies of scale are central to the viability of many solution assemblers, precisely because so many solutions revolve around a physical presence in or near the home. The home delivery-pizza parlour is a classic example. You need enough business within a few minutes delivery time to flourish. Likewise, doordrop densities are crucial to the economics of home-delivered groceries. If you can arrange three deliveries down the same road at the same time, rather than three separate deliveries at different times, you can cut out a massive amount of cost.

For many solution assemblers, therefore, a 'distributed processing' business model – achieving critical mass in many different locations – is far superior to the traditional centralized processing model of mass manufacturing focused on low unit costs. These local economies of scale create an opportunity for many small solutions-focused companies to grow 'bottom up', achieving 'national scale' by replicating the same basic success across many localities.

That doesn't mean would-be solutions have to be small. British Gas owner Centrica has many millions of customers but the same logic applies. Once it knows an engineer is booked to visit the London postcode SW4, it slots in other calls in the same area in the same day. Half the cost of providing home visits is the time spent travelling from one home to another, so the more homes you can visit within a few minutes of each other, the more you drive down costs.

Another angle on the same theme: if a customer buys every one of Centrica's services – provision of gas, electricity, telecoms services, central heating maintenance, plumbing maintenance, electricity maintenance, etc. – economies of scale emerge at the 'local' level of the individual. It's far cheaper to administer eight accounts with the same individual in an integrated, coordinated fashion – single billing, for example – than it is for eight different companies to manage eight different relationships.

6. Information 'logistics'

Effective solution assemblers need to be masters at 'information logistics': getting the right information to the right person at the right time. This is true for internal operational efficiency, as we've just seen, and for their service to their customers. In many areas of life – whether it's when one of your children is sick or wanting to do a 'makeover' to your garden – one of the key sources of hassle is simply getting hold of the right bits of information when you need them.

Information logistics is an emerging art. It replaces the information push of 'publishing' with the information pull of the consumer. The crucial skill: to tackle the twin evils of a lack of the right information on the one hand and information overload, which forces me to waste time sifting through loads of irrelevant or too detailed information, on the other hand.

The Internet and the mobile phone are making information logistics possible both technically and economically. Solution assemblers need to capitalize on this opportunity to the full. In the UK, for example, two Centrica subsidiaries – the AA and British Gas – are making added value information a key part of their offer.

Via its web-site the AA.com, for example, the motor assistance organization the Automobile Association offers access to car insurance, car-purchase loans, breakdown services, driving lessons, 'the complete works' of new car purchasing (including finding the car, buying it, having it checked by a mechanic, etc.), travel information, route planners, and hotel and holiday booking services – even information as to where the lowest price petrol stations are. It is, in other words, trying to offer all the information a motorist needs, all within easy reach.

Likewise, in late 2001 British Gas launched House.co.uk to provide 'everything you need to run your home online'. House.co.uk users could access the complete range of British Gas products and services (plus transaction-cost cutting self-service tasks such as meter reading and bill paying). However, as House.co.uk managing director Alan Higginson notes, many such ingredients do not make a solution. 'There were still gaps'.[2]

So British Gas has recruited a series of partners to round out the offer. Via the web site, customers can now buy home-related products and services (such as gas and central heating); access a wide range of tradesmen (plumbers, electricians, etc.); building contractors for home improvements; home security products and services; all the information and services needed to buy, sell and move home; loans to finance such moves; a product comparison in the guise of its Goldfish Guide, etc.

HomePro, which specializes in sourcing trusted builders for consumers, also offers design and do-it-yourself tips via its web site – and in future, it hopes, an online room design and project management kit. Meanwhile, Rockingfrog.com – a BT offshoot – offers a new type of mobile phone-based route planning service. If you're out shopping in London and you tell it 'I want to buy X and Y, meet so-and-so for lunch at one, and visit the British Museum', it will construct its own bespoke route map for you, and send special offers from retailers selling X and Y along the way, and from restaurant owners too.

Another variation on the same theme are the new 'one accounts' that combine a banking current account, a mortgage, a credit card and other loan services into one integrated package, with an array of online financial planning and budgeting tools designed to help customers manage their personal finances more efficiently and more effectively.

7. A gatekeeper role

By definition, solution assemblers act as a gatekeeper between me and the world of ingredient suppliers. They can use this gatekeeper role to add value and/or generate new revenue streams in a number of (mainly trading agency) ways. By acting as an efficient channel to market for specialist suppliers, they can earn commission and transaction fees. About 25 percent of Ten's revenues come from this source. By collecting more detailed information about what their customers want (from transaction data, queries, requests, complaints, etc.), they also become a source of invaluable market research information, for both themselves and their suppliers. Ten now tutors plumbing and other firms on customer service, for example.

As solution assemblers are a trusted source of information and advice, they also gain 'the ear' of their customers, long before any cold caller would do. By sifting messages and offers from suppliers they can earn contact/advertising fees while adding value. They can also use customers' combined buying power to source products and services more cheaply. The third key 'killer value add' of the packaged holiday (in addition to product expertise and coordinating efficiency) was the ability to bulk-buy flights and holidays, which drove down costs and made holidays abroad affordable for the first time. Likewise, in the long term, Ten UK, for example, hopes to be able to source cars direct from manufacturers at prices much lower than any individual would be able to obtain from a local dealer.

Such gatekeeper functions illustrate another distinguishing feature of new bottom line business models: personal asset utilization. Because solution assemblers help me make the most of precious personal assets such as time and energy, I am prepared to invest other assets – such as information, attention and money – in my relationship with them. They, in turn, use these assets to add further value for me – and as an income stream for themselves. This ability to utilize personal assets, both to add value and as a form of payment, is an essential 'glue' for most new bottom line business models.

FROM BUYING CARS TO PERSONAL MOBILITY?

To see how these seven key ingredients – balloon-squeezing, sourcing expertise, executional expertise, administrative efficiency, local economies of scale, 'information logistics' and a gatekeeper role – could transform the car owning experience, consider this hypothetical case study of a new apartment block near a city centre. Its residents are relatively affluent – you would expect each family to own at least one car – but parking restrictions and traffic jams also make car ownership a hassle. A hundred families occupy these flats. So instead of simply offering underground car parking as a 'perk' the property developer offers a complete personal mobility service.

He purchases (or leases) a variety of different kinds of cars. After careful study (and a few painful experiences) he discovers that having eighty cars on tap means that every resident can have immediate access to a vehicle at any time. He has also adjusted the types of cars he keeps. The vast majority are compact vehicles for inner city chores, but there are also some people carriers and larger sedans for longer journeys and family outings, plus a few pick-up trucks for moving furniture and the like.

Via their always-on broadband based in-home utility service, residents can check to see whether a car is available, signal to the fleet manager when they want to use one, and book in advance if they want to be extra sure that the vehicle is going to be available. Via a deal with a local car rental firm, the property company can also access extra vehicles when demand peaks and give residents access to special vehicles (say, a luxury car for a wedding, or a sports car for a romantic weekend away) at preferential rates.

The service offers many benefits to residents. First, it offers them a much greater variety of vehicles. Most families can only afford one car, and they have to use this car for a wide variety of purposes: going shopping at the supermarket, taking the dog for a walk, taking the family for a weekend away or moving furniture. This involves compromises. By aggregating and sharing across a hundred different families, the property company can provide them with exactly the right vehicle for exactly the right occasion: a much richer match to residents' needs, in other words.

Second, the property company takes the hassle of car ownership off its residents' shoulders. It arranges all car insurance, taxes, road assistance services, vehicle servicing and repairs. It also keeps the cars clean and makes sure they've always got fuel.

Third, it provides these extra benefits at a cost lower than each resident would have to pay to own and run their own cars. Assuming that normally each family would have one car, the fact that a fleet of 80 meets virtually all of their needs means that total costs are cut by 20 percent, immediately. (In its own small way, this way the scheme also helps reduce road congestion.) In addition, the fact that he is operating on a fleet basis (perhaps with many such schemes across many apartment blocks in many cities) means that he has bargaining power with motor car companies, rental companies, insurance providers and so on. This means costs are reduced even further, enabling him to employ a fleet manager to manage servicing, administration, etc. – something that also adds a personal touch to the service for residents.

Charges for the service are related, at least partly, to intensity of use: the more miles you drive the more you pay.

Of course, the service doesn't suit everyone. For some people, ownership of a particular brand of car is a deep personal joy and key to their identity. Simply having access to any old car, chosen by someone else, just isn't for them. Others don't like the fact that moving apartment would also involves rethinking their car arrangements. A certain degree of education is also needed to explain why the service offers such good value for money: most consumers gravely underestimate how much they actually spend on owning and running a car.

There are also a whole series of critical operational hurdles that just must be right. Having a vehicle available instantly, 'when I need it', is vital, for example. Managing the trade-off between such availability and having expensive assets lying idle is key. For this reason, the property company might outsource the whole operation to a local car hire company or even to a manufacturer. By cutting a deal with the likes of Ford or General Motors to provide the complete service from within their range of vehicles and brands, the property company could outsource this risk while offering Ford a chance to boost its 'market share' – while freezing GM out of the picture. Competition between manufacturers for such opportunities may be another factor bringing down the price of the whole service. An added benefit for them: the valuable 'real time' and ongoing market research such a service would provide.

THE LURE OF SOLUTIONS

In terms of sheer size and scale, solution assembly is probably the biggest of our three main new bottom line opportunities. Successful solution assembly represents a classic marketing dream come true. It offers:

■ *Massively increased share of purse.* Just a few solution assemblers who successfully tackle my home, my personal financial management and my car could very quickly 'eat up' 50 percent or more of my total annual spending.

■ *Almost assured customer loyalty:* by definition, a successful solution assembler embeds itself within my life. To borrow a famous phrase from American Express, 'I don't leave home without it'. And as long as it continues to deliver the goods, I'm very unlikely to risk, or bother, changing it.

■ *A strategic gatekeeper role.* Every marketer dreams of 'owning' the customer relationship which clinches the gatekeeper role discussed above. Almost by definition, successful solution assemblers achieve such a role.

However, solution assembly comes at a high price, especially for traditional old bottom liners. It requires nothing less than a complete re-orientation of the business to new bottom line principles. In particular, it requires:

■ *A completely new balance of costs versus revenue streams,* requiring different infrastructure, processes and skills. To be economically viable, the solution assembler will almost certainly need a combination of the key sources of added value discussed here. Miss out on one, and the entire offer may not 'gel'.

■ *The customer relationship is now the company's core asset*, not factories, shops, offices, or infrastructure. For the solution assembler, everything flows from, and depends on, the success and richness of their relationship with their customer. To be sure, successful solution assemblers squeeze every last drop of efficiency out of their assets and infrastructure. But they configure these assets and operations around the demands of their customers' efficiency and productivity. This is the *opposite* of traditional customer relationship management, which is all about building a better relationship in order to sell more of what is made, so that the seller's assets can be utilized more efficiently.

■ *A new level of trust is vital.* Solution assemblers need to deliver on two crucial dimensions of trust: competence trust (the ability to actually do the job well), and relationship trust (me trusting you to be on my side, to act in my interests). Without either, the relationship evaporates, and along with it, the entire business.

■ *Efficient operations.* New information technologies provide the hidden backbone of many emerging solution assembly offerings. Without the ability to offer and organize superb information logistics, self-service to reduce running and transaction costs, efficient, effective customer relationship management, and efficient service coordination and administration, they probably could not get off the ground. That is one reason why the solution assembly challenge is only emerging now.

Solution assembly, then, relies on a new bottom line dynamic which is utterly different to the make-and-sell priorities of the old bottom liner. The question, then, is how can fully fledged solution assemblers emerge?

TWO ALTERNATIVE ROUTES

Companies are addressing the solution opportunity from two very different directions. The first comes mainly from traditional industry incumbents seeking to add value for their customers by 'rounding out' their existing offers. Any of the key elements of solution assembly – specialist expertise, local infrastructure, ability to coordinate or provide information – can be an entry point and springboard for this strategy. The alternative approach is more 'greenfield': to skate above the existing supplier base as a 'virtual integrator', integrating their disparate offers into a new and different package.

Rounding out the offer

The 'rounding out' route is popular precisely because it seems so 'natural' to existing companies – and because incremental revenues seem so easy to gain. In retailing, Tesco's move into home-delivered groceries is a step towards home replenishment, and perhaps even home maintenance, solution assembly. Many financial services companies are racing to bundle ever more financial services products – current account, credit card, savings, loans, mortgages, insurance, pensions – into complete, integrated packages. The customer benefits because the time and hassle spent monitoring account activity, transferring funds from one account to another etc. is reduced. The financial services company benefits from gaining a bigger share of purse.

When Lufthansa formed star Alliance it changed the face of aviation. Without such an alliance no matter how good, or big, its own network, its customers would always be going to other destinations, at other times, where it could not offer a flight. The Star Alliance group therefore rounds out what each individual airline offers by offering a vastly expanded range of destinations, while driving all manner of customer and corporate efficiencies – coordinated schedules and 'single ticket' purchasing, for example. We look at the Star Alliance in more detail in Chapter 9.

Internet flight booking sites such as Expedia and Travelocity quickly branched out, offering hotel and car-hire bookings too – along with weather reports for locations and other local information. Such services save customers time and hassle – making the site a 'one stop shop', while opening up new revenue streams for the provider. Software company Microsoft is meanwhile betting big on 'the intelligent home': integrating computing, telecoms and software services that link and manage all the information needed to run a home.

In addition to promising to 'stamp down on prices' the UK computer retailer PC World offers its unconfident novice customers impartial advice as to the best PC for their particular needs, help with installation and repairs and upgrades – services that relate to 'ownership costs' rather than just purchase costs.

British Gas started out as a one-plank seller of a single commodity: gas. Then it added electricity, to become an energy provider, and telecommunications, to become a multi-utility. It also added a service element: fixing gas boilers, for example. Then it turned these services into annual maintenance contracts: an annual check up plus instant repairs of your central heating system. And it provides similar services for electricity and plumbing too. The ultimate aim? Says marketing director Simon Waugh, to 'move from home services to home management'.[3] Likewise, with Centrica's other subsidiary, the AA, which is seeking to offer 'all the essentials' relating to cars: the full continuum filling the gap between actually making the car and putting petrol in its tank.

Virtual integration

There are two drawbacks to the 'rounding out' approach to solution assembly. First, the 'gravitational pull' of the company's 'core' business may pull it back from investing fully in the skills or infrastructure needed for full solution assembly. Second, it begins to confuse solution assembly with cross-selling (see below).

The alternative is to start with a 'clean sheet', to 'skim' above many, separate ingredient suppliers and to focus on integrating their offers into complete solutions as, and how, their customers want it. One example is Citibank's financial aggregation service MyCiti.com. It doesn't offer any financial service *per se*. What it offers instead, is easier account administration, financial management and planning. The portal allows visitors to have a consolidated view of all their financial accounts (including current accounts, savings, loans, credit-cards, investments, insurance and others) regardless of supplier, including the ability to access them online.

In addition, it allows customers to build in financial news, market prices, email accounts, bulletin boards, etc., into their personal view. It also provides financial advice relating to life events such as becoming a student, getting married, starting a family, buying a home, and planning retirement, plus a series of calculators aimed at helping the customer plan for life events and other financially related matters (e.g., debt consolidation and home equity). In this way, Citibank is placing itself between the customer and its many separate financial service ingredient suppliers, helping her manage her dealings with them.

Other highly successful business models have taken the same approach. Home-delivery pizza parlours have nothing to do with the actual manufacturing of flour, cheese or tomatoes. They simply source and integrate these ingredients from suppliers. Likewise (before vertical integration became fashionable), packaged holiday companies did not own airlines or hotels. They simply sourced them and packaged them. They 'floated above' ingredient supply to focus on coordination and integration (and marketing) instead.

BOX 5.1 THE TEN UK EXAMPLE

Perhaps the most extreme example is Ten (Time Energy Network) which does not specialise in any particular sector or category but instead promises that its teams of lifestyle managers will organize any solution its members want, whatever it happens to be. It may be something mundane like finding someone to do the ironing, or arranging to have their car serviced. It may be something exotic like researching, booking and organizing the holiday of a lifetime. Or it may be taking on a high-risk, high-stress activity like finding a builder for a home improvement project and/or organizing and overseeing his work.

Ten started five years ago with a tiny turnover of £25,000. It now operates in the UK and Germany, boasts 7,000 members and £3 million turnover — and funding from Germany consumer goods giant Henkel. Its core proposition: it does jobs better and more efficiently than its members can.

Ten's services don't come cheap. Members pay £150 a month for its core offer. But for that they get their own 'life manager' who is on call twelve hours a day, and guaranteed to help with any problem. (There is an even more 'upmarket' service for those who want 24-hour access to help, and a stripped down service for £50 which, say, will find a trustworthy plumber for you, but won't oversee his work.)

According to CEO Alex Cheatle, each year the average member asks Ten to do eighty jobs — more than one a week — with some members' requests rising to over 120. With each job requiring an average of three contacts between member and life manager, Ten UK is very much a part of their daily lives.

In its five years, Ten UK has learned some important lessons. One is that human contact is important. People like being able to talk to people they know — and to people who know them. Ten could use more technology to automate customer contacts, but that would undermine the relationship, and as Cheatle remarks, 'We didn't start with products and services we wanted to sell. We started with the sort of relationship we wanted to create.'[5]

Another key consideration is Ten's financial incentives. Ten earns around 25 percent of its income from supplier commissions, but Cheatle doesn't want that figure to grow much larger because then it may become (or its members may perceive it to become) more influenced by the size of the seller's commission than the member's interests. Instead, with its high membership fees, Ten's overriding financial incentive is to maintain the relationship.

Trust is also a vital part of Ten's economics. 'A lack of trust is incredibly inefficient for us,' notes Cheatle. It means members are always ringing up or e-mailing to make sure things are OK. High levels of trust, on the other hand, add value for both sides. It is a simple virtuous circle, he argues. As soon as members are confident that Ten has 'my best interests at heart' then they also feel that 'the more I tell you, the more you can help me'. This information means that Ten 'knows' its members far more intimately than any traditional firm. Says Cheatle, 'once people know we are on their side, they are incredibly honest about their situation.'

The next step has come as something of a surprise. As Cheatle explains 'People are asking us to be far more proactive than we ever thought. They are asking to be led. They want us to suggest things to them.' Thus, for example, busy professional couples who are working all hours during the week often face a weekend with nothing planned: so they ask Ten to organize one in four weekends away. And because Ten's lifestyle manager knows them personally, and their preferences, they trust him or her to come up with good ideas. All they have to do is say 'Yes' or 'No'. The lifestyle manager sorts out everything else for them.

The crucial point is that this simply wouldn't happen without that 'on my side' trust. Says Cheatle: 'They trust us to suggest things with them in mind, rather than suggesting things that the company has in mind to try and sell to them.'

The big question for Ten, however, is whether it can ever become more than a plaything of the very rich. Cheatle estimates that up to 20 percent of the UK population have the money and the psychographic profile (they're 'delegators' rather than 'control freaks') to fit a service like Ten's. 'It will become the common sense solution for anybody who values their time and wants to get expertise,' he suggests. While some people find the whole concept 'really scary', others (especially the under 40s) 'just get it'.

PITFALLS ALONG THE WAY

Solution assembly has many attractions but it also brings many pitfalls. It poses huge technical and executional challenges: when the offer is so intimate to 'my life' you just have to get the service right. It also poses some acute economic and relationship management challenges.

Balloon-squeezing

Cost and price-wise, the degree of pure balloon squeezing versus real added value will determine how far or fast the service is likely to grow. Even Tesco's £5 delivery charge puts many customers off its home delivery service: the vast majority of customers still prefer to do the job themselves. Likewise, when Unilever experimented with a move towards solution assembly with its 'My Home' home-cleaning and clothes-laundering service, it tended to offer a straight trade-off of money for time, without realizing any new synergies. It also found itself on a steep learning curve: managing and coordinating a cohort of cleaning staff – people it wasn't used to dealing with. Eventually, it withdrew.

Chores plc, the UK company that acquired Unilever's My Home cleaning services is now attempting to generate new synergies (more revenue from each customer at less incremental cost) by extending its services to include home security, gardening, etc. Says chairman Tony Hoskinson, 'We have in mind to organize people's homes from top to bottom'.[5]

Cross-selling

Many companies parade cross-selling under the banner of offering solutions, when in fact in many ways the two are at complete loggerheads. Cross-selling is the epitome of seller-centric thinking. It's the attempt to get ever more value out of a customer at lower cost, by selling ever more things to the same customer and ignores virtually every new bottom line consideration.

By simply offering many separate ingredients to the same customer for example, it does little to address the consumer's solution assembly needs in terms of access to information and the time, work, energy and hassle involved in accessing, coordinating and integrating separate services. Under Jacques Nasser, Ford moved into a wide variety of car-related services such as the UK roadside assistance provider Kwik Fit. But it never integrated them in any way, so consumers never experienced any significant financial, time or other benefit. His 'back-to-basics' successor subsequently unloaded the business, at great expense.

Also the focus of cross-selling is added value and convenience for the company, not the customer. Far from sourcing the best product most suited to the needs of the individual customer, the cross-seller is intent on pushing his own product at the customer – usually at a very high margin. The only 'benefit' it offers is actually a disguised form of taking advantage. The cross-seller takes advantage of the fact that the consumer faces additional search and transaction costs looking for a better deal, and so might simply opt for the 'easiest' option.

At worst, aggressive cross-selling driven strategies may actively undermine customer trust, and destroy the very relationships upon which the whole strategy depend. Most financial institutions are still ensnared by the dream of cross-selling. Both of Centrica's attempts to move towards solution assembly – in home management and car management – risk being scuppered by a prevailing cross-sell mentality.

Critical mass

If cross-selling is the big obstacle for established brands, critical mass – in terms of brand recognition, relationship building, trust building and operational infrastructure – is the biggest obstacle facing start-ups attempting to 'float' above the established infrastructure. That is Ten UK's challenge in moving beyond its current well-heeled client base. Likewise Chores chairman Tony Hoskinson insists that his can become a national brand – but only by achieving local economies of scale in one area after another. A slow process, in other words.

RETHINKING 'INDUSTRIES'

It certainly won't be easy, but thanks to a convergence of many forces – growing affluence, new technologies, changing attitudes, and the increasing economic value of customer relationships and trust – the time is ripe for the emergence of a range of different types of solution assembler. Separately and together these solutions assemblers are poised to trigger radical change across every consumer-facing industry. Any product or service related to an area such as personal financial management, personal health and fitness, personal mobility, home maintenance and repair, home replenishment, home operations (such as cooking and cleaning), and personal communications and information could be affected.

Business strategies will also be affected. Solution assemblers challenge the status quo. They require new business models (including costs, revenue streams, operations and assets), skills and areas of expertise, attitudes and culture, and organizational structures. But by saving me time, energy, hassle and stress and boosting my personal productivity, successful solution assemblers put themselves in a hugely powerful position, gaining access to a greater share of total customer spend, preferential attention, greater access to richer customer information, and a privileged gatekeeper role vis-à-vis other companies and brands whose products and services risk being marginalized and 'ingredient-ized'.

Those that get it right – via new kinds of relationship between consumers and companies and new levels of value and trust – will raise consumer expectations, with knock-on effects for all companies. They also blur old industry boundaries and create entirely new value offerings. But there's one thing solution assemblers cannot do. They may save me time. They may ease a lot of stress. They may, sometimes, even save me money. But what they can't do is 'make me happy'. Emotional fulfilment is not their forte. For that, I will have to turn to a different type of new bottom liner.

Summary

The second main form of new bottom line business model is solution assembly. Solution assemblers help individuals maximize the efficiency and productivity of the things they need to do to create value in my life – things like run a home, administer finances, organize personal transport and so on.

They take ingredients offered by traditional suppliers in the form of products, services and information and integrate them to help individuals realize the outputs or results they want.

To achieve commercial viability solution assemblers need to innovate in a number of areas, such as using new technologies to achieve much closer (and cheaper) integration and coordination of supplier activities, generating new local economies of scale and managing relationships to maximize trust and access to information.

The rewards of success are access to a much higher share of 'customer purse' and a trusted gatekeeper role vis-à-vis traditional suppliers.

The rise of solution assembly points to new divisions of labour between producers and customers and promises to blur traditional industry boundaries.

There are two main ways of approaching 'solution markets': by 'rounding out' the value offered by one particular ingredient; or by 'hovering above' individual ingredient suppliers and integrating their separate offers into complete solutions.

6 Passion Partnership

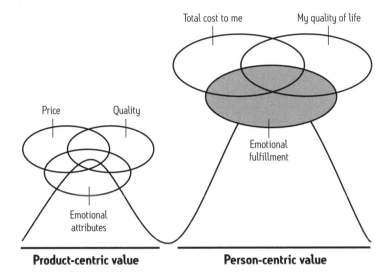

Product-centric value | Person-centric value

'A walk down a wooded trail, the whirr of a bicycle on a winding road, the dip and splash of a paddle into still water, or the moment of quiet at the top of a ski run. Such things allow people to escape, reflect, de-stress and return to their daily lives collected with a greater sense of clarity and purpose'.[1]

If the CEO of a normal retailer came up with such purple prose, it would be dismissed as cynical PR-inspired hype. But somehow when Dennis Marsden, president and CEO of specialist outdoor retailer REI, says his organization's purpose is to 'help people connect to the outdoor', it is at least credible. That's because REI is different.

It was set up 1938 by a group of 23 mountaineers, not because they saw a market niche and a business opportunity, but because they loved

---

TASKS FOR THIS CHAPTER

1. Explore the notion of passion partnership.
2. Explain its enormous potential.

mountaineering and wanted to get hold of the best quality gear at the best price. So they formed a buying cooperative – a business venture designed to make their passion more affordable. They were putting commerce to the service of their passion, rather than attempting to put passion into the service of commerce.

Today, REI employs six thousand people in 60 stores across the US, turning over in excess of $700 million. It still underlines its founders' original message, however – that we're not just here for the money – by retaining its cooperative form and returning a portion of each year's profits to members (linked to how much they've spent at REI in the last year), and by promoting its original passions.

It doesn't just employ people for whom work is 'just a job' – a means to an end. It employs outdoor enthusiasts, who bring with them their own knowledge, expertise and enthusiasm. This creates a bond between customer and employee that goes beyond the simple instrumental relationship of buying, selling and customer service. (We'll return to this in Chapter 10.)

It doesn't only do market research. It also involves both employees and customers in product testing. It encourages them to share knowledge and expertise in its specially created Learn and Share section on its website: so it's also the organizer of a peer-to-peer network of enthusiasts. Sometimes it brings them together by organizing special holidays for like-minded enthusiasts. In addition, it campaigns actively to protect the outdoors its staff and customers value so much. So it's not just a retailer or a cooperative. It's a community organizer, adventure holiday organizer and pressure group too.

THE PASSION PEAK

Trading agents help me maximize the efficiency with which I acquire the inputs of my life. Solution assemblers save me time and help me maximize the efficiency with which I undertake core life processes such as running a home. But it is passion partners who truly help me maximize my personal bottom line, by helping me to do the things I really want to do in my life.

Put it this way: I need the services of the first two to free up and maximize my resources – time, energy, money and so on – so that I can invest even more in what really matters to me.

Passion partners are a new type of business. The old bottom line attitude towards personal emotions is ambivalent, contradictory and ultimately damaging. On the one hand, old bottom liners fear people's emotions, values and passions because they might get in the way of rational decisions to maximize efficiency, productivity and profitability. On the other hand, recognizing the enormous power and potential of the human heart, they seek to corral its power and use it to their own ends: to increase their own bottom line. Neither approach works.

In passion partnership, the passion in question is the business. It is the product. This makes it far more rewarding than any 'normal' commercial activity, even if it is not so financially profitable. Whether they are in it for financial profit or not, the acid test for the passion partner is whether or not they boost my emotional bottom line. The basic rule is: no personal emotional profit, no financial viability.

At the same time, every passion partner has to at least cover its costs, so it must generate a commercially viable business model. That is what gives passion partnership its enormous power: the fusion of passion and commerce. By aligning commerce to passion, rather than attempting to align passion to commerce, passion partnership unleashes the power and potential of both. Combined.

And remember. The potential 'market' (if that is the right word) for such 'emotional added value' is infinite. There are no limits to growth here. You can never have too much fun, fulfilment or happiness, whereas you can have 'enough', or even too much, of most physical products such as food. Yet, old bottom liners are effectively excluded from the full potential of this 'market'. Let's see why.

Instrumentalism

Instrumental attitudes and practices are the main barrier. It is now commonplace for companies to recognize the importance of 'emotional capital' for and within their business. But the imperatives of the old bottom line mean that no sooner is the power of emotion recognized than there's an attempt to 'capture', channel and deploy these emotions: as a means to the *corporation's* ends, not that of the individual.

Thus, when soap powder companies bombard women with 'clean clothes = good mother' imagery, it's not because they want to help women to become good mothers. It's because they want to corral and channel womens' wishes to be good mothers into a good way of selling more soap powder. Old bottom line branding lives and breathes 'emotional added value', but most such 'brand building' merely attempts to use people's emotions to old bottom line ends, not to actually meet people's emotional needs.

The same goes for employees. In recent years, an entire new human resources and internal communications sub-industry has emerged with one core purpose: to unleash the enthusiasm, dedication and commitment of employees – to go that extra mile, provide outstanding customer service and become 'brand ambassadors'. But it's one thing to recognize the power of human emotions for what they can do for the business. It's quite another to ask what the business can do to enrich the emotions in 'my life'. We return to this in Chapter 11.

Instrumentalism rules the roost in old bottom line businesses, but when it comes to human emotions it is invariably counter-productive. This is because, if you treat me instrumentally, then I tend to treat you in the same way. After all, why should individuals invest their most personal emotional assets in a business that seeks to 'sweat' this asset for its own purposes, with little or no thought of the needs or priorities of the investor?

Why Old bottom liners miss out on 'passion markets'

1. Their instrumental attitudes
2. Artificial divisions of labour between 'for profit' and 'not for profit' organizations
3. The nature of old bottom line business models.

In this way, instrumental old bottom line businesses tend to stifle the very emotional investment they seek. There are some hugely powerful win-wins to be had from different parties using each for their own purposes, as Adam Smith recognized many years ago. But they don't even begin to address the power of human passions.

Artificial divisions of labour

The traditional old bottom line response to its fear of human emotions 'getting in the way' of sound business decisions has been to create a clear division of labour between instrumental profit-oriented organizations – focused on bringing products to market for sale at a profit – and other types of organizations and institutions – churches, clubs, charities, political parties, voluntary groups and so on – which deal with the emotional side of things: *values* rather than *value*.

There is a certain logic to this division of labour. It is difficult to serve both masters. Yet at the same time, real people care about all aspects of their lives, and the artificial division of organizational labour has two stunting effects. It constrains people's emotional investment in the commercial side of business. And it relegates not-for-profit, values-driven organizations to a marginal niche.

Ultimately this neat distinction between 'for-profit' and 'not-for-profit' *is* artificial. *Homo economicus* – a rational economic man who carefully calculates the economic benefits of each transaction – is a fictional character invented by industrial age economists. He never really existed.

We can see proof of this everywhere we look. It's now accepted that companies are much more than neat organisation charts: inside, they seethe with passions both positive and negative: pride and greed, ambition and fear, achievement and envy. Huge industrial age markets help address consumers' emotional needs, in passing, in some way or another. Bars and restaurants create an environment where people can meet – we don't only go to them to eat and drink.

Most markets have a definite 'passion segment': groups of consumers for whom the product or service in question plays a major part in their lives. While the main trend in advanced Western economies has been to outsource food preparation to fast food and other suppliers (basically, a solution assembly approach) there has also been a significant counter-trend too: of slow food or 'gourmet' cooking as a hobby. For these enthusiasts food ingredients and cooking – and eating socially – constitute a veritable passion in its own right.

Indeed you can, if you want, redefine most traditional businesses' core offerings in terms of the emotional value they add. Instead of talking about the telephone market, for example, you could talk about the market for 'togetherness'. As Rolf Jensen suggests in his influential book *The Dream Society*, you could place some cars into a similar 'togetherness' category because they help bring people together, while putting others in the 'who am I?' market, because they help to express a person's sense of identity as a badge or status symbol. Yet others address the market for 'peace of mind' (e.g., Volvo and safety). And so on.[2]

On top of that, there are entire industries which sell 'packaged emotions'. Hollywood sells packaged emotions. Disney sells packaged experiences. A thousand and one specialist manufacturers, magazines, television programmes and web sites address the interests and needs of those with hobbies, special interests and enthusiasms.

Ultimately, however, for the reasons we've already discussed, these old bottom forays into 'passion' markets are only scratching the surface. Redefining traditional markets by the emotions they might address can only take you so far: you still end up trying to use people's emotions to help sell the product. And industrial age 'packaged emotion producers' such as Hollywood are still very much stuck within industrial age business models. They all follow the industrial age route of investing in a set of core productive assets (such as film studios, film stars, theme parks and editorial offices) and then sweating these assets to create products and services that (hopefully) sell well. Once my needs for emotional fulfilment stretch beyond these boundaries, however, such models are incapable of meeting them.

SCALING THE PASSION PEAK

By aligning commerce to passions, and recognizing the new bottom line imperative that the purpose of the business is to boost my personal bottom line, passion partners transcend these old bottom line limitations. But how? Here are 'ten secrets of passion partner success'.

Ten secrets of passion partnership

1. A passion asset
2. Partnership
3. Authenticity
4. A different level of trust
5. Involvement
6. Community
7. People/employees
8. Products/platforms
9. Information
10. Integration

A passion asset

The central defining asset of each passion brand is the passion itself. This passion could be almost anything. Obvious candidates include sports, the arts, leisure pursuits such as walking, gardening or cooking, fascinations such as history or fashion, hobbies such as building model boats or collecting antiques, strongly held beliefs and causes such as 'save the whale': any and everything where the prime motivation – and outcome – is emotional rather than practical, operational or instrumental.

The key point about all such passion assets is that they reside first and foremost in people's hearts. They cannot be made, owned or sold by a corporation. They cannot become the private property of any company. Companies may create products or services, or organize events, that appeal to or serve this passion. But ultimately the passion itself is created, owned and controlled by individuals. That is why passion partners have to follow the logic of the new bottom line.

Partnership

Passion partnerships reach beyond traditional buyer/seller relationships. A passion is not a product you buy and consume. It is shared. A passion partner does not have 'consumers' or 'customers'. It has members, fans, enthusiasts and supporters (even if, formally, speaking they are on its 'staff'). It doesn't so much 'make' a product or service which it then tries to sell. Rather, members, fans and supporters 'make' or 'pursue' their passion *with* and *through* the passion partner. The core relationship and appeal, then, is not so much 'Buy Me!' as 'Join Me!'

Authenticity

For such a 'Join Me' appeal to be credible it must be authentic. In a passion partnership, shared commitment to a particular cause, hobby or pastime is an essential ingredient of the relationship. Simply seeing my passion as a means to an end – closing sales, making money – devalues my passion and threatens to undermine the relationship. As Christopher Locke – one of the co-authors of the influential *Cluetrain Manifesto* – puts it: 'It's about transforming the marketing message from "we want your money" to "we share your interests".'[3]

A different level of trust

Passion partners therefore require a different level of trust. Consumers trust traditional brands to keep their product or service promises: to 'do what it says on the tin'. This form of trust is absolutely necessary if marketplace transactions are to be closed successfully. But it is an instrumental, arm's length sort of trust. Passion partnership, on the other hand, requires trust in *people* and their motives, not just trust in products and their quality. If trading agents and solution assemblers rely on 'on my side' trust (as well as 'competence' trust) passion partners rely on 'integrity' trust. Confidence that we are all 'fighting in the same cause' is vital if a pressure group is to campaign effectively, for example.

Involvement

Involvement is a necessary ingredient of partnership. Consumers buying Hollywood and Disney products don't need to be involved. They just have to consume the product. But to flourish, passion partners positively depend on members/supporters involvement, to some degree or another. To truly invest in your passion, you need to invest time, work and energy.

A pressure group or voluntary organization without activists, members or supporters is nothing. A football match without fans is a dull, empty, dead affair.

Community

If something fascinates or concerns us deeply we naturally want to share this fascination or concern with other people. Passions are the gravitational force of communities. Communities form around their shared interests and concerns. This 'peer-to-peer' element is a crucial ingredient of most successful passion partners.

In the industrial age, special-interest publications and television programmes went some way towards bringing like-minded people together, giving them a sense that they were sharing news, views, opinions and so on. Now new technologies such as the Internet and the mobile phone are creating endless, powerful new ways to organize communities to bring people together virtually. But passion partners don't stop there. They also encourage people to come together physically – becoming consummate event organizers too.

People/employees

One of the tests of a passion partner's authenticity is the people it employs. People don't work for a passion partner as a means to an end. You don't choose to work for a passion partner if your basic attitude is 'it's just a job'. You choose to work for that particular passion partner because you are committed to or fascinated by the relevant passion. The sorts of people the passion partner employs, how it treats them, and how it uses them to communicate with and relate to the public are all crucial. The enthusiasm, commitment and knowledge of employees helps the passion partner stand out from 'ordinary' organizations.

Products/platforms

It's almost impossible to pursue a hobby, fascination or leisure pursuit without the necessary 'tools of the trade'. You can't play golf without golf clubs, golf balls and golf courses, for example. Thousands of specialist

Table 6.1 Differences between passion partners and traditional brands

Traditional brands	Passion partners
Address emotional added value as a means of boosting the corporate bottom line.	Accept the logic of emotional added value from the individual's point of view.
Sells passion ingredients and aids: products, content, experiences etc.	Address the passion as 'the product', seeking involvement, building communities etc.
Focus on traditional exchange: money in exchange for goods and services.	Utilise member/supporters' input across all 'optimal' dimensions: work, passion, time, information, money, attention.
Core relationship: with 'buyers' and 'consumers'.	Core relationship: with members, fans, supporters, activists, etc.
Trust: at level of product and transaction.	Trust: at level of motive and relationship.
Employees work as means to an end: 'it's just a job'.	Employees' commitment to cause is key to recruitment and external communication.

manufacturers and retailers already flourish by making and selling the ingredients people need to pursue their various passions. But this, in itself, is not passion partnership. Such manufacturers and retailers have two basic options: a) to use this 'in' as a springboard to a passion partnership role (as in the case of REI) or b) to use passion partners as a crucial channel to market.

Information and content

Likewise, every cause and every hobby generates demand for a vast amount of information: news, views, insight, expert advice, opinion, debate and so on. Specialist media owners have flourished by meeting this demand. Passion partners subsume this service into their overall offers. Their members and supporters also become important sources of new content in their own right.

Integration

All of the above nine are important ingredients of passion partnership, but ultimately the real purpose – and added value – of the passion partner is their ability to fuse them together into a single, integrated, coherent whole. It's how these ingredients come together that matters: in one sense, passion partners are a special form of solution assembler (see Table 6.1).

THE PASSION BUSINESS

Effectively integrating commitment, community and commerce – people, products and information – to truly boost my personal, emotional bottom line is a new type of business. And it requires its own special type of business model. Passion partners may help create and offer far more emotional value than most traditional businesses. But to survive they also need to *get more value* in return. How? To be sure, this is an endless balancing act – and a key skill – for every would-be passion partner. Mixing passions and commerce is difficult, but when done successfully it is hugely powerful.

One answer is that successful passion partners are passed masters at tapping people's OPTIMAL assets. They access and source members and supporters' operations (work), passion, time, information and attention, and deploy them as key parts of their business model both to reduce costs and create extra value. On the cost reduction side, passion partners have many advantages over traditional businesses.

- Marketing. The passion partner's 'customers' tend to be self-selecting, self-recruiting and self-retaining. What's more, they tend to 'spread the word' naturally, on account of their own enthusiasm. Result: formal marketing costs are massively reduced.
- 'The product'. Passion partnership is a classic 'prosumer' business model. Members, supporters etc., go a long way to 'making the product' for each other, whether it is contributing content on a web site or helping to organize and make events happen. Indeed, in many senses, with the passion partner its people are its product.

- Staff costs. With passion partners, people tend to work for love rather than money, so formal employment costs can be lower than a typical commercial organization. Hollywood pays actors millions of dollars. The *maximum* wage for an actor at the Royal Court Theatre in London – which has a reputation for being a writer's and actor's theatre is £320 per week.

On the other hand, passion partners often incur higher costs in areas such as content management (they have to remain at the 'cutting edge' of their passion, investing heavily in identifying and passing on the most up-to-date ideas, commentary, developments etc.) member relationship management and coordination; ethics (which can sometimes mean that costs are higher) and where appropriate, campaigning (which is always expensive).

BOX 6.1 THE BAYERN MUNICH EXAMPLE

One example of so-far successful management of the commerce/passion balancing act is Bayern Munich football club. Twenty years ago it had eight thousand members. Thanks to the media/sporting revolution its membership has rocketed more than tenfold since then, with the number of supporters quadrupling from two million to eight million. Along the way, its finances have been turned upside down. Twenty years ago 80 percent of total revenue came from stadium tickets. Today, that figure is closer to 20 percent, with the rest coming from television rights, sponsorship, merchandising and so on.

The big danger with such commercialisation is that while supporters know that, to flourish, their clubs need to make more money and have welcomed club initiatives to become more commercial, there has also been growing resentment, as many have begun to feel that their club has forgotten its 'real purpose' and is simply trying to exploit 'my passion' to make money.

In such circumstances, feeding the passion as well as the purse is crucial, as Bayern Munich deputy chairman Uli Hoeness has been well aware. Hoeness has been instrumental in keeping the club's eyes firmly on profitability and financial viability – avoiding the huge mountains of debt built up by some of his competitors. But at the same time, he has tried hard to keep members and supporters with him. He calls it 'watching the streams' (of mood and opinion).

He has, for instance, keep stadium ticket prices deliberately low. 'We don't want first class fans [who can afford to see matches lives] and second class fans [who can't],' he says. 'The crowd is very important for the game'.[4] Unlike many other clubs which have sold as many strips as possible, constantly changing them in order to force fans to buy the latest version, Hoeness has also held back from exploiting fans' enthusiasm via excessive merchandising. Bayern Munich only sells two strips (a to-die-for item for children): one for home, and one for away. And it only makes one change a year.

Meanwhile, he has worked hard to improve stadium facilities, not only to boost revenue streams but because they're increasingly part of the total experience. 'People should feel good in the stadium. It's a question of service.' Before, he notes, people would come to the stadium in time for a 3.30 kick off. 'Now they want to come at 12 and leave at six. They want to watch the videos, go to the restaurant. What they want is different.' Even so, Hoeness has been wary about going public to raise funds for a new stadium because, he notes, raising money in this way tends to make football clubs 'greedy'.

Keeping close to the passion is important as much to players as supporters. Unlike many clubs Bayern Munich has avoided active 'trading' of players and focused instead on team building. 'You can have a team made up of the most expensive players, but they won't make the best team,' notes Hoeness. Equally important is a sense of comradeship, a good coach, and a feeling for the club. In other words, players' values, as well as goal-scoring value, matter.

Says Hoeness, 'The criteria for buying a player is not only how good he is on the field but his character, his private life and his personal targets.' Is the player trying to use the club as a platform for his personal ambition, he asks. Or does he have ambitions for the club itself? It is Bayern Munich's people that 'sell' the club, not 'marketing', he insists, 'The best PR is the team and the management.'

A 'growth market'

The Bayern Munich example underlines one of the crucial characteristics of the passion partnership market: its is growing very rapidly. The impetus for this growth takes many forms, but they all boil down to the same fundamental trend. The old bottom line straitjacket – instrumental attitudes and behaviours, artificial divisions of labour between for profit and not-for-profit organizations and the narrowness of industrial-age business models – is being broken by a series of unstoppable tectonic shifts.

One driver of change is the rising power and influence of the media. The media is not only expert at packaging and selling emotions. It has also unleashed important side effects. One such trend is to capitalize on the commercial value of various passions. Sport is the classic example. A strong passion means a large, enthusiastic audience, and large enthusiastic audiences command big advertising budgets. Sports such as football, which were very much the preserve of the 'not-for-profit' enthusiast's club, have, as a result, crossed over into the world of mega-bucks 'for-profits' business – and many struggled to make the transition.

Another side effect of media power is the rise of the pressure group: the rechannelling of protest from mainly political channels into commercial channels too. Pressure groups are a relatively recent invention designed to deploy the power of the media to force instrumentally oriented businesses to address the world of *values* as well as value. In so doing, they are forcing organizations to blur those once-clear boundaries between value and values. Nowadays, we test and judge organizations by a combination of both.

The resulting pressure to 'humanize' money-making machines takes two forms. First, the demand for a sense of affinity. We want to feel (at some level or other) that the people we deal with share our *values* and priorities. We want to feel that it's worthwhile investing in a relationship with them because of what kind of people they are, and not simply because there's some instrumental gain. That's what REI offers and other retailers do not.

The second aspect is ethical. Increasingly we expect companies to provide us with value ... but not at the expense of our values. 'Yes, create superior products. But without destroying the environment or denying a less advantaged group's human rights in the process.' Any sustained failure to win this battle for hearts and minds as well as for purses can spell trouble for even the most mighty corporations and brands – as Shell discovered in its battles with Greenpeace over the disposal of its Brent

Spar oil rig, Monsanto with its failure to introduce genetically modified foods into Europe, and Nike with its battle with human rights campaigners.

(By the way, the reverse is also true: we want *values*, but not at the expense of *value*. So we increasingly expect not-for-profit organizations not only to 'do good' but to do so efficiently and effectively. By raising and spending money with minimum waste and maximum effect, for example, just like every for-profit organization.)

There are other hugely powerful forces driving the rise of passion partnership. One such force is advanced industrial nations' rapid march up Maslow's famous hierarchy of needs. In these societies most of us have the luxury of taking physical sustenance and security for granted. We're amazingly prosperous compared to previous generations. So we now have the privilege of turning our attention to things other than survival, such as emotional fulfilment – what Maslow called 'self-actualization'.

The mirror image of this shift is that companies are also looking for more from their customers and employees. Call it 'contract-plus' for short. Nowadays companies don't only want employees to fulfil the technical terms of a job description: 'a fair day's work for a fair day's pay'. They want to unleash employees' enthusiasm, commitment, creativity and so on. Likewise, companies don't only want consumers to buy their products. They seek brand loyalty, word-of-mouth recommendation, preferential attention, etc. In other words, companies increasingly want to trade in something other than pure financial currency. They want to deal in emotional currency too.

Old industrial-age certainties are breaking down in other ways too – adding to passion partner impetus. Not long ago, our identities and values were very much made for us by institutions such as the church, and circumstances such as class, occupation, region and so on. *Who* we were was very much a product of our lot in life. We were 'made' by our circumstances, rather than 'making ourselves'. But the influence of these institutions and circumstances has declined steadily over the years. This has created a gap in what Rolf Jensen calls the 'Who am I?' market. Increasingly today, we are free to 'make' our own meanings and identities. But this freedom comes at a price: filling the gap left by old sources of meaning and identity is hard work. Many of us look for help.

For all these reasons, organizations that recognize and address the importance of my personal bottom line have increasing relevance. So who's going to do it? The first, and obvious answer, is passion-focused organizations, whether sports and arts organizations such as Bayern Munich and the Royal Court Theatre, or pressure groups and charities. Some are already huge. For example, the German Caritas Association (Deutscher Caritasverband) the charity organization of the Catholic Church in Germany is the biggest employer in Germany with 470,000 full-time and part-time employees, working in 26,000 different charitable institutions. For comparison, DaimlerChrysler, Germany's largest company, has 370,000 employees.

However, there are many other potential candidates. They include special interest media companies, building communities and events around their publications/programmes/web sites and manufacturers serving hobby and leisure pursuit markets seeking to 'round out' their offers. Many more traditional companies may also have the opportunity to migrate towards passion partner roles, in certain specific areas. Not long ago, it would have been laughable to suggest that an oil company such as Shell or BP could be closely associated with environmental causes. But as these companies seek to take environmental issues on board, they are positively reaching out to activists in these areas, and seeking to involve them in what they do.

Meanwhile, even the most traditional consumer markets often have a passion 'segment' – a sometimes tiny group of people who are nevertheless fascinated, and deeply involved in the category concerned. As Procter & Gamble are discovering to their delight, for example, in virtually every market, no matter how apparently mundane, an 80/20 rule (or more like 95/5 rule) applies where a small proportion of the total consumer base invests a disproportionate amount of time, money and energy in the product in question – because it really matters in their lives. Thus for example, at Physique.com P&G caters for a small band of hair fanatics, for whom the latest and greatest in hair care, styling, fashion and so on is a consuming interest. Whether it's hair, cars, food or finance there are some people for whom it really is a genuine passion. Nevertheless, making the move to passion partnership won't be easy.

A CATALYST OF CHANGE

Passion partnership status is a privilege, for a start. I may buy hundreds or thousands of separate products or services, but precisely because of its importance to my emotional bottom line I'll probably concentrate my investments in only a handful of passion partners. In this market, less is often more.

Even though I may allow only a few passion partners into my life, however, they may well set the pace and create the standards other organizations and brands are forced to follow. Collectively, passion partners' influence is set to be all-pervading. Here are some examples.

Marketing

Passion partners upset the marketing and branding apple cart by seizing the high-ground of emotional added value. For decades now, marketers have sought to wrap 'emotional added values' around their products and services. Passion partners expose the emptiness of artificially constructed emotional veneers. To win the battle for 'Join Me!' even the most traditional brands will need to compete on passion partner terms such as authenticity, shared goals and trust, involvement and community. Or else they will have to seek less grandiose objectives.

We can see this already in the world of sponsorship. When big brands like Coca-Cola invest vast sums sponsoring global sports events like the Olympics or the football World Cup they are accepting a harsh truth. The real emotional affinity lies with the sport, not the brand. All the brand can do is try to ride on its coat-tails, by becoming another 'supporter'. The rise of sponsorship is often seen as the triumph of commercialism over passion. The opposite is true. It's evidence that share of purse follows share of heart, not the other way round.

Segmentation

'Passion segments' will emerge within virtually all traditional product and service markets, as we've just seen. Such passion segments may be small numerically, but they can account for surprisingly large proportions of total market spend. The other side of the coin is that in many products, categories and occasions there's nothing consumers want more than a completely emotion-free, arm's length transaction. So markets are dividing, not so much along old bottom line fissures such as traditional quality/value for money trade offs, but along new bottom line fissures such as whether they offer high value for time or low value for time, and high return on emotional commitment or low emotional return.

Corporate social responsibility

In the emerging world of value and values, it's not enough for companies to align what they make to 'my needs'. They must also align their attitudes and behaviours to my values. This pressure should not be underestimated. It is not just to recognize peoples' concerns. It is to actually embrace these values; to 'do the right thing' not only because it helps, say, 'reduce reputational risk' or gain competitive edge, but because it is the right thing to do.

Employment and company culture

Increasingly, successful recruitment brands also appeal to potential employees on the level of values as well as economic value (e.g. wages, terms and conditions). In his studies of 'great' companies – that signally outperformed their competitors in terms of performance over many years – Stanford University researcher Jim Collins notes that they combine a deep understanding of how to make money by doing what they can be 'best' at with a passion for what they are doing: for what 'the company stands for'. Such companies have what he calls 'a core ideology': 'core values and sense of purpose beyond just making money, that guides and inspires people throughout the organization and remains relatively fixed for long periods of time'.[5]

Managing the change

These catalytic effects of passion partnership represent a huge challenge for most organizations. Many, who are still stuck with old bottom line mentalities are flunking it. There are already numerous examples of 'how *not* to do it'. The common mistake: to give a superficial 'nod' towards the need for things like authenticity – and then to revert to old ways, seeing 'passion' in whatever form it takes as just another means of boosting the old bottom line.

Marketers talk a lot nowadays about 'brand experience', for example. Nine times out of ten, the real goal of improved brand experience is simply to close more sales; not to improve the experience of 'my life'. Likewise, many marketers have attempted to organize 'communities' around their brands. Some cult brands such as Harley Davidson have been very successful in this. But in most cases, such 'community building' initiatives are little more than exercises in brand narcissism. The aim is not to create a brand that orbits a community, and that helps that community pursue its shared passion. It's precisely the opposite: to corral and channel consumers' emotional needs so that they orbit its brand, to its advantage.

Likewise, still, too many corporate social responsibility and cause related marketing initiatives amount to little more than glossy PR exercises. They're not authentic. As Jim Collins observes, for every company with a genuine core sense of purpose beyond that of making money, , there are ten saying 'Okay, folks, let's get passionate about what we do'.[6]

Similarly, because the real aim of many human resources and internal initiatives is simply deploy individuals' passions to the benefit of the business – and not vice versa – employees have 'seen through' these initiatives in an instant.

Not-for-profits face other pressures. Every organization, whether profit-oriented or not, has to generate enough revenues to cover its costs. When it faced financial difficulties, for example, REI didn't hesitate to close down or sell loss-making stores and manufacturing facilities. Riding the tide of commercialization for the benefit of the sport and their clubs –

rather than being overwhelmed by it – has been a real challenge for football managers. It's precisely this mix of 'passion and profit' that makes scaling the passion partnership peak so difficult.

The Midas touch?

In the Greek myth, the Gods punished greedy King Midas by turning everything he touched and loved, into inhuman, emotionally sterile gold. Old bottom line businesses have something of the Midas touch about them.

They have been extraordinarily successful at creating value for their customers, and for their shareholders. But passion is one dimension of value that they haven't been able to address: it takes them beyond the elastic 'stretch' of their current business models. By organizing themselves around 'passion assets', passion partners go beyond companies' traditional commercial and operational comfort zone to open up new territory. We're only beginning to glimpse how huge this new territory is.

Summary

Passion partners add value by helping me maximize my personal, emotional bottom line. Their core business is not the provision of goods or services, but 'meaning' and 'fulfilment'.

While trading agents help me source the inputs of my life and solution assemblers help me improve the productivity of my personal operations, passion partners help me maximize the value of my life 'outputs' in the form of the hobbies, causes, past-times and activities that really matter to me.

Passion is not something that can be made in factories and sold in shops. It can only be generated by me, in my life. That's why it requires a different kind of relationship – a *partnership*. Passion partners do not provide passions *for* me, they pursue passions *with* me. They do not have 'customers'. Rather, they have 'members' or 'supporters'.

Passion partners achieve commercial viability by connecting individuals' personal assets (emotional commitment plus time, money, attention etc) with passion-related products, services, information, community-building, events etc.

The potential 'market' for passion partnership is infinite. But it's difficult for old bottom liners to enter this market. The organization must align its goals to those of the individual. To earn the necessary levels of trust, it must be authentic in its commitment to these goals: if you enter a 'passion market' in order to make money out of it, you are unlikely to succeed.

This does not mean passion partnerships will be confined to the not-for-profit sector. In fact, the huge potential of passion partnership lies in its ability to combine the best of both worlds: the for-profit's efficiency and commercial focus and the not-for-profit's emotional appeal. Passion partners may not be 'in business' to maximize profits, but profitability is nevertheless important as a means to achieving their ends.

7 Learning to fly

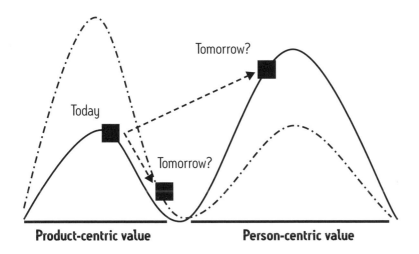

Product-centric value   **Person-centric value**

It's time to draw a few strands together. A new bottom line is moving centre stage, we've argued, because of the collision of some hugely powerful and unstoppable tectonic shifts. The four main forces we have identified are as follows:

- The 'seven deadly sins' of industrial-age business – *systemic* sins which are mostly beyond the control or remedy of individual companies and which mean that old value peaks are sinking.
- The continued neglect of critical value gaps that old bottom line businesses are either unable or unwilling to address.
- The dawning realisation that if we are to successfully address either or both of these challenges, we need to unleash the true potential of the OPTIMAL assets of personal operations (work), passion, time, information, money and attention.

TASKS FOR THIS CHAPTER

1. Outline common attributes of new bottom line business models, and the threat they pose to seller-centric firms.
2. Pose the question: how can old bottom liners make the leap from old bottom line to new?

■ The emergence of new technologies – especially information technologies – which are creating new possibilities for new information flows (e.g., 'upwards' from buyers to sellers and 'sideways' from peer to peer); for much more efficient matching and connecting; and for much more efficient coordination and integration of operational activities.

The collision of these deep tectonic shifts is set to transform the business landscape, thrusting new value peaks in the air: trading agency, solution assembly and passion partnership.

So far, however, we've discussed each one separately. To a degree, that's slightly artificial. As the motif at the beginning of each of the past three chapters has illustrated, in reality they tend to overlap. For example, you could describe a trading agent as a sort of home replenishment or personal sourcing solution provider; or a passion partner as a form of emotional solution organizer. Both solution assemblers and passion partners are, in turn, likely to include some trading agency functions within their overall workings.

NEW BOTTOM LINE FAMILY TRAITS

Looking at the new peaks separately also highlights their differences while ignoring their similarities. But they do share some common, trademark new bottom line themes.

Integration

In one way or another, all three new bottom line models are professional integrators. One of the ways they add value is by combining the separate outputs of different 'vertical' industries – industries organized around the logic of efficient supply – to focus instead on improving the efficiency of my own internal operations: the 'making' of 'my life'.

Specifically, each of the new functions brings the supply of products, of services, of commercial exchange (traditionally called 'retailing') and media (the supply of useful/interesting information) together, to add value at a new level.

Figure 7.1 New Bottom Liners as the New Integrators

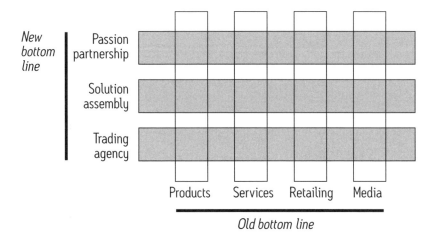

New divisions of labour between company and customer

Under the old bottom line driver of 'value from our operations', companies draw back from taking on tasks which compromise their own internal efficiency and productivity, and seek to pass this hot potato to outside third parties, including the customer. Thus, traditionally, soap companies have made soaps but not helped do the washing. Food companies have made food ingredients but not helped in the cooking. Retailers have made products available but not helped in their delivery. By shifting the focus to 'value in my life', new bottom liners renegotiate such divisions of labour between company and customer – with profound effects on costs, operations and (in the long term) on our very definitions of industries and markets.

A different vantage point

The natural stance of the old bottom liner is to look *down* a supply chain, from the point of view of someone selling to a world of potential customers. Whatever he makes – products, services or information (as in the case of media owners) – his *modus vivendi* is 'make and sell'. The natural stance of the new bottom liner, on the other hand, is to look *up* a demand chain to a world of potential suppliers. His *modus vivendi* is much more 'source and integrate' than 'make and sell'. (To refer back to earlier discussions about the limits of 'customer focus', the new bottom liner is more *supplier*-focused than customer-focused. He is as interested in the potential value of the supplier to the customer, as in the value of the customer to the supplier.)

If we put these three attributes of integration, new divisions of labour and a different vantage point together, they underline how radical a shift is underway. Moving from the old bottom line status quo of *vendor efficient supply* to the new bottom line imperative of **customer efficient demand** is not a trivial matter.

New dimensions of value

The new bottom liner's 'unique selling point' is that he addresses one or more of the value gaps that old bottom line business models are either unable or unwilling to address. Instead of focusing on the making of things, new bottom liners help people make their lives. Neither of the three main new bottom line functions is able to address all seven value gaps in one go, however. But together, they do.

Figure 7.2 Value Gaps Addressed by Different New Bottom Line Models

Value Gap	Trading Agent	Solution assembler	Passion partner
Personal asset (main focus)	Information, Money, Attention	Operations Time	Passion
Transaction costs	■	◪	◪
Integration costs	◪	■	◪
Customization	◪	■	□
Buyer-centricity	■	◪	□
Emotional needs	□	□	■
Failed economies of scale	◪	■	□

Figure 7.2 illustrates how trading agents, solution assemblers and passion partners parcel up the main value gaps between them. Trading agents focus mainly on transaction costs and buyer-centric information; solution assemblers on integration costs, customization and failed economies of scale; and passion partners on emotional needs.

Deploy new assets

A key task for the new bottom liner is to unleash the potential and maximize the value of the main OPTIMAL assets. Once again, none of the new bottom line business functions can do it all alone. Together, however, they do 'cover' all the main personal assets as Figure 7.3 illustrates.

Figure 7.3 Personal Assets Optimized by Different New Bottom Line Business Models

Personal Asset	Trading Agent	Solution assembler	Passion partner
Operations/work	◪	◼	◻
Passion	◻	◻	◼
Time	◪	◼	◼
Information	◼	◪	◪
Money	◼	◪	◻
Attention	◼	◻	◪

Trading agents in particular help me maximize the value of my information, attention and money. Solution assemblers help me save time and work. And passion partners help me make the most of my emotional investments, and the time and attention I devote to them.

Together, the three address the classic marketing dimensions of price, quality and emotional added value, but as applied to 'my life' rather than a supplier's product or service.

New business models

Clearly, new bottom liners require new and different business models to survive and flourish. They differ in the forms of value they add, what resources they draw upon to do so, how they make their money, and how they organize themselves to do so. Generally speaking – though not always – they add more cost in the process of adding more value. To cover these extra costs they have to do one of three things: charge more, monetize more (e.g., turning personal assets such as information or attention into cash), and realize new efficiencies. This is a new and different balancing act, and it won't be easy.

Different mindset

A different mindset and a different business model go together. It's not easy to make the mental leap from 'value from our operations' to 'value in my life'. It's not easy to accept that we make our money *with* and *for* our customers rather than *from* them. Or to really internalize the fact that the long-term strategic value of a strong, trusting relationship with these customers potentially outstrips the value of any (and perhaps even all) the company's traditional corporate assets – and therefore that these traditional assets should serve the relationship, rather than the relationship serve the assets.

New dynamics

These include new win-wins and a new type of virtuous circle. The old win-wins revolved around better, cheaper 'making'. The new win-wins revolve much more around better cheaper 'matching and connecting' – the new key economic 'pinch point'.

The old virtuous circle revolved around growing demand, leading to improved economies of scale, and to better value at lower cost. The new virtuous circle has three very different main steps. First, add a new dimension of value by addressing the core value gaps. Second, in doing so, build new levels of trust ('on my side' trust as well as 'competence' trust). Third, leverage these new levels of trust to gain even greater access to those key OPTIMAL assets, and use this access to generate even higher levels of value.

Figure 7.4 A Virtuous New Spiral

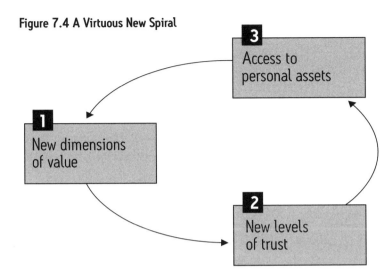

All of which underlines a point we first emphasized in Chapter 2. There is a deep chasm between the old bottom line and the new, and there isn't any easy, straightforward path from the old value peaks to the new. So why bother trying to make such a difficult change?

CARROT AND STICK

The reason companies try to change is simple: carrot and stick. Companies that fail to respond will be penalized by competitive pressures. Companies that respond particularly astutely will climb higher up the new value peaks, to prosper as never before.

Figure 7.5 Tectonic Shifts Force Companies to Migrate to New Bottom Line Forms of Value

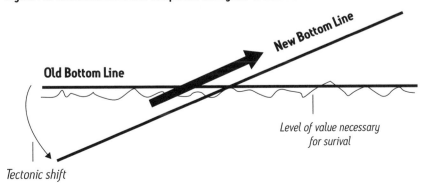

We illustrate the point simply in Figure 7.5. Old bottom line business models flourished at various levels of profitability – above the 'sea level' which marks the transition point from economic viability to non-viability.

However, the tectonic shifts we've talked about mean that some value peaks are sinking below viability, while the potential of other value peaks is rising even higher. Clearly, wherever you happen to find yourself on this map, the impetus is for you to move to the right: to climb the new peaks.

Growth in sales and profits; closer, more trusting relationships with customers; greater customer loyalty; growing market share and a greater share of customer requirement; a more relevant brand; better faster innovation; privileged access to customer information; attention and money. These are all classic goals of traditional seller-centric marketing. The message of the new bottom line is this: they will *never* actually be achieved by seller-centric marketing. If the company genuinely wants to reach these goals, it will have to leave its seller-centricity behind.

Precisely because the new bottom liners are integrators, tending to meet a much greater proportion of the consumer's total requirements and new dimensions of value, they represent a huge opportunity for growth and greater 'share of purse'. Because they both demand – and fulfil – a much higher level of trust (on-my-side trust as well as competence trust) they create much closer *customer relationships* and therefore, preferential access not only to clients' money, but to other increasingly crucial non-financial assets: information; share of attention; share of 'heart' or emotional commitment.

This privileged position brings further benefits. The very nature of the new business models means that they become embedded in my life. I either rely on them for my day-to-day life, or not at all. This 'embeddedness' may take very different forms. With the passion partner, it's probably very high profile. For many trading agents and solution assemblers it might well be a much more low-key platform branding affair: 'there when I need them', valuable precisely because I can take them for granted and don't have to think about them. Operationally close, but emotionally quite distant, in other words. Either way, the role is extremely powerful and should ensure very high levels of *customer retention and brand loyalty*.

In addition, because they do *'own' the customer relationship*, new bottom liners gain a gatekeeper role vis-à-vis other, more traditional, suppliers – rather akin to today's grocery retailers (who risk losing this role). This delivers a hugely advantageous position of 'supply chain' power (with the important caveat that trading agents and solution assemblers need to build strong win-win relationships with suppliers to do their job properly).

If that's the carrot side, the stick side is equally compelling: potential loss of revenues, a closing down rather than opening up of options etc. Some more specific threats include:

- Commoditization. If the focus of differentiation moves to 'value in my life' – realms of value that are difficult to embed in 'the product we make' – traditional brands risk being commoditized.
- 'Ingredient-ization'. When you buy a ready made pizza or sandwich, you rarely ask what brand of flour is being used. By offering value at a higher level, new bottom liners tend to turn traditional suppliers into providers of mere ingredients which are hidden within a much broader value offering. This pushes them down the brand pecking-order.
- Market 'disintegration'. New bottom liners have a habit of slicing and dicing traditional markets along new dimensions. Our current notions of markets are almost entirely seller- and producer-centric. We define them not by the role they play in my life, but by the characteristics of the product and the producer. Thus we have a 'car' market, a motor insurance market, a car loans market, a cheese market, etc.

As new bottom line value considerations move centre stage, these market definitions risk losing their salience. As we saw in Chapter 6, a small proportion of every traditional market has a 'high-passion' end, where the passion partner subsumes the product into a broader passion offering – say, a car and rally club. Solution assemblers might target another segment: personal mobility solutions, and trading agents another: ruthless, instrumental, efficient sourcing of cars and car-related products and services. How does this affect how car makers, car insurers, banks, etc., go to market?

- Loss of trust/relationships. The new bottom line is both cause and effect of an important environmental change: a significant rise in consumer expectations. Any boat that fails to rise with this tide is threatened. Seller-centric attitudes and practices which were once considered quite normal and acceptable – such as intrusive advertising campaigns, cavalier approaches to the use of customer information or wasting customers' time – are quickly becoming anachronistic, even offensive. For a parallel, look at how society's response to racist and sexist attitudes and behaviours have changed over recent decades. What was acceptable yesterday can quickly became unacceptable tomorrow.

■ Loss of access to key assets. Sellers' entire go-to-market agenda has been transformed in recent years by a realization that value flows *from relationships*: value in the form of repeat purchase leading to increased lifetime value; in the form of access to information; in the form of permission to market and preferential attention and so on. This is precisely the territory in which new bottom liners excel, however.

CROSSING THE CHASM

It is a well-documented fact that few established players adapt successfully to disruptive change. Every new vision of value presents a double-edged challenge to the incumbents. First, they have to get their heads around a new dimension of value – one which, understandably, they are not currently addressing. This is difficult if you are already 100 percent committed to your current value focus. Second, they have to overhaul, reconfigure, transform, reengineer (call it what you will) the things they do – skills, processes, assets and infrastructure, cost structures and revenue streams, culture, organizational frameworks, channels, etc., – to address this new dimension of value.

Even so, it can happen. In its early days, Studebaker was a pre-eminent horse and carriage maker. In 1914, for example, six years after Henry Ford pioneered mass manufacturing at his Rouge plant in Detroit, Studebaker churned out three thousand horse-drawn carriages, 20,000 sets of six-horse artillery harnesses and 60,000 artillery saddles for the British government. However, it also had an eye for innovation.

As far back as the turn of the century it saw horseless carriages as a potential market for its core skills. In 1902 it made bodies for electric cabs (which at that time had double the market share of gasoline powered vehicles). And in 1907 (a year before Ford's Model T), it capitalized on its existing strengths in carriage making, sales and distribution (it had a strong nationwide sales network) to combine with the Garford Motor Company to produce a gas-powered car. After the First World War it tackled the market in earnest, going from strength-to-strength in the high-end sector of the market.

Likewise, we believe the new bottom line presents many opportunities for start ups, many opportunities for established businesses to migrate to a new bottom line role, plus many opportunities for established businesses to work with new bottom liners to 're-engineer' their offerings and routes to market (see Chapter 13 for more detail).

Figure 7.6 The Incumbents' Challenge

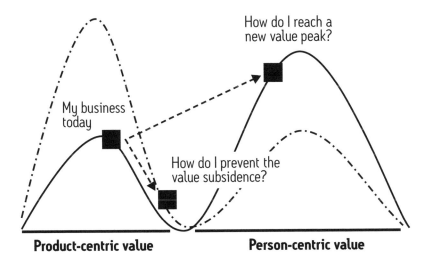

But how can today's old bottom liners, with their sunk costs; legacy systems; fear of cannibalization; and constant pressures to perform, make the leap from the old value peak to the new? As Figure 7.6 illustrates, half-way houses won't do.

Trying to mix old and new bottom line business models and cultures is rather like jumping half-way across a river. You risk falling in and getting the worst of both worlds. Somehow, we need to make a qualitative leap, from one mode to the other.

At first sight, the chasm seems so wide as to be almost impossible, but nature has achieved many such feats before. For land-dwelling animals for example, flight represented a new dimension of value, and nature found not one, but at least three different ways of getting beasts airborne. And it did so by taking up things that it had done in the past, often for very different purposes, and putting them to new uses. Take birds. Birds didn't invent feathers because, one day, a very clever would-be bird sat down and said to itself 'I think I'll start flying. So to do that, I think I'll invent feathers'. That's not how it happened.

What happened – according to today's most widely accepted theory at least – is that feathers evolved from scales which were used by creatures for a totally different purpose: thermoregulation; adjusting the amount of heat the creature gives off or retains to maintain a constant balance. It just so happens that a scale which splits into two (or four, or six) is a more efficient insulator than just a single strand. Many dinosaurs, it appears, were covered with fine downy 'feathers' of this sort.

It also just happens to be the case that if you can move those scales or feathers up and down – to stand them on end or lie them flat – then you can use this movement as a form of temperature control. And if you have a scale with both attributes, then you're half-way to evolving a feather.

'Splitting' scales and being able to adjust their position were incremental innovations designed not for the purpose of flight, but for the immediate, pragmatic goal of better insulation and temperature control. Yet, at the same time, by doing so they also opened up new and completely unexpected and unintended opportunities. As time went on, they discovered that these self-same feathers had aerodynamic qualities, qualities that could help them manoeuvre in – and eventually take to – the air. With the feather, birds managed to build *a bridge to flight* which ultimately enabled them to reach and conquer a completely new value peak.

We believe something similar is happening in businesses today. The pressures – and opportunities – of the new bottom line are hardly new. Those value gaps, and the seven deadly sins of the industrial age, have been around for some time already. It's hardly new to observe that 'convenience' – saving me time and effort in achieving the things I want to achieve – is often a sure-fire way to market success, for example. So firms have been responding to these pressures – *within the framework of the old bottom line* – for some time already.

At the same time they've been doing many things, such as invest in new IT systems and operational infrastructures, not in some premeditated attempt to invent and construct feathers and wings, but simply to cut costs, become more efficient and be more effective. Now they need to use these existing strengths, skills and assets to build a bridge between their existing value peak and the new one. And it just so happens that if we look afresh at many of the things they've done over the past decade or so, they begin to display that feather-like quality. They might not have been invented in order to fulfil the purposes of flight, but they could be applied to this task.

Let's look again at some the basic pre-requisites of a successful new bottom line business.

- It needs to be able to listen to and sense the demands of value in my life, in as close to real time as possible. For this, it needs to develop **information systems** capable of eliciting these signals from customers.
- It needs to organize its **operations and assets** around the efficiency of my life's operations, rather than its own internal productivity measures. For this, it needs to reconfigure these assets and operations around my time, work and other efficiency needs: it needs to make itself more 'convenient'.
- And because it's unlikely to be able to meet the full set of needs on its own, it needs to construct a network of **partnership and alliances**, not around traditional old bottom line goals of improved corporate productivity and profitability, but around this new centre of gravity in 'my life'.
- It also needs to recruit and motivate **staff attuned to this new way of working** – while adding value in their lives too.
- And finally, it needs to transform its **relationship with customers** moving from an arm's length buyer/seller relationship based on competence trust to a client/agent relationship based on 'On my side' and 'Join us!' trust.

This is precisely what many businesses have *begun* – please note, begun – to do: develop a range of skills and capabilities in areas such as information, operations, alliances, and culture which are, in effect, creating the pillars for a bridge from the old bottom line to the new. The challenge now is to complete these pillars and connect them to form just such a bridge. See Figure 7.7.

Figure 7.7 Can Old Bottom Liners Build a Bridge to the New Value Peaks?

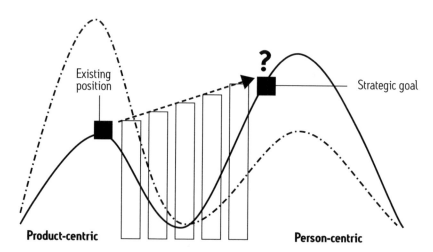

To repeat. Business leaders didn't originally embark upon these initiatives because they had the strategic intent of reaching out to a new value peak. Not initially, anyway. That's not how major evolutionary leaps happen. They embarked upon these initiatives to make their *existing* businesses more efficient, effective and profitable. But having gone so far, these self-same initiatives are opening up new, and originally unforeseen possibilities. The result is that some companies (not all) have the opportunity to seize these 'pre-adaptations' as Charles Darwin called them and to use these feathers to learn how to fly; to make the leap to the new bottom line.

That's our task over the next five chapters: to look at what companies have *already done* to evolve feathers, and to see how these proto-feathers could be adapted to new bottom line purposes.

Summary

Trading agents, solution assemblers and passion partners all 'trade' in different personal assets and all address different value gaps, to different degrees. Together they address value in my life.

Successful trading agents, solution assemblers and passion partners all prosper by creating a new virtuous spiral. By addressing new dimensions of value – the value gaps – they generate a new level of 'on my side' trust. Having earned this trust, they then encourage individuals to invest more personal assets with them – which they can then use to create even greater value.

In the process they achieve all the goals of traditional old bottom line marketing: closer more trusting relationships, greater customer loyalty, privileged access to customer information and attention, greater share of customer requirement and purse, increased growth and revenue generation.

By subsuming old bottom line forms of value into 'bigger, better' value offerings – and by winning the war for consumer trust – new bottom liners transform the market environment for *all* companies. As new bottom line business models mature, traditional old bottom liners will have little choice but to evolve and respond.

Companies started responding to 'value in my life' pressures long ago with a range of changes to information systems, operational infrastructures, partnership strategies and employee and customer relationships.

These initiatives were originally designed to improve the performance of *existing* businesses. At the same time however, they also help build the sorts of infrastructure and capabilities new bottom line organizations need to prosper. In this way, mainstream companies have already begun the journey from improving the old bottom line towards the new bottom line.

8 Let the customer drive your company – literally

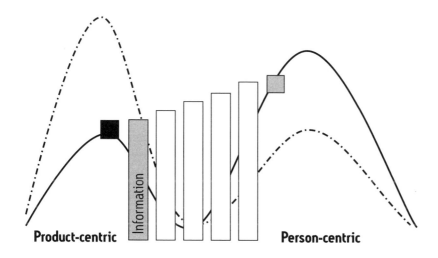

Product-centric | Information | Person-centric

'Find out what your customers want and give it to them'. Thanks to an ongoing revolution in our means of gathering, storing and distributing information, our society is fast developing two, very different meanings for this phrase.

The old bottom line meaning is that of traditional marketing. The idea is to use market research to discover what your customers want, to make it in your factories and operations, and then to sell it – communicating its benefits via advertising and other marketing campaigns. Under this model, information flows just one way: 'down' from seller to buyer. It's a *push* model of marketing.

The emerging meaning takes a completely different tack. It continually elicits signals of demand from its customers, and seeks to respond to what these signals tell it in as close to real time as possible. The primary flow

---

TASKS FOR THIS CHAPTER

Show how some companies are already developing new bottom line capabilities in the sphere of information.

of information is 'up', from buyer to seller. This is a sense-and-respond or *pull* model of marketing.

As long as it is executed well, in nearly all circumstances (*nearly* all, but not 100 percent all) the pull model is better, richer and cheaper than its push counterpart. Old bottom liners work on a push basis; new bottom liners on a pull basis. Many leading edge companies have won their leadership position by moving in the same direction.

BUSINESS' DARK AGE

It's not generally recognized how deeply ingrained 'push' ideas and actions are – or how incredibly wasteful and counterproductive they are. We need to grasp this if we are to comprehend just important this move from push to pull is.

In the early years of the twentieth century when icons of the industrial age such as Procter & Gamble, Unilever, Ford and General Motors were first setting out their stalls, the consumer was a closed book. Zero information flowed 'upwards' from consumers to producers, buyers to sellers.

Manufacturers sold their products through distributors and hadn't a clue as to who the end users of these products were. Retailers sold them on to anonymous customers who paid cash for what they bought and disappeared: no information was gathered at the typical retailer checkout in the 1930s. Or the 1940s, 1950s or 1960s. There were no efficient, effective mechanisms for customers to 'talk' to companies either. Call centres and e-mail didn't exist. A hand-written letter to the customer services department (if it existed) may have elicited a hand-typed reply, but it could have no operational impact on how the business itself worked.

This is the irony at the heart of the industrial-age business system – not only marketing, the complete business system. It invented the whole notion of 'consumer focus and understanding', but it did so because it had none. And it was this *lack* of information from the customer that shaped everything companies did, and how – from R&D (knowing what to offer) through production (knowing how much to make) to distribution and marketing (knowing how to sell it). And it still does today.

Consider some of the effects this information vacuum has. Without a continual stream of fresh insights coming from their customers, companies can easily miss new opportunities to meet customer needs, thereby losing out on sales, profits and relationship-building opportunities. They literally do not know *what* to make. And without the input and involvement of customers during product development, the chances are that they will miss the mark in some crucial way. That's one of the reasons why so many new product launches fail.

The same customer information vacuum also means that companies do not know *how much* to make. Without real time signals of actual demand from the marketplace, production schedules are driven by guesswork, commonly called 'sales forecasts'. In the grocery industry, a 40 percent error is standard; a 20 percent error is 'good'. The result is that either the company makes too little – which leaves it with lost sales and disappointed customers, or it makes too much, in which case it's left with excess stock in its warehouses (which eats up working capital), price mark downs, and extra marketing costs – invested, say, in promotions designed to boost demand for a slow-selling item.

BOX 8.2 WASTE, WASTE, WASTE – JUST IN CASE

To compensate for the absence of accurate, timely, actionable information from customers, companies have been forced to adopt an operating motto of 'waste, waste, waste, just in case'. This motto applies at every stage:

- Production: make stuff via mass production, *just in case* customers want to buy.
- Distribution: distribute it to every possible outlet via mass distribution, *just in case* a customer wanders into the shop and asks for it.
- Marketing: communicate messages about it to everybody via mass advertising *just in case* they notice your message and act upon it.

Many subsequent initiatives, supposedly to reduce waste and improve efficiency, are actually built on top of these foundations of waste, and end up incurring extra costs – extra costs that are incurred in order to reduce other costs that shouldn't exist in the first place.

So-called 'direct marketing' is touted as more efficient than mass advertising, for example, because it addresses named individuals and their responses can be measured. To this end, companies have invested vast sums in building databases, developing analytical tools and undertaking direct marketing initiatives.

Look a little closer, however, and we can see that direct marketing is still compensating for a lack of information coming from customers. Its underlying approach is, 'Given that our customers are not talking to us, how can we target our messages at them more efficiently?'

Now companies are working hard to open up flows of information from their customers, to reduce waste in the areas of new product development, production, distribution and advertising. In doing so, however, they are changing the relationship between themselves and their customers, often in ways they never expected ...

A third effect arises as a consequence of the first two. Given the high probability of 'getting it wrong' and the penalties for doing so, companies become driven by the need to minimize risk and protect investments. As we saw in Chapter 2, under this system marketing – which parades under the banner of 'find out what the customer wants and give it to him' – ends up doing the exact opposite. The aim of most marketing initiatives, including expensive advertising programmes, brand-building initiatives and promotional campaigns is not to get the company to do what the customer wants, but to get the customer to do what the company wants: 'Buy my product'. As Philip Kotler notes in his book *Marketing Moves*, in the industrial age the underlying marketing paradigm is 'one of unidirectional control'.[1]

However, most such attempts at control are counter-productive. Precisely because they revolve around getting customers to do what companies want rather than vice versa, they add little value to the consumer. So consumers soon learn to pay scant attention to them which forces companies on to a treadmill of increased spend to achieve the same or similar results. As Procter & Gamble chief executive A.G. Lafley remarks, 'the mass, push big bang model of marketing is not as effective as it used to be, and it certainly isn't as efficient'.[2]

In fact, looking afresh at marketing in the context of this information vacuum, we can see that virtually every aspect of modern marketing represents an elaborate attempt to *compensate* for its negative effects.

■ Market research, for example, was invented as a surrogate for what happens when customers tell you what they want, directly.

■ Advertising was invented as a surrogate for the information that is exchanged when buyer and seller interact. When the customer is unable to say 'Here I am, this is what I want', it is up to firms to fill the vacuum with their own messages saying 'Here we are, this is what we have to offer'.

■ Branding was invented as a surrogate for the relationships that are created by such exchanges of information: brands are a surrogate for the familiar, trusted faces we look for in a relationship.

The superiority of the emerging value peaks – trading agency, solution assembly and passion partnership – is that they are designed to avoid all this waste, risk and cost from the very beginning. And that's what's driving traditional businesses in the same direction: the opportunity to use information from their customers to reduce the risks and costs that are embedded in the old system.

FILLING THE INFORMATION VACUUM

Dell. Toyota. Wal-Mart. In industries as diverse as computing, car manufacturing and retailing, companies that have embraced 'reverse flow' information – in various ways – have transformed the competitive landscape. Dell and Toyota pioneered 'make to order' – as opposed to 'make for stock' or 'make to sell' – manufacturing systems: systems driven by information from customers in the form of specifications. Wal-Mart has used transaction information from its customers to reconfigure its supply chain. Now an additional third dimension of 'information from' customers is opening up: *volunteered* information which can take a myriad forms of customer feedback such as requests for information, expressions of interest, requests for bids, suggestions, complaints, comments, etc. Let's look at each of these three forms of customer-driven information in a little more detail.

Transactions

Before the barcode, retailers were effectively working in the dark. Manual checking was the only way of knowing what was selling, and what was in stock. In that era of retailing, manufacturers who knew a lot more about consumers (from their extensive market research) had a huge influence over what went on in retailers' stores, and retailing was a firm part of a push marketing system.

Manufacturers told retailers what would sell, retailers purchased this stock, and then worked hard to sell it. Often, the final decision as to what to stock was driven by manufacturer incentives in the form of listing fees and volume overriders, not real consumer demand.

The trouble with this approach to doing business is that it creates waste at every stage. For example, volume overriders encourage retailers to buy large quantities of stock that then sit around in warehouses or stores eating up cash. The retailer and/or manufacturer then have to incur extra costs – in the form of mark downs or special promotions to move this stock. In turn, such ordering patterns create feast and famine orders for manufacturers, who in turn build up large stockpiles of stock to cope with erratic orders from retailers.

With the advent of the barcode this began to change. Retailers began to get a handle on what was selling through their stores, and slowly this information began to influence their purchasing decisions. It has taken decades to sink in, but now most leading retailers realize it's far more efficient to source what sells rather than simply buying the stuff pushed by suppliers and then trying to flog it.

This realization has triggered a retail supply chain revolution, with retailers using information about what was sold yesterday (or even a few hours ago) to trigger orders of just enough stock to cover what has been sold. By eliminating excess stock and related promotional activity, this frees up cash, which enables the retailer to offer lower prices and better service, which in turn encourages greater consumer spend and loyalty – a virtuous circle of competitiveness.

Wal-Mart, with its celebrated Retail Link information and supply chain systems, pioneered this approach, but if anything, other retailers like Tesco and Royal Ahold have picked up the baton to take it even further. With Tesco's loyalty scheme ClubCard, the UK retailer is now able to track not only sales by store, but sales by individual, named customer.

This is enabling it to streamline not only supply chain but marketing activities too. The old 'blind' just-in-case marketing approaches had to send the same message to everyone, because the marketer had no idea who was most likely to take the message on board. But using ClubCard data, Tesco is able to segment its customers by type (in a huge variety of ways, such as whether they have children or dogs, what sort of promotions they respond to, whether they are driven more by price than health or vice versa, etc.). And it's able to direct marketing activities tailored to these individuals' or groups' needs. Customers 'love' it, claims Tesco CEO Sir Terry Leahy, because 'it provides information to consumers about things they are interested in'.[3] Thus it avoids waste for the retailer, and adds value for the consumer.

We saw in Chapter 4 how the ability to gather information from the consumer, and use this information to source value for him or her, is a fundamental building block of trading agency. Companies like Tesco and Wal-Mart didn't start down this road in order to evolve into trading agents. They pursued this path in order to make their existing business more efficient. But having done so, they have constructed some of the prerequisites of a trading agency business model.

Specifications

Dell and Toyota have pioneered another form of customer-driven business model: mass customization. This model has been much discussed so we won't go into detail here. The key point is that by letting the customer specify exactly what he wants in terms of product features and attributes, the company avoids all manner of risk and cost. In the fast moving computer industry (where prices have fallen consistently year on year) Dell's ability to minimize stock levels (by making products only once they have been ordered) has saved it millions of dollars. Ditto: Toyota's approach in cars.

Philip Kotler describes the 'asset-driven' approach of traditional car manufacturers like General Motors and Ford as follows. 'Having developed the assets and capacity to produce a million cars, an automobile company will try to produce this number and charge marketing with the task of selling this number. The disastrous result is that many cars sit in dealer lots for seventy days. And in order to move them, marketers must resort to costly rebates and incentives. Furthermore, the car company's advertising and promotion cost amounts to about 10 percent of the car's price. Thus consumers have to pay around $2,000 for a $20,000 automobile just to help the manufacturer cover its promotion costs'.[4] By avoiding such inefficiencies, Toyota has been able to produce more value for consumers, at lower cost.

Asset-driven companies which are obsessed with sweating their assets to the full by maximizing their output and efficiency only end up creating waste if this asset-maximization does not match and connect with customer needs. The Toyota approach is almost the complete opposite. As Taichi Ohno, one of the pioneers of its 'lean production' process comments, the idea is not to 'maximize' output or efficiency but to *limit* production 'to produce only what can be sold and no more'.[5]

Please note a key point here. Under the old system, 'marketing' and 'making' were separate activities. It was the job of 'marketing' to find out what customers wanted – and then pass the information on to 'making'. Once the goods were made, it was then up to marketing to communicate offers to would-be buyers in order to sell it. In make-to-order systems driven by information (specifications) coming from the customer, this gap is closed. The matching of 'what we make' to 'what the customer wants' is embedded into the very way the company works, at every step of the process. Instead of being a 'bolt on' activity, so-called customer focus becomes a part of the way it works.

Here's how H. Thomas Johnson, one of the early pioneers of management accounting and activity based costing puts it: 'The defining feature of most organizations today is a chronic disconnect between the work and the customer … causing work to be perpetually out of sync with customer needs,' he notes. But 'lean' production systems 'connect every member's work with the needs of specific customers [so that] customer order information and material transformation are joined at every step of the process. ... This linked pairing of information and material unites customer and company – and this union is the fundamental reason any business organization exists.'[6]

Solution assemblers in particular rely on customer specifications to create superior value for their clients. Once again, in their search for better ways to eliminate waste and create greater value, leading edge companies have pioneered the construction of a core new bottom line building block.

Feedback

Dell and Toyota work on a menu basis. They predefine the choices that will be made available to the customer. Tesco and Wal-Mart use transaction data to signal trends and trigger actions such as stock orders. There is, however, a whole world of customer information that falls between both stools. This is the world of volunteered customer information: request for information; comments; preferences; suggestions; complaints; 'if onlys'; and so on.

Once again, leading edge companies are using such information *from* their customers to cut costs and create more value. One of the ways the fashion retail chain Zara stays ahead of its competitors, for example, is by using staff to gather customer preferences and pass them back to designers. Sales staff are in daily contact with customers who come in to shops and say things like 'Have you got this item in that colour, or with longer sleeves?'. By actually capturing this information instead of losing it, Zara keeps a much closer eye on fashion trends.

Likewise, an increasing number of companies involve key customers in 'beta-testing' new products – to fine tune them before they are formally launched on the market.[7] Michael Dell, CEO of Dell Computers once remarked that the most valuable customer is not the one that buys the most, or that has the lowest 'cost to serve' but the ones 'we learn the most from'.[8]

Meanwhile, all manner of companies are going out of their way to generate feedback in the form of 'customer satisfaction' questionnaires. And many are actively harvesting customer complaints. They realize that complaints are not just a nuisance, but an invaluable source of insight into the organization's weaknesses. A growing number of companies are also setting up various forms of customer panel, designed to elicit ongoing comments and suggestions. Procter & Gamble, for instance, is inviting consumers to become P&G Advisors, to comment on everything relating to its brands, from packaging and design and advertising to product formulation and use.

FROM CHOICE, TO VOICE, TO AGENCY

Gathering transaction data, responding to customer specifications, eliciting customer input and feedback: they each require and express a different type of company/customer relationship, one which moves from data harvesting, to 'permission marketing' to the customer as investor.

When a retailer like Wal-Mart uses barcode transaction data to streamline its supply chain, it is using this data without its customers' knowledge or permission. The data is gathered as a by-product of its routine day-to-day business, and requires no further customer input. Likewise, when direct marketers acquire 'lists' of potential customers for targeting purposes, these lists have been generated and sold with neither these individuals' knowledge nor permission. The first you get to know that you are on a list is when a piece of junk mail arrives through your door, from a company you have never heard of. At this stage, companies harvest and trade information about customers as a corporate asset over which the customer has no ownership or control. Data is gathered *about* customers but used *for* companies.

When companies like Dell elicit customer specifications, or retailers like Tesco set up loyalty schemes, they are moving to a different level. They are gathering information *from* their customers, and *with* their permission. And the customer is offered an explicit extra benefit in return. Often this permission – and the related benefit – is pretty perfunctory and rudimentary. But it's a start. And it begins to recognize that this information is the customer's to withhold or give.

Under the next step of volunteered information the customer has to proactively invest time and effort in the relationship. This volunteered information is extra-valuable to the company: it cannot be deduced, gathered or gleaned in any other way; it's unlikely that any competitor will have access to it. But in return for this investment, the customer expects a much greater reward. In the process, the relationship between the two sides changes. They're not only exchanging money for goods or services, they are trading value for information too – on the understanding that the company will use this information in some way *for and on behalf* of its customer. The company's appeal to the customer is not only 'buy me', there's also an element of 'invest in me', 'join me'.

In the first stage of information harvesting, companies simply used new information technologies to achieve 'more of the same': to streamline costs and to extend and deepen control. At this stage, their priority vis-à-vis customers is the same as it always has been – to boost the old bottom line by influencing customer choice in their favour.

During the next phase they go beyond simple take-it-or-leave-it choice to give customers a voice, with some influence over what information is gathered and what it is used for – how the company itself behaves. The

Table 8.1 Approach to Information Under Old and New Bottom Lines

Attribute	Old bottom line	New bottom line
Company mode	Information *about* the customer	Information *from* the customer
Information gathering	Implicit, without customers' knowledge or permission	Explicit, with customers' knowledge and permission
Nature of information	Aggregated, anonymous	Personal, specific
Customer	Buyer of goods and services	Investor of personal asset
Customer mode	Passive, 'target'	Active participant
Requirement	Value for money	Return on investment
Purpose of data use	Maximise value of, and return on, corporate assets	Win-win use of joint assets

underlying incentive remains exactly the same, however: to cut costs or improve 'customer life time value' by encouraging repeat purchase. This is the core territory of 'permission marketing' and Customer Relationship Management.

In the next phase of *volunteered* information, however, a new dynamic emerges. Control over what information is volunteered in what circumstances passes to the customer, and the value of their input becomes much more explicit. And as customers become more aware of their role as active investors, pressure mounts on the company to deliver a return on this investment. So at some stage of 'relationship building' the dynamics change, and the momentum towards new bottom line attitudes and practices intensifies.

The information 'feather'

We ended the last chapter noting how the feather was 'invented' for one purpose – insulation and temperature control – but was then deployed for a completely different purpose; that of flight. Without the feather, birds could not have made the leap from one peak (the land) to another (the air).

We started out 'featherless' – in the dark ages of the industrial age when the customer was a closed book. Thanks to an ongoing information and communications technology revolution, however, we have started to develop these feathers; we have started to fill the customer information vacuum. Along the way, companies have started to develop:

- The technical ability to gather, store and analyze information coming from customers.
- The operational ability to respond to what it says, in as close to real time as possible.
- Customer relationships which provide permission to gather and use this data.
- and (in a few rare cases) a 'consumer agent' culture and mindset which recognizes the value of the customer as an information investor.

Along the way, some companies have already reached a crucial flexion point: it's one thing to gather information *about* customers and use it to pursue the same old corporate goals more efficiently and effectively; it's quite another to elicit flows of information *from* the customer and to use this information for and on behalf of that customer.

But that doesn't mean we've reached take-off yet. Feathers alone –a technological capability – do not guarantee 'flight'. Nor does a mindset that says 'I want to fly'. Gathering information from customers is relatively easy. Getting the organization to 'dance' to its tune – to use this information to really add value – is a different matter.

Gathering information *from* the customer is rather akin to inserting a nervous system into a lifeless machine. It may become a lot more aware of its surroundings, but without parallel changes to its muscular-skeletal structure – the ability to actually act in response to these messages – its real potential will be wasted. Changing the way the organization itself works is the subject of our next chapter.

Summary

Old bottom line business models evolved in an information dark age. When today's great businesses were formed, there was no efficient, effective mechanism for customers to tell companies 'Here I am. This is what I want'.

This information vacuum shaped companies' operations (e.g. high 'just-in-case' stock levels) and go-to-market practices, which are based on top down 'Here we are. This is what we have to offer' messaging.

Now, however, new information and communication technologies are eliminating the circumstances that originally made these practices necessary. In countless different ways – from the use of retail scanning data and data-capturing loyalty cards through to make-to-order production systems – companies are learning how to tap 'Here I am, this is what I want' information from their customers. They are using this information to cut waste and costs, and to improve their value offerings.

The ability to gather 'bottom up' information from customers is a defining feature of new bottom line business models. Ongoing corporate attempts to 'reverse the flow' of information form the first pillar of a bridge from old bottom line to new.

9 Organize your operations around your customer

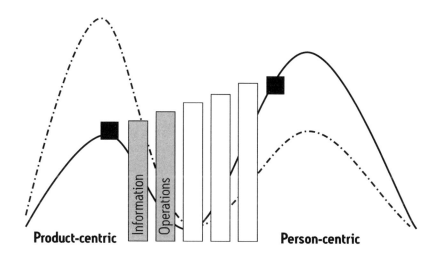

Product-centric   Information   Operations   Person-centric

Look at virtually any major consumer-facing business you care to choose. The chances are that over the last few years it will have faced an upheaval in what was once loosely called 'distribution', especially in advanced industrial countries in Europe and America. Here are just a few examples.

In the case of cars, there are many large question marks over the role and purpose of motor dealers. Financial service industries are in turmoil over who gives which advice, over which channels companies should use to go to market, and over the whole notion of customer self-service.

Huge retail sectors such as groceries are being reshaped by format proliferation. A few years ago, most major grocery players were almost exclusively focused on superstores. Today they're opening all manner of

---

TASKS FOR THIS CHAPTER

Show how some companies are already developing new bottom line capabilities in the sphere of operations.

outlets, from home-delivery grocery services through petrol station forecourt convenience stores, to local and town centre convenience stores, to huge warehouse-style hypermarkets.

In travel, the future of the travel agent is under review, as airline and holiday companies seek to establish direct Internet sales. In music, a rearguard action by the powers-that-be might have scuppered the ambitions of Napster, but a host of smaller peer-to-peer music distribution outfits have filled the gap: there is now more peer-to-peer music file sharing taking place than when Napster was at its peak.

In each case sometimes profound questions are being raised over the future shape of the industry, what forms of value and access it offers, and how to charge for this value. Clearly, the Internet is an important ingredient of this particular value stew. Other factors such as regulation also have their role. However, one common factor unites them all: the growing consumer demand for easier, faster, cheaper and better quality access to the products and services they want; a shift in value focus, from better quality products to better use of my time and my work. What we're seeing here, in other words, is new bottom line pressures making themselves felt on old bottom line businesses.

E-commerce guru Patricia Seybold sums the old bottom line response up perfectly with this eminently sensible piece of advice: 'Make it easy for customers to do business with you'.[1] Such blindingly obvious advice is only helpful because, historically, so many businesses have focused their attention on the complete opposite – organizing customers to make it easy for the for company to do business with them. As Tesco's lean process manager Barry Evans notes 'most value streams are geared towards value for the company, not the convenience of the customer'.[2]

NEW BOTTOM LINE OPERATIONS

'Convenience'. Now there's a word that virtually everyone in business underestimates. We talk glibly about 'the convenience revolution' in sectors such as retailing, but even then most of the time we don't recognize its full import. It really does represent a fundamental sea change; a tectonic shift.

Old bottom line businesses, which are focused on 'value from our operations', naturally make internal operational efficiency the sun of their particular universe. Everything they do is driven by the quest to cut costs, maximize productivity, etc. Everything they do, in other words, revolves around their own convenience: the old bottom line logic of vendor-efficient supply. Only now are some leading businesses recognizing that by moving towards the new bottom line logic of customer-efficient demand – by adding value for customers along new dimensions of 'life quality' such as better, more efficient use of time as well as product quality – they can beat their more traditional competitors hands down. This is the second pillar of our bridge to the new bottom line.

BOX 9.1 NOT JUST CONVENIENCE

As a word, 'convenience' is loaded with hidden, producer-centric value judgements. Convenience is always used in relation to consumers and my life, never to companies. Companies never do things for the sake of 'convenience'. They have a much grander word for it: 'productivity'.

In fact, they are exactly the same thing. You could argue that the first 'convenience' product was the wheel.

The real challenge of convenience is that its puts the new bottom line agenda of personal productivity ahead of corporate productivity, requiring companies to reorganize assets and operations around consumer- rather than company measures of value.

The 'convenience revolution' has hardly begun.

Coca-Cola is a classic example. When Coca-Cola started investing vast sums in pursuit of its maxim 'within an arm's reach of desire' it was implicitly accepting the logic of customer-efficient demand. It was adding value for consumers in a way that went beyond the value it could embed in its product: it was addressing the consumer's go-to-market problem of easy availability; having it when and where I want it. This 'simple' insight – and the enormous investment in distribution infrastructure that was necessary to bring it alive – went a long way to making Coca-Cola the premier icon global brand that it is today.

In the Introduction we saw the incredible power of fast food. It has gained a 50 percent share of stomach mainly by addressing consumers' value for time, as well as value for money and product needs. For another demonstration of the power of 'convenience' just look at the world of telephony which has been turned upside down by the mobile phone. Mobile phones bring communications to the person, rather than expecting the person to go searching for communications – and they've taken off like a rocket. Likewise, in financial services, 24-hour access via 'the channel of my choice', is fast becoming a core consumer expectation. Amazon is a case-study everywhere for its easy, efficient one-click ordering system and efficient distribution.

Now, even the biggest corporate giants are responding to the same overall trends. We've already seen the example of format proliferation in grocery retailing. Here's another example: Nestle chief executive Peter Brabeck's slogan of 'wherever, whenever'. Guided by this slogan, Nestle has been busy taking its products to consumers wherever they happen to be, rather than expecting consumers to come searching for its products, at its convenience, in traditional shops. Already, in Europe, 30 percent of total revenues come from outside traditional channels.

Tesco is using ClubCard data to go even further, to reconfigure what each store stocks, and how this stock is displayed, according to the shopping habits of the people who frequent that particular store. The supply chain implications and complications are huge. It changes the content of negotiations with suppliers for example, because a particular brand may no longer be sold in certain stores. But the end result, Tesco hopes, is that each customer will see Tesco as 'my store' – the store that somehow seems to know exactly what I want.

Internet home shopping data is taking this process even further by closing another gap. Loyalty card data – which is based on barcode scanning – can only tell you what customers have actually purchased. It cannot tell you what these customers would have liked to have purchased, given the opportunity. By tracking the items consumers ask for but cannot buy (because they are out of stock, for instance) Tesco is gaining new insight into customer needs that it is failing to fulfil. It's going beyond shaping its marketing and merchandising by what customers *actually* buy, to shaping them instead by what they *want* to buy. As Leahy remarks, 'We try to operate our business as a genuine pull system'.[3]

Meanwhile Centrica, the UK utility provider is using its massive investment in a database which gives it a 'single customer view' to approach this same task from another angle. When and if a customer telephones, the call centre operative checks to see if the customer has, for instance, a central heating maintenance contract, and if so, whether a routine maintenance visit is due soon. If the answer is 'Yes', the customer is asked when they would like the engineer to visit. Instead of sending out a notice telling the customer when the engineer will be arriving – and forcing the customer to make arrangements around it – Centrica is organizing its visits around the customer's diary. 'People are amazed we can do that,' says marketing director Simon Waugh.[4]

In each and every case, companies are prospering by accepting a simple but fundamental truth. They need to organize how they go to market around customers' personal productivity, rather than expecting consumers to organize their operations around corporate productivity.

CUSTOMER RELATIONSHIP MANAGEMENT

'Convenience' doesn't stop with physical distribution, however. It also applies to all my interactions with companies. That is what lies behind the rise of customer relationship management (CRM).

CRM requires companies to recognize individual customers, even when they are buying different products or services from different divisions, via different outlets and channels – and to treat them accordingly. At the most basic level, it means customers don't have to explain who they are many different times over, to different people within the same company.

At more sophisticated levels, it means customers have seamless access: a choice of many different ways of dealing with the company, according to what is convenient for them at that particular time. In other words, it requires the company to reconfigure how it goes to market to suit the customer's go-to-market needs, rather than expecting the customer to reconfigure how he goes to market, to suit the company's needs.

As we write, there is something of a backlash against CRM with many companies claiming it's not generating a satisfactory return on investment. There are two prime causes of this dissatisfaction.

First and very simply, it's so very difficult. Reconfiguring operations around those of your customer isn't easy. Creating 'a single view' of each customer across many separate product and divisional databases can be a nightmare. Reconfiguring how the company goes to market in order to give customers channel choice creates all manner of operational (and sometimes strategic) dilemmas. The organization needs a central database that can recognize the same customer on the Internet and at the call centre, for example. Giving the customer channel choice may upset long established distribution partners: channel conflict is fast rising up the board agenda as a major headache.

Likewise, actually using personal information to be able to respond personally – to treat each customer as an individual – flies in the face of everything old bottom line companies were trained to do: seek standardized routines, processes, products, messages etc., in the quest for minimum unit costs and maximum efficiency. It also demands not only sophisticated information infrastructure and software, but the right culture, extensive staff training, clear managerial guidelines, etc.

The net result is that effective CRM is difficult and complex, expensive and time-consuming. But for many, it's also necessary. The UK utilities group Centrica, for example, has committed £340 million to its multi-year CRM programme involving 700 full-time staff, including 50 human resources professionals focused solely on changes to education, training, incentives, career paths, etc. As Centrica remarks, CRM is a 'comprehensive business philosophy'. It's about 'integrating people, processes and technology' – not around the company's core operations – but around its customer relationships.

The second reason for dissatisfaction with CRM is that customers have been underwhelmed by its benefits: it hasn't delivered the 'delight' of increased revenues and loyalty it was supposed to. That's because many of the potential customer benefits of CRM are being missed, compromised, distorted or even rendered counterproductive by managers' attempts to shoe-horn them into 'old bottom line' priorities.

How many CRM programmes, for instance, are driven mainly by companies' attempts to cut the cost of dealing with customers or to cross-sell and up-sell (i.e., driven by a focus on revenue benefits for the company rather than additional benefits for the customer)? Time and again, the corporate mindset is to use richer customer information for the purposes of better control – i.e., to *manage* customers' attitudes and behaviours in the company's favour – rather than improved service. The very fact that companies are measuring success by their own internal measure of return on investment – rather than the return their customers get from investing in them – shows they're still looking at marketing from the wrong end of the telescope. We return to this in Chapter 12.

PRODUCTION

Reconfiguring operations and assets to meet new bottom line requirements doesn't end there, however. Another crucial arena is production. Reconfiguring operations around the dictates of customer pull, rather than marketing push, can take many forms. They include:

- *Flexible manufacturing.* As we write, Ford's core 'blue oval' car business in the US is in the doldrums. Historically, this icon of mass manufacturing has built single, inflexible production lines that can only make huge volumes of one car model. One part of its recovery programme is new manufacturing capacity that can switch quickly and easily between car models in response to fluctuating customer demand.
- *Synchronized production.* Procter & Gamble is developing new software systems with Microsoft. The aim: to synchronize production of its main brands to retailers' sales – thereby avoiding the problems of over- and under-production discussed in the last chapter. 'With demand as the catalyst and the key to solution, the ultimate aim is to create a system that captures real-time data at the point of sale that is able to automatically trigger the necessary restocking, resupply and manufacturer responses in the supply chain,' says Jake Barr, associate director of Supply Chain Innovation at the company.[5] In each case, operational decisions are driven by the consumer rather than the company (in this case, implicitly, by aggregated sales data).
- *Mass customization.* This concept was pioneered in high value categories with knowledgeable, demanding buyers. When Dell started out, for example, it avoided low-end consumer markets to focus on high-end corporate markets. But the concept is spreading from this core. Reflect.com, a Procter & Gamble offshoot that offers customized beauty products over the Internet, is one example.

■ *Solution assembly* is never far away from customization. As we saw in Chapter 6, by definition, solution assemblers organize their operations around value in my life.

Lean thinking

A more subtle variation on the same theme is so-called 'lean' thinking. The word 'lean' is usually associated with concepts such as 'just-in-time' and 'continuous improvement' as pioneered by Japanese manufacturing companies such as Toyota. These notions are important, but they are only part of a much bigger picture.[6]

At the heart of the 'lean' approach is the simple idea that anything that does not add demonstrable value for the end customer is waste: to be avoided and eliminated. That sounds obvious and simple, but its ramifications are enormous. Waste – or 'muda' as the Japanese call it – is very different to cost. Almost exactly the opposite, in fact.

Companies incur costs when they do things which add value for a customer. The cost of a product's raw material, for example, is integral to that product's ability to deliver value. Cost is therefore a Good Thing. Customers are happy to cover the cost of costs because that's how they get the value they want. New bottom liners often add a lot more cost.

Waste, on the other hand, is a Bad Thing, because waste is anything the company does that incurs costs without adding value to the customer. When an item is handled more times than is necessary, that is waste. When it lies idle, waiting for somebody to do something with it, that is waste. When somebody has to do extra work to make good a mistake, that is waste.

Ruthlessly, relentlessly pursuing this line of inquiry throughout the entire business often leads to radical conclusions. For example, when Tesco asked itself 'what value does stock add to the customer', it came up with a disturbing answer. Some stock is necessary to cope with variations in the rate of customer demand. But most stock is just institutionalized waste – the product of systems set up to paper over the cracks of non-value adding processes and practices such as poor information flows, push marketing programmes, or batch and queue production processes.

With these thoughts in mind, Tesco has set about eliminating all non-essential stock from its system. This is a massively complex task. It requires accurate, real-time information to flow 'up' the chain to suppliers, to trigger a constant flow of the right amounts of stock back to the store, with as few stopping, holding or handling points as possible.

BOX 9.2 HOW FAR CAN 'CONVENIENCE' GO?

Reconfiguring operations around customer convenience isn't without its dilemmas. The easy part is where the win-wins are obvious. Always available, 24-hour Internet banking fits the trend towards customer efficiency perfectly. It offers customers better service in terms of 24-hour access, flexibility, easier access to more information and so on. It also benefits the bank greatly if it can slash its costs by getting customers to digitally input transactions on the Internet (work that is normally done by paid backroom staff).

But what happens when, and if, the move towards improved customer efficiency begins to compromise and endanger corporate efficiency? When the customer's win is a lose for the company? Then, ultimately, a 'leap' towards a new business model becomes necessary.

Take the familiar example of convenience foods. Traditional ingredient manufacturing prioritizes internal efficiency, not consumer convenience. The main ingredient of pizza is flour, for example— and the flour manufacturer concerns himself mainly with maximizing the efficiencies of his core assets and processes: sourcing grain, getting the most out of his milling machinery, efficient packaging and distribution, and so on. That is how he adds his particular form of value to the consumer.

As the consumer demand for more convenience weighs in, he can respond by moving 'downstream': by moving beyond selling packets of flour, to selling pizza bases; perhaps even making and selling frozen, or chilled, ready made pizzas. But at some point along the convenience spectrum – the home-delivered pizza – he actually needs to become a completely different business. Not a few big, central, remote, efficient factories but many, small, local outlets working on a make-to-order basis. This, in turn, means different infrastructure; skills; processes; cost structures; culture; human resources policies (for the pizza parlour, the employee is a brand ambassador and not just a factory 'hand'), and so on.

That's where trading agency, solution assembly and passion partnership step in: where, to keep on going, a 'leap' to a new business model becomes necessary.

What have stock holding or handling points got to do with the value in my life? At first sight, there's hardly any connection between the two. But on closer inspection they are closely linked. If a company's operations do not orbit value as defined by the customer, then they must orbit something else: value as defined by the company. If the company is not focused on customer-efficient demand or customer convenience, then it is focused on vendor-efficient supply, or its own convenience. The old bottom line, in other words. This is how the new bottom line reaches up supply chains to inside what companies do, as well as how they interact with customers. But it doesn't stop there.

CORPORATE SOCIAL RESPONSIBILITY

Yet another way in which some companies are responding to consumer demands to reconfigure their operations and assets around 'value in my life' is via cause-related marketing and corporate social responsibility. A subject worthy of many books in its own right, we'll restrict ourselves to one simple observation. With the rise of corporate social responsibility consumers – or perhaps 'citizens', or just 'people' – are looking beyond the value of the products and services companies offer, to the broader, overall value and contribution of their operations; to the value of the organization itself.

Mounting pressure to change, say, labour practices in South-East Asia, environmental practices or sourcing policies all add up to one thing. Yesterday, companies looked out to people and saw an extension of themselves. When you 'build a brand' you extend your presence into the minds of the people around you. Now people are looking to companies as an extension of themselves. With corporate social responsibility people are extending their presence into its policies and priorities; thereby changing corporate attitudes and behaviour. People are attempting to get the company to organize its operations and assets around their own personal priorities instead.

AFTER CONVENIENCE

Distribution, marketing, production, corporate social responsibility. The examples of operational alignment are diverse but the core message is the same.

- Level 1 Pure 'product value' isn't enough any more. Easier, simpler access to this value is important too. So are easier, simpler interactions. Companies need to pay attention to the quality of my life when they deal with me, not just the quality of their product. As we've seen, in their quest for improved competitive edge, many companies have recognized this new bottom line imperative and started to travel down this road.
- Level 2 is more subtle. Whereas the old bottom line sees the company 'selling to' the customer, the new bottom line increasingly sees the company 'acting for' the customer; as a 'tool' in the hands of the customer. The new bottom line places the company – its infrastructure skills, resources, influence and so on – at the disposal of the customer. This is a new attitude, but with latest developments in lean thinking and corporate social responsibility it is beginning to take root. Yet another pillar of our bridge is at least under construction.

Summary

Companies do not add value for their customers by being inefficient in the way they supply products or services. So the go-to-market watchword of the old bottom line business is 'vendor efficient supply'.

But what is efficient for companies is rarely also efficient for customers. So the go-to-market watchword of new bottom line businesses is 'customer efficient demand'.

In a thousand different ways, traditional companies are discovering the need – and the benefit – of reconfiguring their operations around *customer* efficiency and productivity. Invariably, this involves changes to infrastructure and processes. For example, bringing the supermarket shop to the customer (in the form of home delivered groceries) requires very different skills and infrastructure to expecting customers to travel to and from stores.

Companies' ongoing attempts to add value for customers in this way – to reconfigure their operations around their customers' 'bottom line' – is another crucial pillar in the bridge towards new bottom line value.

10 Build partnerships around your customer

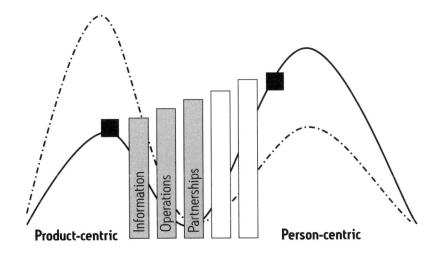

Product-centric — Information — Operations — Partnerships — **Person-centric**

'The consumer is the federator of our industry.' This comment from former Marks & Spencer chief executive Luc Vandevelde sums up the essence of business partnerships and alliances under the new bottom line.[1]

As sourcers and integrators, new bottom line businesses live and breathe 'partnership'. They understand that no single company can go it alone. By definition, trading agents need supply partners. Like traditional retailers, if they cannot connect their customers to good sources of value, they can't do any trading on their customers' behalf.

Likewise the whole point of solution assembly is to provide an extra dimension of value over and above that provided by traditional ingredient suppliers. This can only be done by bringing the offerings of many

---

TASKS FOR THIS CHAPTER

Show how some companies are already developing new bottom line capabilities in the sphere of partnerships.

different companies together. And few passion partners will have the skills to supply the many different passion 'ingredients' of their own accord. So partnerships of various sorts are also a 'must have' for all new bottom liners.

PARTNERING AROUND VALUE IN MY LIFE

The difference is that these partnerships are formed around value in my life, and not the usual corporate logic of value from our operations and vendor efficient supply, such as geographic or product category extension, rationalization, vertical integration or technology access.

Recently the notion of constructing partnerships, alliances (whatever you want to call them – see Box 10.1) around the customer has started to gain ground. It's not our job here to discuss the secrets of successful partnership – our task in this chapter is simply to point out the two main forms such partnerships are taking: 'horizontal' and 'vertical'.

BOX 10.1 'PARTNERSHIP'

We use the word 'partnership' generically, to cover every conceivable form of business combination – from mergers and acquisitions, through joint ventures and alliances, electronically-enabled virtual networks or Kieretsu-style business formations, to supply chain relationships, to outsourcing (which creates a new partnership between two entities where once there was just one) – because the boundaries and borderlines of business entities are always changing, and always will.

This is not just because markets, technologies and regulations are always changing, or because corporate activity is always rife. It's also because the fundamental economics of what generates the communities we call 'companies' are also always changing.

As economists like Ronald Coase have pointed out, the fundamental 'make' or 'buy' decision that defines the firm's boundaries is driven primarily by transaction costs: the relative cost of sourcing what you want 'externally' and coordinating its production 'internally'. And thanks to the ongoing information revolution, transaction costs are changing rapidly. As a result, we can expect sometimes radical reshaping of corporate structures and boundaries to continue long into the future.

The new bottom line will be a major influence on the specifics of such restructurings because, as we show in these two chapters, the demands of 'value in my life' often cut right across existing departmental, corporate and industry boundaries. For this reason, we expect pioneers in this field to be innovators, not only in marketing, but in organizational forms too.

Trading agents reach vertically upstream to particular suppliers while solution assemblers reach out horizontally, across many different sectors, to create a complete solution. Similar vertical and horizontal 'customer-focused' partnerships are already proving their power within the context of the old bottom line.

BOX 10.2 THE CONSUMER AS PARTNER

Supply chain partners may have a lot to learn from the focus of consumer agents on 'value in my life' over 'value from our operations'. But consumer agents also have a lot to learn from supply chain partners.

Key characteristics of successful supply chain relationships include:

- Information sharing — to avoid surprises, direct activities, aid coordination and deepen mutual understanding
- 'Mutual process reengineering' — both sides being open to changing what they do, or how they do it, in order to avoid waste, reduce total costs and enrich final outcomes
- A search for win-win interactions and outcomes
- Transparency: about costs, profits and aims, without which it's difficult to build ...
- Trust. Not just trust in a product, 'to do what it says on the tin', but trust in other people's intention to achieve a common objective

These essential ingredients of supply chain partnership apply almost as well to the consumer/agent relationship as to inter-company relationships. In fact, one way of describing the new bottom line is in terms of recruiting the consumer as a supply chain partner, rather than as a mere consumer.

'HORIZONTAL INTEGRATION'

Horizontal integration happens when different companies come together (or the value they offer is integrated by a third party) with a view to rounding out the value they offer their customers, and making it easier for their customers to access this value. Package holiday companies started doing it decades ago, bringing the air travel, hotel and airport transfer businesses together into a single offer. The home-delivery pizza parlour combines manufacturing, retail and logistics functions.

Familiar stuff? Yes, it is. So familiar that it's easy to forget how such 'customer-focused' aggregations have a habit of transforming the industry concerned. Another example is the rise of global alliances in air travel. When airlines were seen as 'national champions' any traveller wanting to travel beyond their national airline's reach faced an administrative and coordinational nightmare. If the journey required, say, three 'legs' the traveller would have to buy three separate sets of tickets. Timetables were not coordinated so large amounts of time were wasted in transfer lounges. Baggage handling was a nightmare. As each airline was focused on its own operational efficiency, in other words, the fact that their separate services came together in a completely customer inefficient way was irrelevant (and invisible) to them.

In 1997, the Star Alliance began to change all that by enabling customers to buy one single ticket for that three-legged journey and encouraging member airlines to coordinate arrival and departure times, to eliminate duplicate routes, work together to fill destination gaps, and so on. This new layer of customer efficiency (along with the incentive of a single set of frequent flyer rewards across all member airlines) has since reset the industry's competitive agenda, forcing other airlines to form their own rival alliances in order to compete. Indeed, the effect on the industry has been so profound there's probably no going back.

One airline may drop out of one alliance to join another, but the thought of dropping out to 'go it alone' is almost inconceivable. All the impetus is in the opposite direction, towards what Lufthansa chairman Jurgen Weber calls 'vertical' as well as 'horizontal' integration: integration of IT systems, common web pages, common reservation systems, common checking-in systems, etc. 'If you have common systems, you are practically bound to the alliance,' observes Weber.[2]

We believe many more such horizontal partnerships will emerge, across many different sectors, to take them to new 'no going back' levels of value and convenience. They make take different forms. In the case of packaged holidays, a 'virtual integrator' hovers above separate ingredients to provide coordination on behalf of the customer. In the case of the Star Alliance, members of the same industry come together 'as equals' to jointly serve their common customer.

There are also other permutations and combinations. The word of sport has been transformed by effective alliances between sporting organizations, media companies, corporate sponsors and merchandisers to build audiences and promote the sport in question, round-out fans' overall experience, and share the benefits. Roland Berger calls such initiatives – which inevitably reach beyond any one organization's assets and infrastructure – 'co-revolution': because only by joining together can they revolutionize the offering for everyone's benefit.

Yet another permutation is the emergence of a 'system brand' whose power to attract customers gives it the muscle to act as a system organizer and coordinator. Coca-Cola is one example. One hundred percent own-label retailers such as Marks & Spencer, Migros and Aldi act a bit like this. M&S, for example, organizes a complete web of suppliers in a wide variety of categories from fashion to food to furniture into a single overall offer, represented by a single brand targeting its particular customer base.

VERTICAL CO-OPERATION

'Companies don't compete. Only supply chains compete.' That sort of insight is common now across many industries and quite rightly so. No matter how efficient you are as a company in isolation, if your supplier or distributor is inefficient, then the chances are, you won't be able to offer superior value to your customer.

Vertical cooperation is crucial for new bottom liners in three ways. First, without executional excellence, even the most basic of customer expectations will not be met. If I order a washing machine via a trading agent, for example, I expect it to arrive on time. Obvious and basic? Yes. Absolutely. But amazingly difficult to achieve.

Second, one of the core win-wins offered by new bottom line business models to both their suppliers and their clients is that they reduce total go-to-market costs. Quite simply, this is not possible if trading partners are not working together to align practices and processes, share information, plans and forecasts, etc. Once again, obvious and basic but incredibly difficult to do well.

Third, as we've just seen in our discussion about operations, moving from push to pull efficiently and effectively is a supply chain issue, not a company issue. For the full benefits to be achieved, trading partners have to work together. Here are two simple examples.

'The long term benefit lies in getting control of our total supply chain to create value for our customers'. This comment from Barry Evans, lean process manager Tesco is hardly designed to make them feel warm and cosy inside, especially considering the context.[4] As we write, Tesco is trying to introduce 'primary distribution' and 'factory gate pricing' with its main suppliers. Meaning: it's trying to renegotiate the division of labour between itself and its suppliers, so that instead of suppliers sending trucks out from their factories to Tesco's distribution centres (DCs), Tesco sends its trucks out from its DCs to collect stock from its suppliers, whenever it wants to.

The reason: Tesco believes that by gaining control over the activity, it can eliminate all sorts of waste (such as trucks travelling back to suppliers carrying nothing but air), thereby cutting costs and improving margins. The consequence: the suppliers' long and painful investment in efficient distribution (infrastructure, skills, etc.) risks being written off. Prices will have to be renegotiated downwards, to reflect the fact that Tesco is doing a job once done by the supplier. And suppliers are pushed one step further back up the supply chain, away from end consumers – and away from any influence or control over how they are reached, or marketed to. So Tesco's initiative is not particularly popular among its suppliers.

On the other hand, if we follow the 'lean' logic embraced by Tesco, of always looking at value from the customer's point of view, and of eliminating everything else as waste, you can see the sense of what it is doing. This 'lean' logic has zero respect for any corporate boundary: it flows, potentially, right the way back up the supply to farm and mine. Hence lean process manager Barry Evans' comment above.

Take another example: the secondary packaging used by soft drinks manufacturers like Coca-Cola to wrap up two litre bottles for movement through the supply chain. Following the 'eliminate anything that does not add value for the customer' mantra, Tesco has analyzed its pros and cons. The cons weigh heavy. Tesco staff have to bring the packs out onto the shop floor, wrestle with them on the aisles, pick out each bottle one by one to put it on the shelf, scrunch up the left over plastic and cardboard tray and store it neatly for disposal (another, additional task).

Why not have a form of reusable packaging that can take the bottles in the factory, go on and off trucks, and be rolled out into the aisle and simply placed there – to let customers take bottles out when they want one? It would eliminate all manner of wasted handling, labour, time and materials. But to do so requires not only a change to what Tesco staff do in its own stores, but what the supplier does in his factories, and the forms of packaging material supplied by the supplier's supplier. Eliminating waste, in other words, requires following the 'value stream' as Evans calls it, all the way back up the supply chain, changing processes at every step.

Such initiatives are becoming increasingly common, even within the most traditional old bottom line supply chains. The point: they are fast becoming 'best practice', and no company – whether old bottom line or new – that fails to keep with such best practice will be able to compete effectively.

'Owning' the customer

So what about Luc Vandevelde's comment about the consumer as the 'federator of our industry'? When it comes to driving partnerships – whether horizontal or vertical – the crucial question is, 'who is the lead integrator?' Who has the power and influence to actually lead the process? The answer, of course, is that increasingly it is the company that 'owns' the customer relationship (to use yesterday's customer-controlling language). In future, the new bottom liner in other words.

This strategic positioning – the ability to 'call the shots' in industry reorganizations – is a 'must' for any ambitious company. The work that has already been done in these areas represents crucial building blocks for any efficient and effective new bottom liner. The quest to 'represent' the customer is propelling traditional businesses in the same direction, because increasingly he who represents the customer wields supply chain and partnership power. With this, another pillar in our bridge is under construction.

Summary

Every business is constantly conducting a series of relationships with other businesses – as trading or technology partners, as merger or acquisition targets, etc.

So far the driving force for most such 'partnerships' (in the broadest sense of the word) has been in pursuit of old bottom line logic: increased economies of scale, penetration of new markets, application of new technologies, etc.

Increasingly, however, companies are discovering the need to work with each other to 'round out' the value they offer their customers. This rounding out can take the form of 'horizontal integration' of many separate ingredients to create a broader solution, or 'vertical integration' to cut costs and be more efficient.

Recasting alliances and partnerships around the requirements of 'value in my life' forms the next pillar in the bridge to new bottom line business models.

11 Become a company that works for me

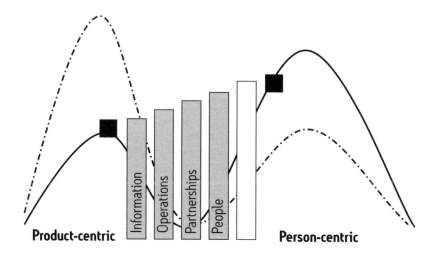

Product-centric — Information — Operations — Partnerships — People — **Person-centric**

Throughout this book we have talked about 'value in my life' almost exclusively in terms of company/customer relationships. But there is another dimension to 'value in my life' that we've hardly touched upon: the world of work and of employee/ employer relationships.

The fact is, work is a hugely important source of personal value. Not only is it a source of income, it can also be an immensely important source of self-esteem, identity, prestige, meaning and so on. And everything we've talked about so far – in terms of the consumer/producer relationship – applies equally to the employee/employer relationship.

This chapter's subject is worth many books, so all we do here is outline some basics. A hugely important tectonic shift is unfolding within the workplace. This shift is fundamentally changing the relationship between

---

TASKS FOR THIS CHAPTER

Show how some companies are already developing new bottom line capabilities in the sphere of employee relations.

employers and employees. Until very recently, it was employees who worked for companies. But increasingly, the tables are being turned. Employees are looking for companies that work for them. The inversion of the relationship between buyer and seller discussed in the rest of this book is being paralleled by a similar inversion in the workplace. Both inversions are just different manifestations of the same underlying trend: the new bottom line and value in my life.

The search for a company that works for me is not new by any means. Like all such tectonic shifts, it goes back decades, but now it's accelerating fast.

THE ASSERTIVE EMPLOYEE

In the classic industrial age firm, the role of the employee was clear. The worker was a 'hand'. He was an appendage to the industrial machine and he worked under a clear command and control environment. He was told what to do and, if he did it he earned a fair day's pay for a fair day's work.

Over the decades, employees' expectations have risen far beyond that. From the 1950s and 1960s – the era of 'organization man' – a growing number of employees started to look for 'careers'. They wanted some sort of progression and advancement over time, not just a dead-end 'job'.

More recently, expectations have risen even further. People don't want to give their complete working lives to an organization in exchange for the odd promotion. They want work that they find interesting and satisfying. They want to feel that their skills and talents are being developed. Many also want to feel that the job they do is 'worthwhile' in some broader social sense – that the company they work for not only 'does well' but 'does good'; taking care of the environment, for example, or contributing to good works and causes. At the same time, we don't want to be consumed by work: we want a good 'work/life balance'.

The further we move along this spectrum, the more the company has to work for its employees if they are going to work for it. The trend is by no means complete. Fear and greed, carrot and stick, are still the main management tools in many companies. In some sectors, employees are still very much treated as 'factory fodder', but the trend is deepening, for a very good reason that reflects deep-seated changes in the very nature of work – and of organizations themselves. It is a product of the information age.

The information age time bomb

In the mechanical age, people had to be appendages to machines if firms were to achieve optimal efficiency. In that era, corporations tried to automate everything that could be automated. As Geoff Armstrong, director general of the UK's Institute of Personnel and Development explains, to this end, managers sought 'to commoditize and standardize job descriptions and work instructions into interchangeable parts'. And workers were positively encouraged to leave their brains – and their hearts – outside the factory gate.

With computers, the onward march of automation was extended from manual tasks (captured by clever bits of machinery) to routine administrative and clerical tasks. These early days of the information age simply accelerated and extended the same underlying corporate logic. 'From steam engines to software programs, companies have invested in technology to improve productivity – and thought up linear models that put people last, and only in the gaps where machines don't fit,' argued *Fortune* magazine in an article on this subject. Even the most radical revamps such as business process reengineering have followed the same path. 'Decade after decade, management theory and practice have been reinvented – but always in a direction that has put the business process first, and the individual second'.[1]

As the computer reaches further and further into every conceivable dimension of working life, however, it is creating a counter-intuitive side effect. As we saw in Chapter 2, the computer quickly replicates everything that can be automated. And the more this happens, the less these 'replicated routines' can provide firms with a competitive edge. By their very ease of replication, they are no longer a source of differentiation.

As a result, the focus of competition is shifting inexorably away from the things computers *can* do, towards the things computers *cannot* do: people-things such as sense, judge, imagine, create, invent, envisage alternative futures, set goals, formulate plans, empathize with others, build relationships, joke, inspire, motivate, and so on.

That's the unexpected effect of the information age. Slowly but surely, it is transforming companies from industrial factories into 'factories' – or communities – of imagination and emotion. Companies don't want 'hands' any more. They want people to bring their hearts and minds into work, because these are the assets that matter. And those who let old command and control practices get in the way find they're losing out (see Box 11.1).

BOX 11.1 PROCTER & GAMBLE IN TRANSITION

Procter & Gamble has a long history of being 'a good employer'. In an era when companies simply hired and fired workers at their convenience, P&G was the first major U.S. company to guarantee steady employment (through the seasons) of its workers. It was the first company to introduce a profit sharing plan for its workers (in 1887), and to introduce the first employee stock ownership programme (1892).

But over the years, attitudes and practices that P&G had developed for positive reasons began to turn sour. One early P&G rule, for example, was that the CEO had to personally agree to any consumer-noticeable product change to an existing brand. As P&G grew, this began to slow it down considerably.

In its understandable quest to minimize the risks involved in new product launches and marketing campaigns, P&G also tended to become risk averse. Says former head of global fabrics Wolfgang Berndt, 'We created a culture of second-guessing and of perfectionism: a sell and inspect relationship between bosses and subordinates.' This, in turn, put a break on innovation. At one time, P&G's growth was powered by new products which created complete new consumer categories, such as diapers and fabric conditioners. But by the early 2000s P&G hadn't created a new category for ten years.

Meanwhile, as P&G's operations spread from category to category, and region to region it developed a sprawling top-heavy bureaucracy. Says Berndt, 'We had a very unwieldy, multi-layered, multi-sign-off process'. And in its well-intentioned attempts to spread new learnings and best practice around the organisation 'We best-practised ourselves into a very, very tight configuration – into lockstep'.

In such an environment employee creativity (and satisfaction) were being stifled. That's why, over recent years, P&G has been attempting   an internal cultural revolution. P&G tends to be 'linear, analytical, predictable', says CEO A.G. Lafley. Looking back, the company 'was not as strong as we felt we needed it to be in our ability to take risk, or stretch, or think in a more discontinuous way. We wanted to be less predictable, more discontinuous, more capable of creating a business strategy that was breakthrough.'

So, in recent years, it has attempted to drive a culture change with – as European president Paul Polman puts it 'less hierarchy, a higher degree of autonomy, and empowerment in decision making which is much lower down the organization.

Says Berndt, 'We need to find the right balance between exploiting the known – which is best practice – and exploring the unknown. In order for that to happen you have to be fairly constrained in terms of the number of rules you impose on the system. You have to move from a very rigid command and control system to one based on commitment, collaboration and cohesion.'

The difference, says Berndt, is between 'seeing ourselves as a pyramid with a commanding management at the top when we wanted to be more like a tree. The tree and the soil is the company and the management is the trunk, feeding the branches and leaves with resources. Then the branches – out there in the sun – can move with the wind.'

P&G's attempts to drive a root-and-branch culture change have proved painful, especially in Europe. Taking place parallel to, and as part of, P&G's structural upheaval Organization 2005, a period of rapid staff turnover and fading performance followed. 'Did we have growing pains?,' asks Polman. 'Yes. Did we make mistakes? Yes. Did we get the balance between global, regional and local right? No.'

But now, he insists, the changes are working through, 'We are getting the balance right' and performance is improving as a result. 'We have a very strong culture, and changing a culture takes time,' says Polman. But he adds, 'We were a very insular company. Now we are much more externally focused, and external focus is key to innovation because it creates a connection between what's needed and what's possible.'[2]

The parallel with our earlier discussions is direct. Consumer agents address the value gaps old bottom line industrial age firms are unable or unwilling to address. They do this by unleashing the consumer assets old bottom liners are unable to nurture and tap.

The traditional industrial age firm is constrained by a one-dimensional exchange with its customers: of money for goods or services. It is similarly constrained by a parallel one-dimensional exchange with its employees, that of wages for work; a form of exchange that neither addresses nor taps the wealth of potential that resides in employees' hearts and minds. With consumer agency, consumers aren't only buying products from companies. They are investing assets such as information, time and attention in them. The same is true for the agent corporation, its employees don't only sell work to it. They invest in it. They invest information and knowledge, time, attention, emotional commitment and so on. And they naturally expect a return on this investment.

Indeed, it's increasingly accepted in corporate circles that in companies where the most important asset now comes in the form of skills, knowledge and ideas, a critical part of the company's 'capital' comes, not in the form of financial capital from shareholders, but as human capital from employees. As the British social philosopher Charles Handy notes, if ideas, skills and knowledge really are becoming the key asset of most organizations, 'We can no longer expect the owners of this property, the individual employees, to be so ready to concede all their rights of ownership to the company in return for a contract of employment.'[3]

Thus, Science Applications International Corporation, a major contractor to the US defence industry, rewards staff who develop valuable ideas with stock options worth (sometimes) hundreds of thousands of dollars. 'Those who contribute to the company should own it,' declares CEO J. Robert Beyster.

Likewise, the UK telecoms giant BT is one of many large corporations to embrace internal corporate venturing. When employees come up with bright ideas that could be the basis of separate revenue and profit streams, BT encourages them to set up their own company – with BT funding – so that both BT and the staff concerned share the spoils if the venture ever goes public.

Even where employees are not contributing hugely valuable intellectual capital, they may still be investing a hugely important personal asset. In industries where high levels of personal service are required, staff act effectively as 'brand' and corporate ambassadors with customers and the public. Here, these employees are providing the company with 'emotional capital', without which the company could not prosper. And this 'emotional capital' is becoming increasingly important. BT futurologist Ian Pearson calls this the rise of 'the care economy'. As automation of physical and intellectual labour brings its cost and value ever lower, the value of human qualities – 'caring' – comes to the fore: and the pressure on companies to recognize the value of this employee 'investment' is growing.

This pressure – from both sides – to get 'more' from the employer/employee relationship is not some fad or affectation. It reflects some of the deepest dynamics unfolding at the heart of the modern economy and the workplace. It is creating the impetus for the 'agent corporation'.

THE 'AGENT' CORPORATION

The growing demand for the corporation to act as the agent of its employees takes many forms. At its very heart lies the question: who is working for whom? Take executive search. A familiar feature of the corporate landscape, it's all about finding the right person for the company. Now, however, the big growth area is career agents: agents who work for the individual to find the right company for the person. Comments Professor Maury Peiperl, director of the careers research initiative at the London Business School, 'The idea of fitting people into jobs is slowly shifting towards finding jobs to fit people.' Career management, he argues, should start not with asking what jobs are available, but with what drives the individual and what skills and relationships are most important to them.

Sometimes, the agent corporation mirrors the models we talked about earlier. As we've seen, I may look to my employer to act as a sort of trading agent for me: to help me maximize the value and output of my skills, knowledge and work – and, of course, my income. If not, I may turn to another form of employee trading agent: a trade union.

My employer may also be one of my passion partners. This is clearly the case if you work for an organization like Greenpeace, for example. As

Lord Peter Melchett, director of Greenpeace UK remarks, 'There is a unity between Greenpeace values and the values of the individuals joining it'. But it can also be true of more traditional companies which inspire employees by aligning with a good cause, or even by the nature of their skills and work (see below).

Companies can also address such agency roles indirectly. Some companies, which invest heavily in highly skilled senior staff, already employ solution assembler concierge services like Ten UK (see Chapter 5) to take the hassle out of senior employees' daily lives – if only so that they can concentrate better on their jobs.

But 'value in my life' in the work arena has its own special characteristics. These fall into five main areas: of rewards, respect and control, achievement, ethics/meaning and work/life balance. Below, we look at each of these areas briefly, illustrating just how far they can go with some 'extreme' examples of commonplace trends.

Rewards

It is increasingly accepted that staff should share in the prosperity of the firm beyond their salaries. This mainly takes the form of various profit-sharing and share option schemes – many of the companies making it to *Fortune*'s Best 100 Companies To Work For list feature this benefit prominently. But profit-sharing can be as long as a piece of string. In a world where employees 'own' the key assets of intellectual capital, argues Charles Handy, 'My guess is that we shall, eventually, have to abandon the myth that shareholders own a business. They will be more like mortgage holders, entitled to a rent for their money.'[4] Thus each year, for example, the Brazilian publisher Prensa, allocates a 'wage to capital' of, say, 10 percent of profits and splits the rest 50:50 with its staff.

In most cases, however, the proportion of profit made available to the ordinary employee (as opposed to senior management) tends to be small. And experience seems to suggest that profit-sharing in itself rarely reaches management's aim of aligning employees to the firm's objectives. For that a different style of management is necessary.

Respect and control

The traditional command and control workplace accords no respect to the worker and 'requires no trust between workers and managers', notes US policy thinker Frances Fukuyama.[5] Now, however, companies are realizing that to get respect and trust, they need to give it. 'If you treat people with integrity and dignity, they will be more than prepared to align with you,' says Wal-Mart CEO Lee Scott.[6] Like rewards, how far companies go in conferring respect and control varies enormously.

One particularly extreme example is the Brazilian industrial company Semco. It lets its staff choose their own salaries (everyone's salary is made public knowledge) and their own working hours and times (as long as they keep their commitments). Profit sharing – set at 23 percent of all profits – is administered by the staff, not the managers, of each business unit. They decide who gets what. (The most common outcome is that everybody, from top manager or lowliest cleaner, gets the same).

Semco lets its factory workers design their own work cells, set their own production quotas, redesign the products they make, and help formulate marketing plans. If a factory or office is being relocated, it lets its staff vote on where. If it's taking over a company, the final decision goes to a ballot of its employees. Board meetings are open to employees (the first two who happen to turn up), financial information is open to all to see (and workers are trained in accounting in order to understand it). Workers, not managers, interview and hire their own co-workers. And to get a management job, you have to be interviewed by the people you are going to lead.

Most companies would run a mile before introducing such practices, but Semco seems to have gone from strength to strength since it first started down this road in 1981.[7]

Achievement

Rarely, if ever, have people worked 'only' for the money. Everyone, at some level or other gets some satisfaction from a job well done, or a new skill learned. Traditional careers offer a form of achievement. But the idea that work should be 'an extension of me', rather than the worker being an extension of the corporation, is now being taken to new lengths.

One of the basic principles of Wal-Mart, says CEO Lee Scott, is people development. Over fifty per cent of Wal-Mart's managers started out in jobs such as unloading trucks. Says Scott, 'We caused them to be more than they could be.'

German drugs retailer DM-Drogerie Markt follows a similar philosophy. According to Götz Werner the corporation should be seen as 'an enabling area for the biographical development of people, with work as an opportunity for self-improvement.' The job of managers is 'not to ask how can I achieve the greatest output at minimal cost, but to design this work as a process of biographical fulfilment; a positive stage for each person.' This isn't a matter of making working 'fun', or simply providing a pleasant working environment. Nor is it about developing incentives or 'psychological tricks to get better results. It's about growing beyond one's own ability.'[8]

Ethics/meaning

However, some people are still looking for even more from their working lives. They want work not only to generate value but also to express their values. Companies increasingly worry that a 'bad' corporate reputation will undermine their ability to recruit new talent. If a company is deemed to have suspect values it may find it hard to attract the best people, no matter how good its pay and benefits package.

Once again, there's a huge spectrum here. For some companies, certain basic ethics are crucial. Among Wal-Mart's prescripts, says Lee Scott, is that every employee should be able to say 'I am never once asked to say or do anything that I would not feel comfortable with. And I am always required to tell the truth.' And now his biggest challenge, he says, is 'to put a human face on the company.'

'We believe in belonging and giving back,' he says. 'If we don't, we simply become a large entity. There won't be any human-ness about us. The store manager has to end up being who Wal-Mart is, so we are not seen as a company that comes in and takes money out for the select few. You can earn a profit while you serve. But if you don't serve, in the end you won't make a profit.'

Some firms go much further, however. Patagonia, the US retailer of outdoor sports and clothing is a good example. Its stated purpose is 'to use business to inspire and implement solutions to the environmental crisis.' Part of corporate training, for example, is in non-violent civil disobedience – and part of the benefits package is bail for those arrested. As identity consultant Nicholas Ind observes, 'this is a campaigning company with a campaigner's zeal.'[9]

Notes Ind: 'For risk athletes and environmentalists Patagonia provides the opportunity to find meaning through work'. And it seems to work. Since it was first set up in 1966, the company has grown steadily to become a $200 million business which consistently ranks in *Fortune* magazine's Top 100 Best Companies To Work For.

Not every would-be passion partner needs to wear its passion on its sleeve like this, however. The passion can be much closer to home. Researcher Jim Collins, author of *Built to Last* and *Good to Great*, argues that a common hallmark of companies that really stand out from their peers in terms of performance over the longer term is that they not only know what they can be best at and how their particular economic model works, they also do something about which they are deeply passionate.[10]

This is not about inventing or simulating a passion – but 'discovering what makes you passionate,' he stresses. One of the knock-on consequences of doing so, he observes, is that the organization then attracts like-minded people with similar passions who are committed to 'the cause' (whatever it happens to be) as well as wanting 'a job'.

Work/life balance

The other side of this coin of personal development, self-expression and commitment, however, is not being consumed by one's work. This, too, is rising up the agenda of 'value in my life'. 'There's an increasing unwillingness for people to sacrifice their whole lives for the sake of their careers', notes Elizabeth Klyne, founder of personal career agency

Careers by Design. Next to sharing in the company's prosperity, corporate flexibility – such as a willingness to accommodate working hours and times to the stresses and strains of individuals' every day lives – is one of the key factors in *Fortune*'s Best Companies To Work For list. It's the employee equivalent of 'organize your operations around your customers'. Yesterday, companies expected employees to organize everything they did around the company's convenience and efficiency. Now, both sides recognize a more equal balance is needed.

THE GREAT BALANCING ACT

Recognizing the need for companies to take on an 'employee agent' immediately raises a crucial issue, however. If both employees' and customers' expectations are being raised within a new bottom line environment, can both sets of expectations be met at the same time, or does one come at the expense of the other? CEOs are only too well aware that they've got shareholders breathing down their necks. Now, to win the war for talent, they are discovering the need to remould themselves into companies that work for their employees – even as, at the same time, they struggle to redesign themselves as customer agents. The potential conflicts are clear. Doesn't customer convenience translate into employee inconvenience, such as unsocial working hours? Don't higher salaries and benefits translate into higher prices or lower profits? And can such circles be squared?

BOX 11.2 THE INTERNAL COMMUNICATIONS BANDWAGON

Since the 1990s a massive new industry has mushroomed into existence out of almost nothing. Driven by the conviction that 'our staff are our most important asset', companies have been experimenting with an armoury of new techniques and concepts – internal communications and marketing; recruitment brands; staff motivation; team building; the promotion of visions; missions and values. They all revolve around the same basic questions: how can we get more from our staff? How can we go beyond that old one-dimensional exchange of money for labour, to tap the rich resources that lie in people's hearts and minds?

Yet, for all the activity, interest and investment, for the most part the results are disappointing. It's not just because of incompetence. It's because much of the activity is misdirected and misconceived. As Edgar Schein, professor of management emeritus at Sloan School of Management points out, the parallels between most of these programmes and the 'brainwashing' techniques developed by the Chinese during the Korean War, are striking. So are the results. Generally speaking, around 10 percent of individuals respond by becoming converts. They're pointed to as 'proof' of success. Another 80 percent react by going through the motions without changing their real beliefs at all. They hope that, in time, the storm will pass and they can get back to normal. The remaining 10 percent become active resistors.[11]

The trouble with most of these programmes is that, even as they attempt to listen, involve and persuade rather than simply 'tell', they miss the point. For them, the central question is how to get staff working harder/better for the company. But they don't address what's fast becoming the central issue: how to get the company working harder and better for me. Just as the traditional marketing mindset, with its focus on helping sellers to sell, is blind to the need for consumer agency, so the traditional human resources mindset is blind to the need for employee agency.

Take Wal-Mart, for example. One of the secrets of its success is the fact that its staff costs are low – its operating costs (around 17 percent of sales) are much lower the US retail industry's average of 21 percent. Traditionally, people have accepted lower wages at Wal-Mart partly because its historical roots lie in southern rural areas where wages are lower than the northern urban centres it's now moving into, but also because Wal-Mart has a history of treating people well. Its open-door policies – letting any employee 'let off steam' with a senior manager without having to go through a formal chain of command; its flexible employment practices that recognize individual's family circumstances; the good chances of promotion; the profit-sharing all 'represent real payments in a meaningful currency', notes a recent *Fortune* article.

But the same *Fortune* article suggests that Wal-Mart's attempts to focus ever harder on its customers – and to reduce costs ever further – are now beginning to undermine its employee-friendly policies (despite CEO Lee Scott's claims). 'Employees no longer believe Wal-Mart and its managers are on their side,' says *Fortune*. If so, longer term, one of the biggest employers in the world – with over one million employees – may be storing up trouble for itself.[12]

As new bottom line pressures intensify, we predict companies will need to innovate on many fronts – policies, culture, organizational and ownership structures, etc. – to manage such potential conflicts.

Some may seek alternatives to 'pure' shareholder capitalism. If we look across the complete spectrum of employment, for example, we find a huge range of different beasts, including:

■ Governmental, public sector and not-for-profit organizations and institutions.
■ Pressure groups, charities and various forms of foundation, such as Claritas the largest employer in Germany (see Chapter 6).
■ Private companies – 80 percent of German companies are private, and they account for over half of gross national product.
■ Partnerships, which are still common in many professions such as law.
■ Cooperatives, both customer-owned and employee-owned. Customer-owned cooperatives include the 'Co-op' and the mutual building societies and life assurance companies in the UK, REI in the US (see Chapter 6) and Migros in Switzerland. Employee-owned firms such as the UK IT firm Xansa, the UK retailer John Lewis, the US plumbing, heating and air-conditioning contractor TDIndustries, the $5bn hi-tech firm Science Applications International, and Scott Bader the chemical manufacturer.
■ Hybrids, thanks to mechanisms such as stock options, many classic industrial shareholder oriented corporations are evolving into hybrids. Procter & Gamble, for example, is now 26 percent owned by current and former employees.

Another alternative may be to seek new and better forms of alignment. Thus Tesco's 'corporate steering wheel' is designed to link staff rewards and satisfaction to customer satisfaction and improved business performance. Likewise, Virgin founder Richard Branson runs his empire on the philosophy that if you look after your staff they will look after your customers, who will, in turn, 'look after' your profits.

Indeed, according to Stanford University professor Jeffrey Pfeffer while many companies still see the employee as a cost to be managed down rather than as an asset to be nurtured, if you compare companies that have the same technologies, size, strategies and so on, it's the ones that 'put people first' that tend to be the most profitable.[13]

The most successful attempt to measure this relationship is US retailer Sears' now-famous employee-customer-profit chain, which works on the simple realization that employee attitudes and behaviour affect customer attitudes and behaviour which, in turn, affect profits. According to Sears' research, a five-point improvement in employee attitudes (to things like 'I like the kind of work I do', 'My work gives me a sense of accomplishment', 'I am proud to say I work at Sears', 'I understand our business strategy'), will drive a 1.3 point improvement in employee attitudes, which in turn will drive a 0.5 percent improvement in revenue growth. Anthony Rucci, vice-president of administration at Sears estimated that in one year alone its initiatives to improve employee satisfaction boosted revenues by $200 million.[14]

There are also potentially powerful win-wins between staff and customers. There is growing evidence that consumers increasingly judge companies at least partly by how they treat their staff. At the same time one of the keys to staff satisfaction is the sense of worth that comes from being of value to someone else. As Götz Werner remarks, 'When people think to themselves 'I am here for the corporation' you get a problem with motivation.' The command and control corporation makes work 'a necessary evil'. On the other hand, 'real' work is 'being active on behalf of others. If the individual perceives that their work is needed by others, is recognized and valued, that becomes a decisive basis for motivation. It comes from within.' And work begins to move from 'management push' to 'employee pull'.

Another way of putting it – formulated by management accounting pioneer H. Thomas Johnson – is that 'The rationale for the whole organization is the union between customer and company': every person's work should focus on this.

We saw earlier how, in the sphere of company/customer relationships, both sides are looking for more, and how this is propelling us towards consumer agent business models. In this chapter, we've seen the same forces at work on the employee/employer relationships. Companies want greater 'customer focus', innovation and commitment and to unleash these extra dimensions of employee value they have to offer new layers of value to employees too.

Companies like Sears, Procter & Gamble, Tesco and Wal-Mart want to improve staff satisfaction and empower employees because they believe it's going to increase their profits. They're still focused on the old bottom line. Nevertheless in their quest to boost the old bottom line, they're beginning to address the demand for employee agency via ingredients such as rewards, respect and control, achievement and 'meaning'. A win-win between employees and companies is driving both sides along this path: towards becoming a company that 'works for me'.

Consumer agency is a major spur of innovation in terms of business models, marketing and so on. Employee agency is emerging as an equally powerful spur of innovation in the fields of management styles and philosophies, reward and motivation systems and organizational forms. What's needed, however, is something that brings it all together.

Summary

The quest for 'value in my life' is as strong in the workplace as it is in the home.

Companies are under increasing pressure to become a 'company that works for me'. This pressure takes many forms, including demands for a better work/life balance, for more personally rewarding work (however that is defined), for more autonomy and control at work, for the company to reflect my values as well as offer me wages, etc.

At the same time, companies are discovering they need employees to invest more personal assets with them. Firms don't want mere 'hands' to act as appendages to machines any more. They want 'the whole person' to come to work, bringing her heart (motivation and commitment), and her mind (creativity, the ability to spot opportunities, etc).

In order to persuade individuals to invest these precious personal assets with them, companies are having to offer them more. Hence the trend towards 'a company that works for me'.

Achieving this isn't easy, however. It runs counter to traditional command and control attitudes and practices (fear and greed still prevail in many corporate cultures). And there is a need to balance – and if possible, align – increased employee expectations with the value in my life demands of customers.

Such win-wins are possible. Just as the search for new win-wins in company/customer relationships is driving radical innovations to business models, so the search for new win-wins in the workplace is driving innovation in organizational forms, structures and cultures.

This search constitutes a fourth pillar in the bridge towards the new bottom line.

Chapter 12: Make marketing a service

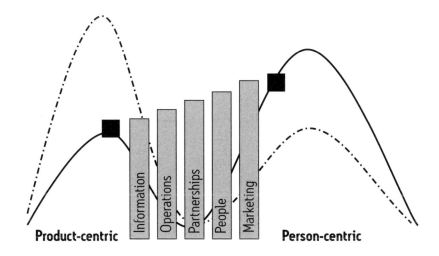

Product-centric — Information — Operations — Partnerships — People — Marketing — Person-centric

If there is one thing new bottom liners understand implicitly, it's the economic value of relationships. Traditionally, superior value products and services act as magnets for transactions. So sellers focus everything on improving and communicating this product and service value.

Under new bottom line business models of trading agency, solution assembly and passion partnership, however, potentially much greater value flows through strong, trusting relationships. So these businesses prioritize the building and maintaining of such relationships.

Many old bottom line companies have also recognized the value of relationships. They see stronger more trusting relationships as a means to close more transactions and have begun the move from a transaction focus to a relationship focus for their own old bottom line reasons. Nevertheless, in the process, they have started to build new bottom line capabilities. Here are some examples.

TASKS FOR THIS CHAPTER

Show how some companies are already developing new bottom line capabilities in the sphere of marketing and customer relations.

THE CHICK IN THE EGG

One-to-one marketing

Trading agents and solution assemblers take it for granted that they conduct their relationships with their customers on a one-to-one basis. This would have been impossible even a decade ago, because the necessary skills and technologies in data gathering, analysis, storage and distribution had not been developed. Old bottom liners embraced one-to-one marketing back then as a better means to achieve the goals of seller-centric marketing. These systems and skills are a 'core competency' for trading agents and solution assemblers.

The difference: under seller-centric marketing, the first 'one' in one-to-one was the seller, selling to the buyer. In the emerging model, that's reversed. The first 'one' in one-to-one is the buyer. But the underlying skills, tools and techniques are basically the same.

Customer relationship management

CRM and one-to-one marketing go hand-in-hand. As we saw in Chapter 9, the operational challenge of actually implementing a CRM programme to achieve new levels of customer service is huge. It requires companies to recognize individual customers and adapt corporate responses, communications and channels to their specific needs. These same skills lie at the heart of new bottom line business models. Trading agents and solution assemblers do little else than manage customer and business partner relationships: CRM 'is' their business.

As we also saw in Chapter 9, the trouble with too many CRM programmes is that they have been usurped by seller-centric attitudes and priorities: the over-riding aim being to cut the cost of dealing with customers and to extract more value from them; to manage customers' attitudes and behaviours in the company's favour.

Now however, leading edge companies are going beyond CRM to let their customers take control of relationship management – when to contact the customer, about what, via which channels. For them, 'customer managed relationships' or CMR is moving centre stage. This is a further step along the journey, away from push, campaign-driven marketing to 'sense and respond' information and business systems.

Of course, there's still a seller-centric heart to old bottom line CMR. Companies are not investing in CMR systems to enable their customers to manage relationships with many competing suppliers, as trading agents and solutions do. They are doing it to make their particular relationship richer and cheaper to manage. But still, CMR tools, processes and technologies are an operational 'must' for trading agents and solution assemblers and its technologies and processes are maturing within the confines of old bottom line marketing.

Lifetime value

One of the big breakthroughs in old bottom line marketing has been the realization that the 'lifetime value' of a customer is more important than a narrow focus of transaction value. The seller-centric take on this, of course, is that the value of a relationship is judged by how many transactions you can cross-sell and up-sell within it – and that this is the purpose of relationship building.

Even so, it's not a huge practical step (even if it is big mental leap) to realize that the value of transactions needs to be judged by their effect on the long term value of the relationship. This is the new bottom line view (always remembering that for the new bottom liner 'value' is not measured in purely monetary terms, but also in terms of the exchange of other resources such as information and attention).

Cross-selling

Cross-selling is closely linked to lifetime value. One of the best ways of increasing a customer's lifetime value is to persuade him to buy two or three products from our portfolio rather than just one. This, of course, is entirely seller-centric in orientation. But cross-selling can be an entry point to solution assembly: where marketers attempt to 'round out' their narrow product offerings and meet a greater 'share of total requirement' by selling a broader range of products and services. Some, like Dell and

Centrica, have even taken the next step. If we are into cross-selling, do we always have to cross-sell our own products or services? Couldn't we 'cross-sell' even more, if we were offering other companies' products and services too? In this way, cross-selling can open a path towards solution assembly and trading agency.

Permission marketing

Many marketers now realize that good-old-fashioned intrusion marketing – grabbing as much of the consumer's attention as possible in order to ram your particular message down his throat – is increasingly ineffective and possibly even counter-productive. The pressure is on for marketers to *earn* consumers' attention. Giving consumers the chance to say 'yes' or 'no' to receiving messages both increases their involvement and helps reduce marketing waste. That's the big win.

As ever, the notion of permission has been interpreted in a thoroughly seller-centric way (it's all about gaining permission to sell) and 'permission' has sometimes been reduced to little more than a promotional gimmick or consumers ticking a box for 'more information', which then opens the floodgates to spam.

Nevertheless, new bottom line business models effectively trade in 'consumer permissions': permission to do various things for and with them, such as send a message to potential suppliers. Thus, the notion of permission is crucial – and so are the tools and mechanisms of so-called permission marketing: various forms of text messaging, e-mail messaging, box ticking and so on.

Corporate reputation

Over the past few decades, the rise of corporate branding has broken the umbilical chord between 'product' and 'brand'. By definition, corporate brands cannot be reduced to product qualities and attributes. They work at a different level, often relating to the values and purposes of the organization, what sorts of relationships it tries to build with its stakeholders, how it contributes to the wider community, and so on.

Corporate branding has sometimes been interpreted by old-fashioned marketers as an opportunity to take 'spin' to even higher, greater levels. But the main trend is very different. Ultimately, reputations are built not by what you say about yourself in communications you control (such as paid-for advertising). They're built by what other people say about you. And the best way to 'control' (or at least influence) what other people say about you is to earn their good opinions: through your behaviour.

Powerful corporate reputations, therefore, are built not only by selling good products and services, but by overall organizational behaviour. Getting the organization – including its employees – to embody the brand's values becomes an imperative. Trading agents, solution assemblers and passion partners all find their natural home in this broader notion of branding.

Recruitment and employee branding

'The war for talent' is now a common phrase on many executives' lips. Companies realize that to flourish, they not only need to sell their products successfully, they also need to attract the right calibre and type of employee. Having recruited these people, they need to retain and motivate them. The notions of employee branding and 'internal' marketing have therefore become hugely important: an organization which cannot align its staff behind what it is trying to achieve is by definition dysfunctional.

Of course, this quest is easily undermined by old-fashioned, top-down, command and control assumptions and attitudes. Many companies have tried to 'sell' themselves internally as they do externally – by attempting to insert the 'right' message into employees or consumers' heads in the hope or belief that they will change their attitudes and behaviours accordingly. But as we saw in Chapter 11, this quest for closer alignment between company and employee is a stepping stone to creating a company that works for me.

Total brand experience

There are two aspects of 'brand experience'. First, there's our overall experience of buying and using the brand. Second, there's the selling of branded experiences such as a ride at a Disney theme park.

Traditional marketers have rushed to embrace the first type for classic seller-centric reasons: 'If we can improve our customers' experience of our brand, they'll come back for more'. Nevertheless, the quest has broadened their vision of customer needs – taking it beyond the product offering to the experience of dealing with the company, for example. This is a step towards looking at markets and marketing from the customer's point of view. The skills and insights learned here are crucial for trading agents and solution assemblers whose 'product' vis-à-vis their clients is really an improved overall go-to-market experience.

When it comes to branded experiences, the passion partner's purpose of maximizing members' emotional bottom lines is achieved via the experience of pursuing their particular passion. The skills learned here by traditional businesses such as Disney will also be useful to many, if not all, such passion partners.

Brands as 'religion'

Traditional marketers have long stressed the fact that brands offer emotional as well as functional benefits. Some of these emotional benefits flow out of functional ones: a sense of reassurance about quality, for example. But many are 'additional'. The brand acts as a 'badge' which says something about myself to other people, or is 'aspirational' for example. In a world where traditional sources of identity such as region, class and even religion are fading, some brands help fill the vacuum. People use them as social markers, expressions of identity and even personal meaning.

The manipulative side of this is the growth of 'smoke and mirrors' image-driven marketing – where companies seek to maximize the badging and other elements of their brand to justify ludicrous margins. This sort of brand strategy focuses on making money *out of* customers rather than creating value *for* them. On the other hand, it's a genuine insight that as human beings we are not the rational benefit calculating machines invented by classical economics: we naturally react emotionally to things and people. This is the essence of the appeal of passion partners: passion partnership is the next logical step for 'brand as religion'.

Segmentation

Many – indeed most – tools and techniques invented by old bottom line marketers retain their usefulness under the new bottom line. It is a crucial insight, for example, that different groups of customers want and need different things. Understanding new forms of segmentation – for example, between inveterate control freaks and natural 'outsourcers' – is essential for successful new bottom line initiatives.

BREAKING THE SHELL

In its early days, no chick can survive without the egg which nourishes and protects it. Without the egg, the chick would die. But at a certain stage of development, the chick needs to transcend the confines of this shell if it wants to survive and flourish. From now on, if it accepts the limitations imposed by this shell, it dies.

Marketing now needs to break the shell of seller-centricity to fully realize its mission of customer focus, and of identifying and meeting peoples' needs. Looking back at the evolution of marketing we can see how it has passed through some clear and definite stages, each of which has laid the foundations for the next. While, in many ways, the new bottom line perspective of buyer-centricity rather than seller-centricity represents the complete opposite of traditional marketing, if we look again we can see that it is also the continuation of a long evolutionary trend.

Figure 12.1 Marketing's Journey from Seller-Centric to Buyer-Centric

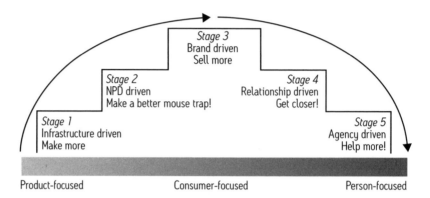

- **Stage 1: Infrastructure focused.** In the very early days of consumer goods manufacturing, the very fact that a product was being mass manufactured gave it a competitive edge in terms of quality assurance and the price/value equation.

- **Stage 2: New product development focused.** As such infrastructure became 'normal', however, manufacturers had to do something extra to gain an edge. In addition to constantly upgrading their infrastructure they also found the need to offer consumers better value through new product development. This was the era of New! Improved!

- **Stage 3: Brand focused.** New! Improved! is a hugely powerful marketing weapon, but at some stage merely having a better mousetrap isn't good enough any more. People have to know you have this better mousetrap. This was when the marketing focus began to shift to marketing communications and building brands as vehicles of innovation.

- **Stage 4: Relationship focused.** As the number of brands proliferated, and consumers' ability to choose between them grew, the game began to shift once again. Sellers wanted to focus ever more on 'loyalty' – which delivers repeat revenue and lower marketing costs. Consumers began to exercise choice, not only between products, but in the media they consumed, what messages they paid attention to, which channels to market they used, and so on. This forced companies down the road of relationship building.

- **Stage 5: Agency focused.** The fact is, however, consumers have a choice between many different relationships. And increasingly, they are only prepared to invest precious time, money, information, attention and energy in a relationship if that relationship delivers a high 'return on investment'. The buyer of products also becomes an investor in relationships, and the new bottom line begins to move centre stage. Today, we are just beginning to enter Stage 5.

Standing back, we can see three important ways in which marketers have helped prepare the way for new bottom line business models.

- **New technology** Marketers use the power of the *database and interactivity* to the full, to gather data as well as broadcasting it, and to create relationships and not just messages. This technological infrastructure and skill-set provides an essential building block for new bottom line business models.
- **New attitudes** Choice is a hugely powerful force, but it extends beyond choice between competing products to choice between which relationship to invest in. Realizing this fact changes the dynamics of marketing, and points to the new bottom line.
- **New notions of value** This has two dimensions. First, time – the shift from one-off transactions with anonymous buyers to 'lifetime value' or relationship value. Second, the shift from a one dimensional exchange of money for goods or services to multidimensional trading of OPTIMAL assets.

BOX 12.1 REINVENTING MARKETING

Nowadays, even those companies most embedded within old bottom line marketing – companies that actually helped to *invent* it like Procter & Gamble – are realizing the need for far-reaching change.

P&G is a classic product marketer that helped to invent push marketing as we know it. As the CEO A.G. Lafley puts it, 'In the past, it was mass marketing and it was push, basically. Push packaged product, push the advertising on to the telly, turn it on as loud as you can, keep it on as long as you can. Sample as broadly as you can for as long as you can. That's the way we did it.'

P&G has had some tough times of late. It has struggled to reorganize to achieve global economies of scale and faster, better innovation and at one stage shareholders hammered the company for not keeping to growth targets. In recent years, however, its performance has improved with a 'back to basics' marketing approach, focusing on the strengths of its top brands.

Nevertheless, even as P&G makes the most of these traditional old bottom line strengths, it recognizes the need for change. Says Lafley, 'We have to reinvent branding. We have to reinvent marketing ... What we are trying to do now is find different business models, different launch models, different branding and marketing models.'[1]

The essence of this reinvention, says Lafley, is a new 'consumer-is-boss' approach: 'Bottom line: the fundamental relationship between consumers and brands is changing – and the balance of power is shifting to consumers.'

Consumers, he says, are 'becoming activists ... They demand more control.' They also expect more. Marketing is moving from its mass marketing model 'away from advertiser push to consumer pull'. And this pull is based on the fact that consumers expect more: 'more personal attention – communication, products and services that are tailored to their wants and needs'. Which, in turn, means companies have to move beyond their traditional 'one-dimensional, product-myopic marketing'.

'We have to reinvent brands in which functional product benefits are transformed into solutions; shopping and product usage are transformed into experiences; transactions are transformed into relationships; and brands are transformed into trusted friends.'

For a company with P&G's history and its strengths, moving its current position to this projected future implies root-and-branch change. To find a way to make such changes, P&G is exploring – on the edges. It is recognizing the power of the 80/20 rule to move beyond mass marketing, for example. It's attempting to establish stronger, closer links with individuals who buy more P&G products. Via its 'golden household' programme it's discovering who its most important consumers are, and working out ways to communicate with them directly, for example.

Generally speaking, it notes, in each market and category a tiny proportion of consumers (around 5 percent) will account for a surprisingly high proportion of sales, so it's attempting to identify these people and address their needs at a much higher level, including information, advice and service as well as products.

Physique.com, for instance, isn't only a platform for promoting the Physique hair care range. Targeted at the tiny percentage of people (mainly young women) for whom hair care, styles and fashion are supremely important, it provides all the standard elements of community including fashion-related news, chat facilities, expert advice, product sampling, etc.

P&G's customized beauty care brand reflect.com meanwhile adopts a more 'buyer-centric' approach to branding. Rather than talking about the attributes of the product, reflect.com is supposed to be a mirror for the consumer, and reflect her own attributes back to her. Likewise, P&G is increasingly thinking of marketing communications in terms of providing information that consumers want and need, rather than the 'Look at me!' obsessions of traditional advertising. As chief marketing officer Jim Stengel notes, 'You have to do this, otherwise nobody will take any notice of you'.[2]

Put such developments in the context of other initiatives discussed elsewhere – the move from push to pull supply chains, towards synchronized production, closer more information-sharing relationships with retailers plus the attempt to spark employee creativity – and we can see a company struggling to build new bottom line pillars on many fronts.

Of course, such initiatives are still very much side shows compared to P&G's main marketing engine. And as a 'technology' company and manufacturer P&G itself is not well-placed to move towards a new bottom line role. Yet at the same time it is recognizing new bottom line imperatives and building new bottom line capabilities, in an attempt to enrich its offerings and reduce its go-to-market costs. Here's a suggestion: if P&G really wants to 'reinvent marketing', as Lafley put it, it needs partners who understand emerging 'consumer-is-boss imperatives'. Even if it cannot become a new bottom liner itself, it needs to work *with* new bottom liners to achieve its goals.

OF BRIDGES AND PILLARS

Over the past five chapters we have looked at five crucially important evolutionary developments within business. They are:

- The move from push to pull business systems, driven by information from the customer.
- Reconfiguring operations around value in my life and not just efficient supply.
- Reconfiguring partnerships around the requirements of the first two.
- Becoming a company that works for its employees, rather than a company that simply expects people to work for it.
- Recognizing that creating relationships 'worth investing in' is usually far richer than products and services as magnets for transactions — and that if you 'own' the relationship you have the 'supply chain power' to get other companies to work with you to achieve your (or better, the customer's) goals.

Old bottom line companies have embarked upon such journeys, not because they had a vision of the new bottom line in mind but because, like that feather, it helped them achieve their immediate goals better, quicker and/or cheaper.

These journeys have, nevertheless, required significant changes to both their operations and their attitudes and assumptions. What's more, at each step of the way, they have created an incentive to go further. Taking a step back would mean you become less competitive, not more competitive.

Nevertheless, to progress, each of these journeys requires a 'leap' at some stage. As we saw in Chapter 9, for example, you can only build so much more added convenience into your food products via existing operations and infrastructure such as centralized factories and shops. At some point, you need a completely different infrastructure (of many, local, convenient outlets and delivery points) to reach the next dimension of value in my life.

Likewise with marketing. Marketers can only go so far in building closer, more trusting, more valuable customer relationships within the confines of their seller-centric attitudes and goals. At some stage, if you want to really achieve these objectives, you need to break the shell of seller-centricity to embrace a new bottom line approach.

On each of our five journeys, leading edge companies are now coming face-to-face with the need for such 'leaps'. Thus, ultimately:

■ If you want to unleash the full power of information from your customers, you have to use it for them and on their behalf.

■ If you want to add value via your operations and not just via the value you embed in your products, you need to reconfigure these operations around value in my life, not just vendor efficient supply.

■ If you want to leverage the full value of the move from push to pull, and of person-centric operations, you need to organize your partnerships around the same logic.

■ If you want a workforce prepared to go that extra mile for you, you have to become a company that works for them.

■ If you want to 'own' that customer relationship – the precious resource that gives you the power to organize complete supply chains and value networks around your offering – you have to make it a relationship that's designed to maximize value for that customer.

However, at the same time, few companies have travelled equally far down all five roads. They have pursued some with more enthusiasm and dedication than others. Also, they have pursued each initiative as a separate project. After all, on the surface, each one addresses very different issues and goals, tackling very different aspects of what the business does, using very different methodologies and tools, under the tutelage of very different departments, e.g., IT, operations and logistics, strategy, human resources and marketing.

In fact, without the perspective of the new bottom line it is very difficult to see what unites them: the common centre of gravity of value in my life. The result is that while some companies may have evolved proto-feathers, they certainly can't fly yet. So far, we have five separate pillars at varying stages of construction, and they're not yet aligned to build a bridge from A to B; from old bottom line to new. We still need a new 'vision of value' to bring these pillars to completion, and to bring them together so that we can build that bridge from old to new. Building this bridge, and this 'vision of value', is the subject of our final chapter.

Summary

At root, the old bottom line approach to marketing is simple. 'Meet customer needs' rhetoric notwithstanding, its core aim is to get customers to do what companies want them to do – buy our product or service! Companies attempt to achieve these goals by inserting compelling 'buy me!' messages in customers' heads via advertising and other marketing communications. The desired end result: another transaction closed.

However, the intensifying quest for market benefits such as increased brand loyalty, word of mouth recommendation, access to customer information, and 'cut through' in marketing communications means that companies now need to do more than close transactions. They need customers to invest precious time, information, emotions and attention (as well as money) with them. And they are having to work much harder for such customer investment.

Marketing concepts such as customer relationship management, permission marketing and life time value reflect this pressure.

When shoe-horned into seller-centric marketing strategies, they frequently disappoint. They nevertheless recognize the direction of future success, which lies in maximizing the returns individuals earn for investing their personal assets in companies' marketing programmes.

New bottom line business models go one step further: to help individuals achieve their go-to-market or life objectives.

As the buyer of products and services morphs into an investor in relationships, companies are beginning to learn how to respond to these emerging new bottom line imperatives. This creates a fifth pillar in the bridge to the new value peak.

13

13 A New Vision of Value

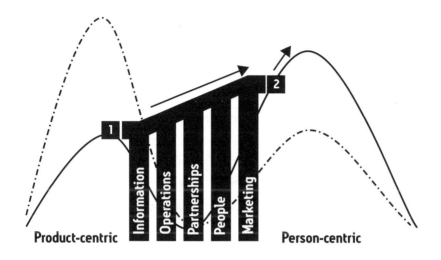

When Christopher Columbus sailed the seas in 1492 he didn't set out to discover America: he was looking for a better route to China. And when, at last, he set foot on his first Caribbean island, he didn't believe he had stumbled upon a new world. He thought it was an island off India: hence the name West Indies.

Columbus did all the hard work. He actually got his ship there. But he went to his death bed denying his discovery. He had set out to find a better route to China and that, he insisted, was what he had found. That's why early maps of that time mark the west coast of America as 'Cathay'. It was only later that cartographers put two and two together and concluded that this was a New World indeed – a New World that would emerge to be the world's greatest superpower.

Many a consumer-facing business now finds itself in a similar position. Companies have introduced all sorts of changes and developments in their search for a better route to China – faster growth, higher margins, greater customer loyalty, stronger brands and so on. And this quest has brought them a long way, to the verge of the new world. Table 13.1 sums up our discussion over the last five chapters, showing how each one of the recent developments in those core areas of information systems, operations, relationships with business partners, employees and customers help pave the way for new bottom line practices. A lot of the hard work has already been done, or is at least under way.

Incredible as Columbus' feat was, however, it was still just a half-way house. It took an extra, mental leap – putting two and two together to recognize the existence of a New World – to trigger the next operational leaps: a frenzy of exploration, discovery, occupation and settlement. The

Table 13.1 New Bottom Line: from Feather to Flight?

Business area	Immediate purpose	'Pillar' function
Information	Improved responsiveness Lower costs	Create infrastructure and culture for a move from 'push' to 'pull'
Operations	Add value e.g., convenience	Create skills and infrastructure that move beyond vendor efficient supply towards customer-efficient demand.
Partnerships	Add value Cut costs	All new bottom line business models aggregate/integrate value from many sources. This is impossible without strong partnerships.
People	Attract, retain, motivate staff	■ A company that 'works for me' is the employee's version of the new bottom line ■ In outsiders' eyes, treatment of employees is a test of the company's authenticity ■ New bottom line goals give additional meaning/purpose to work
Customer relationships	Sell more, at lower cost	Rams home critical importance of personal assets, and the need for 'on my side' trust

same goes for the new bottom line. Only when we recognize the importance of this new world can we truly begin to explore its opportunities. Each of the pillars discussed in the last five chapters is important, but they only represent a half-way house. What's needed is a new Vision of Value which triggers a determination to bring the new business models we discussed earlier – trading agency, or solution assembly, and passion partnership – to fruition.

Back in Chapter 7 we noted how birds first evolved feathers for one purpose and then used them for another, revolutionary purpose – that of flight. Not every bird that evolved feathers ended up taking to the air, however. A whole sub-species – the ratites, including ostriches, emus and dodos – stayed firmly land-bound.

To reach take-off, a whole further set of evolutionary changes were needed. Birds needed to reduce their body weight, which meant they had to hollow out their bones. They needed to develop pectoral muscles strong enough to push their body weight into the air when they beat their wings. They needed a new thermoregulatory system to cope with the huge amounts of heat all this effort generated. And they faced difficult trade-offs. The strengthened pectoral muscles needed strengthened arm and shoulder bones to attach to, even as these bones were being hollowed out.

One way birds coped with the heat problem was by pumping air in and out of these hollowed bones. In other words, only when all these challenges were seamlessly addressed, in an integrated way, did birds take to the air. (It's now believed that Archaeopteryx, the first known feathered beast, never actually took off.)

As far as the new bottom line is concerned, we're still at an early stage. We need a new bottom line vision of value to integrate many different developments in information, operations, partnerships, marketing etc. into a seamless whole: to turn a series of separate pillars into a complete bridge to the value peaks.

A NEW CONVERGENCE

Mastery of the air presents some huge opportunities for 'competitive advantage'. That's why nature invented flight in at least three completely different ways: birds with feathers, bats and pterosaurs with extended skin flaps, and insects. Eyes evolved separately at least fifty times, with the core design challenge – how to capture the use of light and shade – solved in a dozen different ways.

We anticipate something similar with the new bottom line. Many different types of player   – firms of many different sizes, shapes, industries and categories will converge on the main value peaks we've outlined in this book.

Figure 13.1 A New Convergence?

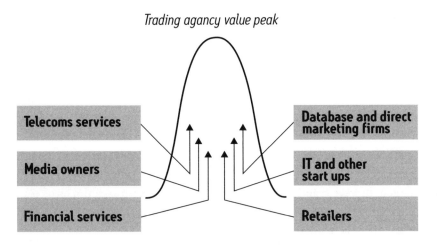

Figure 13.1 illustrates, for example, how numerous different players from many different industries might all converge on the trading agency role. Database and direct marketing firms would see it as a natural extension of their core customer data business – with the added benefit that they are eliciting even richer, better responses from target customers.

IT firms could see a market opportunity for new pieces of enabling software and infrastructure. A retailer like Tesco might see trading agency as a natural extension of its existing core trading skills and relationships. A telecoms company might offer trading agency services to existing subscribers as a way to add value (thereby boosting loyalty) which also encourages incremental usage of its core offerings in fixed line and mobile telephony, Internet, etc.

Similarly, a financial services company such as a credit card operator might regard trading agency as a chance to add a relevant new layer of value to both its customer base and its merchant base: one which connects the two in a more efficient manner and which, happily, also encourages incremental use of its cards. A media owner might seek to use its impartial editorial expertise as a platform for the provision of additional buyer-centric information – with transaction services added on to complete the service.

We're likely to see similar convergence with all new bottom line business models. In solution assembly, for example, many different players – car manufacturers, car insurers, car rental companies, roadside assistance organizations, property companies, etc. – might see an opportunity in personal mobility services.

The other side of the coin is that while many different players may converge on the same value peak from many different directions, each individual player has a choice of many options.

Figure 13.2 Many Evolutionary Options

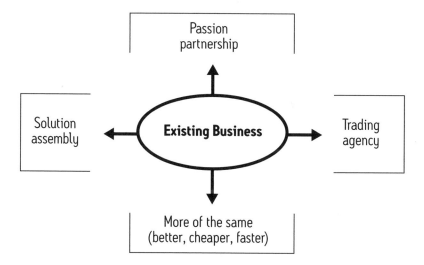

Figure 13.2 sums these options up. Do we want to continue ploughing the same basic furrow? (This may be the best possible option, but it may also be the worst – see below). Or do we want to migrate to a different new bottom line business model?

Some retailers might reach out for a trading agency role by offering extra layers of buyer centric information, creating new reverse market mechanisms for certain product areas, and seeking to become their customers' 'sourcing partner' of choice. Others, however, might seek to add new layers of service in a quest to become a domestic solution assembler – e.g. offering to repair household appliances purchased from the shop, and extending these services towards a general home maintenance role. Yet others, especially in high-expertise and high involvement sectors (like REI), might seek a passion partner role.

Financial services companies might also opt for solution assembly, via complete personal financial management services. Or they might plump for the complete opposite, and become specialist, low-cost ingredient providers to such solution assemblers. A few, at the high end, might even evolve into a passion partnership role – for those who see personal investing as a hobby, for example. And as we've seen, some, such as credit card operators, might add trading agent functions to their core business (see below).

A car company might take on a personal mobility solution assembly role (we saw a possible example in Chapter 5). In certain glamour segments (e.g., off road, or sports cars) it might seek out a passion partner role. Alternatively, in mainstream markets it might work with trading agents to access richer, more up-to-date customer information and streamline go-to-market costs, perhaps even using trading agents as a platform to move towards mass customization.

All of which raises some important questions: who is best placed to seize which opportunities? And how best to seize them?

Monday Morning Answers

There is one thing all companies can do straight away: review your existing value offering from a new bottom line perspective.

Using our *existing* information systems, operations, partnerships, staff and customer relationships:

- In what ways do our current products, services and go-to-market practices fail to address, or actually increase, the key value gaps introduced in Chapter 1. And how can we avoid this?
- In what ways can we start closing these key value gaps, to mutual benefit?
- In what ways do we currently ignore, waste or abuse customers' OPTIMAL assets?
- In what ways can we help our customers increase the productivity and value of these assets?

Even a most cursory review of this nature is likely to throw up an enormous range of *immediate* opportunities to improve *current* performance in these areas. These improvements weren't made before simply because the right questions had not been asked.

But the real message is that as soon as you start asking questions, the need to *change* existing information systems, operations, partnerships, staff and customer relationships becomes glaringly obvious. These changes need to be made in an integrated fashion, with a coherent end view in mind. And the question has to be addressed: are we making these changes in order to add value to our *existing* products and services – to make it easier to sell what we already make? Or are we making these changes to transform this core offering? If so, we need to evolve towards a new business model.

Let's review these options in a little more detail.

We see four main options:

- To evolve an already-established business towards a chosen new bottom line model.
- To start with a clean sheet; addressing a new business model with new start up business.
- To stick to your knitting, e.g., focusing on good old-fashioned making and selling, while adapting to a new bottom line environment by working with trading agents, solution assemblers and passion partners as new channels to market.
- To resist the whole trend.

Option 1: Evolve your existing business

We see three main evolutionary trajectories, as illustrated in Figure 13.2.

Figure 13.3 Possible Migration Strategies

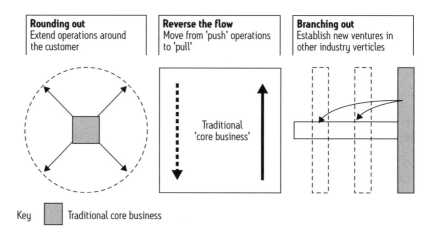

Rounding out
Extend operations around the customer

Reverse the flow
Move from 'push' operations to 'pull'

Branching out
Establish new ventures in other industry verticles

Traditional 'core business'

Key — Traditional core business

Rounding out

Here, the company uses an existing base – production of an important ingredient for example – as the platform from which to extend its offer, adding layer after layer of extra products and services (and integrating them along the way) to move from ingredient production to solution assembly. This is the sort of route currently being followed by a player like Centrica – and by most players wanting to take on solution assembly/passion partner roles.

It is also a route adopted by players like Amazon. It started off as a straightforward e-retailer with the 'added value' of clever buyer-centric devices such as reader reviews plus the bonus of very low transaction costs (e.g., 'one click' purchases). With its use of profiling (comparing my personal shopping basket to those of people who purchased some of the same books) Amazon has edged towards an expert sourcing/advisory role. And by opening up second-hand markets, it is enabling its own customers to participate as sellers as well as buyers.

Critical point: 'rounding out' is not just cross-selling and up-selling, or brand extension. For companies seeking to evolve towards a new bottom line business model, the central purpose of such 'rounding out' is not simply to make more money out of the customer by selling more to them, but to address a targeted set of value gaps with a complete, integrated offering. The acid test: is the company still measuring (and operating according to) sales and margins per product line, or by the overall value of the customer relationship? And does it focus this critical calculation of 'return on relationship investment' *for both sides: both* client and company? After all, if one side is not getting a superior return on investment, trouble is brewing.

Reversing the flow

This migratory route is open to retailers like Tesco who have long been shifting their operations from a 'push' mode to a 'pull' mode. This shift is both psychological and operational. Where does the heart of the business lie? In buying and (then) selling? Or in sourcing on behalf of the customer?

The acid test here: does the business earns its keep from margin on sales? Or from fees for sourcing? As we saw in Chapter 4, the material difference may be slight. However, psychologically, the implications for future development are huge.

Branching out

Many companies may see an opportunity to move into a new bottom line market which is parallel or complementary to their existing core business – a chance to invade another industry's back garden. We mentioned some examples above. If a telecoms provider starts offering trading agency services which help its customers source, say, electrical goods, that telecoms company is 'treading on the toes' of traditional electrical goods retailers. If a bank offers loans for customers sourcing cars via fleet operators, it is treading on the toes of car dealers.

For the telecoms company or bank, however, these incursions into other companies' back yards are not a threat to its core business. Buyer-centricity only makes business people quake with fear when it addresses their own core business – not when it is an opportunity to grow an incremental revenue stream and win plaudits from their existing customers.

Ultimately however, 'branching out' will remain a mere promotional exercise so long as its main purpose is to defend/boost the company's traditional core business. The acid test is whether the company begins to see and treat the venture as a separate, viable business which must add enough value to both company and customer in its own right.

The common theme uniting all three evolutionary trajectories is this: the shift to the new bottom line finally happens when the company realises that its core asset is not its infrastructure, property or other operational assets but its relationship with its customers and the flows of value that are funnelled through this relationship. Whether it is rounding out, reversing the flow, or branching out, at some stage the business has to cross a threshold, to leave old bottom line priorities and considerations behind to embrace a new bottom line business model. It is precisely business leaders' reluctance to let go – and their fear of what they might put at risk – that makes crossing this threshold so difficult. That is why many successful new bottom liners will take the opposite, start up route.

Option 2: Create a stand-alone start up

The start-up's big advantage is that it is not held back by legacy attitudes and systems, or a fear of cannibalizing existing 'core' businesses or revenue streams. Its big disadvantage, of course, is that by definition it lacks critical mass: infrastructure, an established customer base, a recognized, trusted brand, resources, etc. Its key challenge, then, is how to survive the daunting journey to such critical mass (see Box 13.1).

Option 3: Accommodation

The next option is accommodation. For many businesses, evolving towards a new bottom line business model is not a serious option. If you have not already evolved to walk on two legs, your chances of evolving wings are virtually zero: you still need your arms for walking. Likewise, for reasons of history and circumstance many companies are simply not in a position to adopt a new bottom line strategy.

There's nothing wrong with this. When the industrial revolution occurred, that didn't spell the end of farming. Yes, farming was no longer the centre of economic gravity. But nevertheless, in one sense it became even more important, because the farms now had to feed the cities as well as the countryside. Likewise, all the new bottom line business models depend implicitly on the existence of a mature, efficient supply base. Making and selling doesn't disappear with the new bottom line. It just becomes part of a much bigger picture.

BOX 13.1 HOW START-UPS GAIN CRITICAL MASS

There are three basic routes to critical mass for start-ups. The first one is to enter a niche that everyone else is ignoring or avoiding. The first steam engine – a huge, dangerous and unwieldy beast of a machine that wasted 99 percent of the energy it used – found use in only one place: pumping water deep underground in mines where men and horses could not work. But having established itself in this niche, it then had a platform to start perfecting its operations, and with each improvement in its capabilities it extended its reach and use, to become the dominant energy industry.

Wal-Mart started out in the backwaters of retailing, in regions completely ignored by the brand leaders. It was seven years before Sam Walton even opened his second store – it took so long for him to get his first model right. But in the particular niche where he was operating, he had the chance to learn and improve. Once he had perfected his business model he moved in from the margins towards the centre.

The second approach is 'trickle down': start with a service that's so expensive that only a tiny minority of extra-rich people are prepared to pay for it, but then use this as a basis to build technical expertise and economies of scale, thereby bringing down prices and expanding the market. That's how gas lighting, the telephone and the motor car started out. It's also the route chosen by would-be solution assemblers like Ten.

The third approach is to simply rely on a subsidy from a 'sugar daddy' parent who sees the long-term benefit of building critical mass. The telegraph and the airplane would not have survived years – decades in the case of the aeroplane – of unprofitable operation if their development had not been subsidized by the military. Likewise, players like Tesco and Procter & Gamble are subsidizing the development of their on-line operations with a clear vision of future benefit. We anticipate a few successes – and many failures – from each of these three main routes to critical mass.

For companies whose continued expertise lies in 'making', the new bottom line opportunity remains huge. This is their chance to completely reengineer their marketing and go-to-market strategies. By working closely with the new business models as more efficient channels to market, they have the opportunity to enrich the insights they generate from their customers and to streamline their costs of going to market, dealing with their customers, etc.

Option 4: Resist

Some companies, however, may decide to resist the entire trend. These fall into two categories. If the company relies on customer inertia, relative ignorance or strong market power (e.g., monopoly control over certain distribution channels) for its profits it may decide to resist the rise of new bottom liners, seeing them as a threat. They are quite right. For these companies, the writing is on the wall. Their value peak is sinking and new bottom liners will take pleasure in helping to sink it even further.

There is another group, however, for whom new bottom line strategies may simply be inappropriate. These are companies for whom the traditional industrial age win-wins – driven by innovation and/or still-improving economies of scale – remain paramount. Pharmaceutical companies developing new blockbuster drugs. Entertainment companies developing new blockbuster films and shows; pop stars; blockbuster authors; designer furniture or clothes companies; inventors of fabulous new electronic gizmos. If you are a superb intellectual property creator then the best strategy for you might be 'back to the future' with ever, better 'New! Improved!' products. The crucial question is: does our intellectual property creating ability really reach this stratospheric level? Or do we just wish it does?

So here, in sum, are seven 'no brainer' steps for responding to the new bottom line challenge.

1 Understand which of the seven value gaps are most important to your particular business and its customers – which ones do they miss the most?

2 Given the current state of your operations, value offerings, culture, brand, etc., which of the value gaps is easiest for you to tackle?

BOX 13.2 ARE THE NEW VALUE PEAKS FOR EVERYBODY?

Not every traditional company or brand will want to start the journey: not every traditional value peak is sinking, or has sunk low enough yet to warrant a forced migration. One group of industries and categories whose value peak shows no signs of sinking is those driven by 'intellectual property' creation (in its broadest sense): creating value by giving me things I didn't know I wanted or could have.

There are many, varied candidates for this role. Industries driven by cutting edge technology research – creating new electronic gizmos or pharmaceutical products – continue to offer enough value 'from our operations' to hold their own. In fact, their contribution complements that of the new business models. Likewise, creators of to-die-for editorial and entertainment content. The blockbuster musician or author driven by his own creativity doesn't make his money sensing and responding to consumers wants and needs. He makes his money by creating things I didn't know I wanted or could have.

A second important set of 'bystanders' are those players who by virtue of their technical expertise or economies of scale can continue to shore up traditional value peaks. If your company is continuing to reap additional economies of scale benefits from, say, globalization – so that you can continue to offer your customers better value at lower prices, then extending and deepening that existing business model may be far more attractive than attempting any sort of migration.

The dividing line between these positions is far from clear. Many a manufacturer talks innovation but actually lives in me-too land. Many a media owner pretends his 'content is king' whereas, in reality, most of his editorial content is becoming commoditized. Many companies are looking for growth by traditional means such as geographic expansion. But not all of them are growing as fast, or as profitably, in these directions as they would like. So companies have real choices to make.

3 Understand which of the OPTIMAL assets you are in a best position to leverage on behalf of your customers – which of these assets are you *already* trading?

4 Understand which of these assets are most important to your particular customers (again, probably segment by segment).

5 Work out if there is a coherent way of bringing these different strands together. It's no good tapping into say, the richness of information from customers if the key value gap is 'passion'.

6 Decide how to respond. Do we want to lead the charge, be a quick adapter, or resist the flow? If it is 'lead the charge', then decide on a migration strategy.

7 Identify which pillars (e.g., information strategy, operations, partnerships, people, customer relationships) you are currently weak on, and how you can reinforce/extend those pillars that you already have. For this, a simple new bottom line maturity scorecard might be helpful.

A NEW BOTTOM LINE MATURITY SCORECARD

Not every company is in a good position to cross the bridge to the new value peaks. If the company hasn't yet begun to reconfigure information, operations and relationships with suppliers, employees and customers around the demands of the new bottom line it will almost certainly find trading agency, solution assembly and passion partnership beyond its reach.

Figures 13.4-13.6 give a crude top-of-the-line assessment of three companies' new bottom line maturity. A traditional manufacturing company like Ford has yet to develop any new bottom line capabilities. It is focused strongly on its own operational efficiency and the value generated by these operations, and it deals with its end users via a third party – dealers. A substantial move towards mass customisation, however, would open up flows of information from its customers and enable it to offer personalised value, and perhaps even evolve towards solution assembly. Hence the 'possibles' marked on the scorecard.

As we've seen, in most cases, the biggest new bottom line opportunity for companies like this is accommodation: working closely with would-be consumer agents as a supplier, to access richer sources of information to understand their customers better, enrich the value they offer and streamline go-to-market costs.

Figure 13.4 Ford's New Bottom Line Scorecard

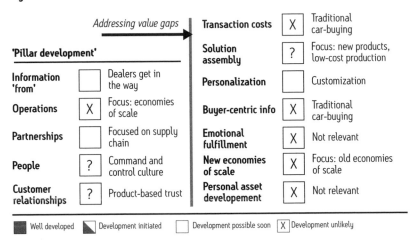

Figure 13.5 Tesco's New Bottom Line Scorecard

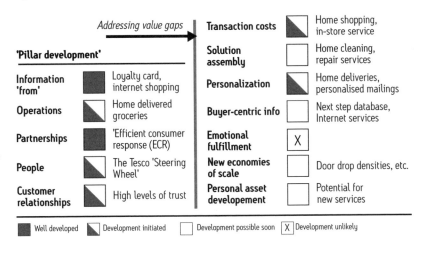

Most traditional retailers wouldn't fare much better than Ford. But with its loyalty card and home shopping operations Tesco's ability to elicit information from its customers (with their explicit permission) is now well established. By introducing home-shopping operations along with large-scale changes to shopping formats aimed at increased convenience, it has begun to reconfigure its assets and operations around its customers' go-to-market efficiency, rather than just its own. It has well-developed relationships with many suppliers, many of which are explicitly driven by customer data and demands. Also, compared to most UK brands, it has high levels of 'on my side' trust.

Tesco has a relatively high maturity score, then. It also has important 'possibles' revolving around next steps such as solution assembly (in home services) and trading agency. Whether Tesco chooses to prioritise these opportunities remains to be seen, of course. It has many competing priorities, including expansion into non-food and into international retail markets. The opportunity to evolve is not the same as a decision to do so.

The same goes for the Centrica subsidiary British Gas. It has moved beyond traditional energy supply into areas such as maintenance contracts and home management services, as we saw in Chapter 5. Owing to these developments, Centrica is already offering a degree of personalisation and solution assembly – and because these services are based on the home, it has had to organise its operations and partnerships accordingly.

Figure 13.6 Centrica's New Bottom Line Scorecard

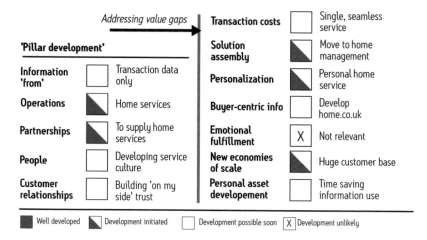

So far, however, it is not gathering transaction (or any other data) from its customers with their permission. While it could conceivably offer customers home-related buyer-centric information and transactions in the future, it hasn't done so yet. Certain old bottom line attitudes could also hamper its progress towards a fully fledged solution assembly role. While it has high levels of 'competence' trust, unlike Tesco it has low levels of 'on my side' trust, for example. And a strong 'cross-selling' culture stands in the way of strong moves in this direction.

OBSTACLES ALONG THE WAY

The existence of such legacy barriers underlines a key point. Companies that do decide to address the new bottom line opportunity will have to surmount many obstacles along the way. This is new territory so, by definition, it involves a steep learning curve. Critical challenges include:

- Understanding critical new bottom line customer segments: e.g., which value gaps are most important to them and what sort of relationship do they want? Are they control freaks or relaxed outsourcers? Category novices in search of expert reassurance or connoisseurs in their own right? Are they looking for a 'close' or an 'arms length' relationship?
- Crafting the right vision/business model to connect your particular company's skills and capabilities with these segments.
- Evolving, or changing, culture internally to embrace new bottom line principles and objectives.
- Balancing new costs with new revenue streams over time, to create a clear, viable pathway to critical mass.
- Creating different types of relationship: e.g., moving beyond seller/customer to 'investor' and co-producer.
- Educating customers as to what you're doing and why – because they're as unfamiliar with this world as you are, and without such an education process the necessary levels of trust may not be realized.
- Educating shareholders and business partners as to why such a move makes sense for them, too.
- Building the necessary consumer trust to 'close the loop' and unleash new win-wins.

CONCLUSION

Is the gain worth the pain? We believe it will be, for two reasons. First, the climate is changing anyway. The tectonic forces we began discussing are unstoppable. Every consumer-facing company, from utilities through food, property, financial services, non-food merchandise, financial services, travel, retailing, media, telecoms and computing will, over the coming years, be fundamentally affected by the shift towards the new bottom line. Whether to respond is not a choice. The only question is how.

Second, this is 'a new world' and it does hold out unthinkably huge opportunities. Name any prized goal sought after by any traditional old bottom line business:

- Innovation and growth
- Accessing and tapping new assets and revenue streams
- Achieving higher levels of trust, loyalty and customer retention
- Gaining greater share of purse/requirement and becoming 'embedded' within the customer's life.

Unfortunately, as we've seen, old bottom line priorities and competitive conditions positively undermine the achievement of these goals: the price of achieving them is accepting the logic of the new bottom line. And here, the opportunities are huge.

Summary

New bottom line pressures are already prompting businesses to respond and adapt.

Companies have pursued sometimes-radical changes in information systems, operational infrastructure, partnership strategies and employee and customer relationships, not because of a deliberate strategic intent to migrate towards new bottom line business models, but to make their existing businesses more efficient, effective and profitable.

Nevertheless, the net effect of such responses is that new bottom line infrastructure, skills and perspectives are being established.

Meanwhile it is becoming clear that traditional corporate goals of revenue growth, increased share of customer purse, closer customer relationships, higher levels of trust, increased 'brand loyalty' etc are often best achieved by new bottom line rather than old bottom line business models and practices.

This trend can only be compounded as new bottom line upstarts raise consumer expectations of value, shake up industry boundaries and competitive sets, reconfigure channels to market, and sap traditional sources of margin and brand strength.

For some companies 'more of the same' may still be the best response. Such a strategy can work where there is significant potential for product or service innovation or new economies of scale to unleash.

Existing suppliers of products and services, on the other hand, can realize huge win-wins by working with emerging new bottom liners to reduce go-to-market costs and to increase information flows to drive better, faster innovation.

Others will use the pillars discussed in Chapters 8-12 to construct a bridge from their old value peak to the new. To do so, they will need to connect these pillars with a comprehensive new bottom line 'vision of value'.

They also need to identify a viable migration path. The three main options are: 'rounding out' from existing products or services; 'branching out' from the current core business to adjacent ones; and 'reversing the flow' within the existing business to turn it into a consumer agent.

Such migration strategies may take the form of 'bet the business' strategic shifts, or limited-risk experimental skunk-works and start-ups. A simple 'new bottom line maturity scorecard' can help identify the best options for companies' particular circumstances. But the ultimate message is simple. The question is not whether to respond to the rise of the new bottom line, but how.

Chapter References

Introduction

1. Stengel, Jim, Interview with authors, June 2002.
2. North, Douglass C., *Institutions, Institutional Change and Economic Performance*, Cambridge University Press, 1990.
3. Lafley, A.G., Interview with authors, June 2000.
4. Fitzgerald, Niall Interviewer with *Market Leader*, Autumn 1998.

Chapter 1

1. Tomkins, Richard, 'Science and Utopia', *Financial Times*, 3 October 2002.
2. North, Douglass C., *Institutions, Institutional Change and Economic Performance*, Cambridge University Press, 1990, p28.
3. Butler, Patrick, et al., 'A Revolution in Interaction', *McKinsey Quarterly*, 1997, Number 1.

Chapter 5

1. Cheatle, Alex, Interview with Authors, September 2002.
2. Higginson, Alan, Interview with Authors, July 2002.
3. Waugh, Simon, Institute of Direct Marketing presentation, May 2002.
4. Cheatle, Alex, Interview with Authors, September 2002.
5. Hoskinson, Tony, Interview with Authors, July 2002.

Chapter 6

1 Marsden, Dennis, President & CEO of REI, Annual Report, 2001.
2 Jensen, Rolf, The Dream Society, McGraw Hill, 1999.
3 Locke, Christopher, Gonzo Marketing, Perseus Publishing, 2001.
4 Hoeness, Uli, Interview with Authors, August 2000.
5 Collins, James C. & Porras, Jerry L., Built to Last, Century, 1994.
6 Collins, James, Good to Great, Random House, 2001.

Chapter 8

1 Kotler, Philip, Jain, Dipak C. & Suvit, Maesincee, Marketing Moves, Harvard Business School Press, 2002.
2 Lafley A.G., Interview with Authors, June 2000.
3 Leahy, Sir Terry, Interview with Authors, February 2002.
4 Kotler, Philip, Jain, Dipak C. & Suvit, Maesincee, Marketing Moves, Harvard Business School Press, 2002.
5 Johnson, Thomas H. & Bröms, Anders, Profit Beyond Measure, Nicholas Braeley, 2000.
6 Ibid., p2.
7 Thomke, Stefan & von Hippel, Eric, 'Customers as Innovators: A new way to create value', Harvard Business Review, April 2002.
8 Dell, Michael, Direct from Dell, HarperCollins Business, 1999

Chapter 9

1 Seybold, Patricia, 'Customers.com', Times Business, 1998.

2 Evans, Barry, Presentation to Institute of Grocery Distribution, May 2002.

3 Leahy, Sir Terry, Interview with Authors, February 2002.

4 Waugh, Simon, Institute of Direct Marketing presentation, May 2002.

5 Barr, Jake, Interview with Authors, July 2001.

6 Womack, James & Jones, Daniel T., Lean Thinking, Simon & Schuster, 1996.

Chapter 10

1 Vandevelde, Luc, Speech at an ECR Europe Conference, Barcelona, May 2002.

2 Weber, Jurgen, Interview with Authors, March 2000.

3 Sorrell, Martin, Interview with Authors, June 2001.

4 Evans, Barry, Presentation to Institute of Grocery Distribution, May 2002.

Chapter 11

1 Fortune, 30 July 2001.

2 Material in this box is based on a series of author interviews with senior P&G personnel over the last three years.

3 Handy, Charles, The Elephant and the Flea, Hutchinson, 2001.

4 Ibid., p86.

5 Fukuyama, Francis, The Great Disruption, Profile Books, 1994, p224.

6 These quotes comes from a speech given by Lee Scott to the GDI conference in Switzerland, July 2001 and a subsequent interview with one of the authors.

7 Semler, Richard, Maverick!, Century Book, 2001.

8 Werner, Götz from a speech to the GDI, July 2001.

9 Ind, Nicholas, Living in the Brand, Kogan Page, 2001, p6.

10 Collins James C, & Porras Jerry L., Built to Last, Century, 1994. Collins, James C., Good to Great, Random House, 2001.

11 Schein, Edgar, ' The Anxiety of Learning', Harvard Business Review, March 2002.

12 'Wal-Mart's People Problem', Fortune, 25 March 2002.

13 Pfeffer, Jeffrey, The Human Equation, Harvard Business School Press, 1998.

14 Rucci, Anthony J., Kirn, Steven P. & Quinn, Richard T., 'The employee-customer-profit chain at Sears', Harvard Business Review, January-February 1998.

15 Johnson, H. Thomas & Bröms, Anders, Profit beyond Measure, Nicholas Brealey, 2000, p72.

Chapter 12

1 Lafley, A.G., Interview with Authors, June 2000.

2 Stengel, Jim, Interview with Authors, June 2002.

Index